D1083995

BETWEEN FREEDOM AND EQUALITY

# Between Freedom

TOPOGRAPHICAL

Map

OF THE

DISTRICTS COLUMBIA

# and Equality

## The History of an
## African American Family
## in Washington, DC

BARBARA BOYLE TORREY *and* CLARA MYRICK GREEN

Georgetown University Press / Washington, DC

© 2021 Georgetown University Press. All rights reserved. No part of this book may be reproduced or utilized in any form or by any means, electronic or mechanical, including photocopying and recording, or by any information storage and retrieval system, without permission in writing from the publisher.

The publisher is not responsible for third-party websites or their content. URL links were active at time of publication.

Library of Congress Cataloging-in-Publication Data

Names: Torrey, Barbara Boyle, author. | Green, Clara Myrick, author.
Title: Between freedom and equality : the history of an African American family in Washington, DC / Barbara Boyle Torrey, Clara Myrick Green.
Description: Washington, DC : Georgetown University Press, [2021] | Includes bibliographical references and index.
Identifiers: LCCN 2020029548 | ISBN 9781647120818 (hardcover) | ISBN 9781647120825 (ebook)
Subjects: LCSH: Pointer, George, 1773-1832. | Pointer, George, 1773-1832—Family. | African Americans—Washington (D.C.)—Biography. | Washington (D.C.)—Biography. | Washington (D.C.)—History.
Classification: LCC F205.N4 T67 2021 | DDC 975.3/020922 [B]—dc23
LC record available at https://lccn.loc.gov/2020029548

♾ This paper meets the requirements of ANSI/NISO Z39.48-1992 (Permanence of Paper).

22  21      9  8  7  6  5  4  3  2  First printing

Printed in the United States of America

Cover design by Jeff Miller, Faceout Studio
Interior design by Erin Kirk

RELATED WORKS

*Facing Georgetown's History: A Reader on Slavery, Memory, and Reconciliation* edited by Adam Rothman and Elsa Barraza Mendoza

*A Georgetown Life: The Reminiscences of Britannia Wellington Peter Kennon of Tudor Place* edited by Grant S. Quertermous

*George Washington's Final Battle: The Epic Struggle to Build a Capital City and a Nation* by Robert P. Watson

This book is dedicated to our husbands,

whose support and interest in our work have been heroic:

E. Fuller Torrey and Richard C. Green

# Contents

# Illustrations

# Foreword

I was in my mid-fifties when Barbara Boyle Torrey and Clara Myrick Green introduced me to my eighth-generation grandfather Capt. George Pointer, an incredible man who rose from slavery to place his unique imprint on the building of this nation we call the United States. My first feeling was a full sense of overwhelming pride. Then I felt almost angry, and a collection of questions about why things happened as they did and why things didn't happen as they should have filled my mind. Why did I not know George Pointer's story, and why didn't the average American know his story? His life and accomplishments in Washington, DC; Virginia; and Maryland unquestionably earned him the right to be acknowledged and honored.

After a grueling search on the internet to find out more about George Pointer, I discovered another thing that invoked the question, Why? In his June 2005 report titled the *History of Slave Laborers in the Construction of the United States Capital*, the architectural historian in the Office of the Architect of the Capitol William C. Allen states that given the lack of biographical documentation of the contributions of the many slaves and freed Blacks who labored, he had only enough information to mention two men by name: the first was my ancestral grandfather, Capt. George Pointer, and the second was Philip Reid. In reflection, I have heard the name Philip Reid in association with American history but not ever a mention of Capt. George Pointer. The "only two" names resonated with me and added other questions to my list: Why couldn't history make room for both? Why weren't George Pointer's achievements elevated to the heights of other deserving Blacks in history? Clearly, he was a man unique in his time—perhaps too unique. He had proven an extraordinarily strong asset to George Washington and his Potomac Canal Company throughout its existence. He began his association with the Potomac Canal Company as a rented slave and general laborer; then he purchased his freedom and rose through the ranks to the highest level in the company. In 1816 when the Board of Directors of the company appointed him the superintendent engineer to direct a full multicultural workforce, he became the first Black man to rise in a white company nearly fifty years before slavery ended. Given the stereotypes of Blacks and the obvious challenges they faced, how could he be explained?

To understand my excitement over the publication of *Between Freedom and Equality: The History of an African American Family in Washington, DC,* you must understand my journey: a little about my childhood; about learning of my ancestral grandfather, Capt. George Pointer; and about helping introduce him to a country that should have known of him and his contributions long before now. My journey began in my early years. It was at St. Augustine Catholic School on V Street, Northwest, in DC that I was first enrolled in school. I was an extremely quiet child but very observant. I was there for three years, and the only memory I have is of a sister's daily beatings, which lasted until she tired. It seems that I had a problem with repeating the pledge of allegiance to the flag. I stood up, hand over heart, and just silently moved my lips. She watched me, and when she realized I was not being compliant, she made it her mission to have me speak it. Need I mention, I failed her class. Yes, even as a child I had serious issues with America.

In the late 1950s, my loving, hard-working mother uprooted my three sisters and me from Northwest Washington and moved us to Southeast Washington, where I enrolled in the District of Columbia's public school system. It became apparent very quickly that my three-year enrollment in Catholic school had advanced my learning years beyond those of my public school classmates, so I was insanely bored. My favorite classes were PE and, surprisingly, history.

American history, however, came from books written by white people about white superheroes and with only one insert listing their choice of Black achievers on one side of the page and a picture of raggedy Black slaves in cotton fields on the other side. This got old fast. This telling of history was repeated year after year throughout my schooling. It made me disinterested in American history as I marched to adulthood. This experience with American history did, however, greatly influence my stronger interest in world history, as I pursued truth, lesser recorded truths, or, more likely, truths of history. Today, in 2020, the study of American history should include the study of the building of America, adequately covering the history and contributions of African Americans, the hardships every person encountered, and the stories of those who impacted its success the most. Our history books, however, continue to be a prime example of whitewashed lies and purposeful omissions. More alarming is how the purposeful omission of African history also contributes to the challenge of instilling pride, self-esteem, and dignity in young African Americans. If you don't know where you've come from, it's more difficult to know where you're capable of going. Should this be an African American child's challenge?

Every handful of years since age twenty-five, I have had a fast moment of thought as to what my family tree would uncover if I researched it. In more recent years, I wondered if my family had ever been a cohesive, loving entity. I was extremely skeptical about what I would find before I even started. Much of this was due to the fractured dynamics of my extended family. My grandmother and grandfather had eleven children. While there was a resemblance of a familial support system, they often divided themselves into separate camps, over trivial matters and old hurts, with a few divides lasting a lifetime. Alcoholism, drug addiction, incarceration, and, surely, depression plagued more family members than I care to mention. With no father or male family role model and no example of family unity, I was deeply skeptical that I would find anything marginally positive from researching and constructing my family tree. Further, for some reason, I felt sure that my research would come to an end and hit a wall after discovering only three or four generations of family information. I since have learned from the research conducted and written about in this book, however, that the displacement of my family from our farm village and land on Broad Branch Road in Washington, DC, ultimately played a major role in the disruption within my family and the later conditions they found themselves in.

Early in 2012, I visited my best friend in the world and partner, Tanya Hardy. I listened as she spoke passionately about several friends' and associates' families, which she had researched and for whom she had developed family trees as a hobby. On that day, I casually mentioned my thoughts of researching my own tree. Before the final words had left my mouth, she paused and then lit up with questions while she opened her laptop. Thus, the journey began.

After three weeks of constant researching on numerous genealogy databases, we had populated nearly four generations of my family tree, and my enthusiasm was mounting. Yet I held my emotions at bay because my earlier skepticism still lingered. Shortly after these discoveries, Tanya and I received emails from Clara "Tiggy" Myrick Green and Barbara Torrey, two people we did not know, concerning our work on my family genealogy on Ancestry.com. The email I received stated that they had been looking for me and my family, and they asked if I knew that I had a famous ancestral grandfather who was born enslaved in 1773. I sat looking at the computer monitor in shock and disbelief. I read the email several times before thinking, "*My* family?" Could they be mistaken?

Tanya responded to the email and asked questions about this revelation, including how these two researchers had come upon this information. Their

responses made it clear that their information was truly legitimate. We celebrated the news and made plans to continue the conversation during lunch at
Tiggy's home. The chance that total strangers were able to locate and contact
me through a family tree on Ancestry.com was astonishing. To learn during
our conversation at lunch about my ancestral grandfather Capt. George
Pointer and about his accomplishments and contributions was very surprising. Furthermore, that he could have purchased his freedom and written an
eleven-page letter (see appendix 1) in perfect writing style and beautiful cal-
ligraphy was mind-blowing. When I asked Tiggy and Barbara why they were
attracted to researching George Pointer, they shared that finding his letter was
so amazing that it compelled them to find out more. As we looked through the
pages of research and primary sources they had that day, there was no doubt
in my mind that they had connected the dots and built a bridge between the
work that Tanya and I did reaching back into history and their work moving
forward from history. My skepticism slowly melted away.

The journey to discovering more about my family was enriched even further by learning Tiggy and Barbara felt confident that their research had revealed that the location of George Pointer's cabin was close by Tiggy's home.
After lunch they invited Tanya and me to take a walk with them down to the
cabin's remains. As we arrived at the site, I saw the remains of a stone chimney
as well as that of a stone powder magazine (a structure that once stored gunpowder). I gazed at the Potomac River from the site, and a sense of calm came
over me. I spanned the scene and noticed a structure rising out of the water.
As I walked toward the shore for a closer look, I realized it could have been
the remnants of the fish pots wall, mentioned in Pointer's letter, that he had
constructed to provide food for his family and to sell for profit at the market.
I saw the island where he planted his crops, and I marveled at how organized
he was in his planning. This elevated my respect for his genius. After working
all day, he could stand on the shore, enjoying the tranquil view, and listen to
the calming sounds of the water. He could see the fruits of his labor. This was
his sanctuary.

Our next trip with Tiggy and Barbara took us to Lafayette Park in the Chevy
Chase neighborhood of Washington, DC, to see the land where my great,
great, great-grandmother, Mary Harris, started the family farm. We walked
onto the land and stopped under a huge tree that had been rising there well
over a hundred years. I could envision my family living on this land they
owned, working the fields, and watching the younger ones run and play. The
image of two of those children growing into manhood and being of the first
to enlist in the US Colored Troops to fight for the freedom of their enslaved
brothers and sisters came to mind. A sense of pride once again swelled up in

me, but just as quickly I became saddened. This was ours. This could have still been our "home place," our "family village." My family could have continued to enjoyed unity, support, and prosperity had it not been taken from us. With the influence of a private development company, the city had taken it by eminent domain to build a school and a park as part of an established community for white people, as was way too common at the time. It was our land and should have stayed as such from the time it was acquired to the present.

So began my new friendship with Tiggy and Barbara. We had many more wonderfully engaging lunch meetings. We spent many hours reviewing research, studying documents at the National Archives' repositories in both Maryland and DC, and comparing notes during our research of George Pointer and his descendants. We traveled to libraries and museums to discover more information about my ancestors. At times when meeting to discuss findings, different points of view led to debates on the true perspectives. We always came away with a better understanding and looked forward to our next meeting. I am on a mission to be sure that my grandfather's story is told, and I want to gather as much information as I can to support the process of getting him into the history books and museums where he belongs.

Part of this journey also included attending lectures about the history of the Chevy Chase community in Washington, DC. One evening, Tanya and I attended a lecture about the African American community near Fort Reno at the old Reno School for Colored Children. During the lecture, the host recognized me as a descendant of the Harris and George Pointer families that owned land on what was now Lafayette Park in Chevy Chase. At the end of the evening, I was approached by a gentleman and his mother. His name was Tim Hannapel. As he introduced his mother, he was full of energy and excited about uncovering the truth about the land that many had never known to be occupied by the Harris and Pointer families. As he talked with me, he shared that he had been losing interest in history, but after hearing about the Harris family, Lafayette Park, and George Pointer, he was eager to learn more and help in whatever way he could. He asked if Tanya and I would meet him for lunch one day soon to talk more about the Lafayette Park community, where he grew up, so that he could learn about the families that had lived there.

We joined him for lunch a few weeks later. At the meeting he shared a booklet that was made when he was in high school. In the booklet was a picture of an old African American woman smoking a pipe and another sitting in front of an old house. Until meeting me and hearing my story, Tim was not sure who this woman may have been. After getting more information, he said he believed that picture was one of my great-great-grandmother, Mary Moten, and he was going to help me find proof of it. There were many times when I became tired on this journey. Tim proved to be a constant gust of optimism and a stabilizing voice of patience, a never-ending source of energy and hope. He would constantly bring new paths for us to travel on if a different one seemed blocked. My band of friends was growing at an amazing pace. I could not have felt more blessed.

When Tiggy and Barbara mentioned that they wanted to write a book about George Pointer, I was thrilled. This is what I had envisioned. This was the beginning of getting the word out about Capt. George Pointer. In one of our meetings, they mentioned a wax figure representing Pointer was at the Great Falls Park Visitor Center in Great Falls, Virginia, a national park across the Potomac River from where George Pointer lived and certainly along his route as he captained boats down the river. The wax figure was not formally identified as Pointer. Yet when the audio button at the exhibit was pressed, a male voice spoke excerpts from Pointer's letter.

The thought that my ancestral grandfather had an exhibit in the National Park Service's visitor center at Great Falls was exciting, and it more strongly confirmed to me that his story needed to be told. When Tanya and I arrived at the park and entered the center, I anxiously looked for the exhibit. As we approached the back of the museum area, we saw a large display with four wax figures. One was dressed as a white male surveyor, one as a white woman, and another as a white laborer. On the far right was an African American man dressed also as a laborer. There was no identifying signage about who these persons were. Tanya pushed the audio button, and each figure began to tell his or her story. When we got to the African American figure and the audio began, I was shocked at what I heard. It was the voice of a man telling about the work he was doing, and he spoke the exact words from the letter that Pointer had written to the Chesapeake and Ohio Canal's board members. It was very apparent that this wax figure was a representation of Capt. George Pointer.

Upon hearing the words being spoken, I had mixed feelings. My first feelings were of elevation and pride that he had accomplished so much and that his accomplishments were evidence that nothing could keep him buried. My frustration continued to build, however, because, once again, I was being presented with more questions—my "whys" and "why nots." Why did they have this nine-year-old exhibit with a nameless figure even though the Park Service knew very well that the African American wax figure was a representation of Capt. George Pointer? The evidence was in the audio it shared each time the button next to him was pushed. I decided that I would not let this continue, and I asked the Park Service for a meeting. When we went to meet with the rangers about the exhibit, they expressed that they already knew about Pointer and his contributions to the construction of the locks and other projects at the falls. When I confronted the visitor center's management about why Pointer remained nameless, I was met with silence.

Not too long after this visit to Great Falls, another meeting was scheduled at my request with three of the rangers, including management, to discuss the righting of the wrong of not identifying George Pointer in their museum. Barbara and Tanya accompanied me, and the meeting went well. The rangers agreed that some changes needed to be made and that George Pointer should be identified. A discussion was also held about having a plaque made to address the importance of his presence as the last superintendent engineer overseeing all work and labor for building the locks and the Potomac Canal. During the meeting, I also spoke about other changes that should be made, including moving the Pointer wax figure to its own space. More meetings were held, and tasks for the rangers were agreed on. Two of those tasks were to provide signage identifying Pointer in the museum and to dedicate a page to the story of George Pointer and his contributions on the National Park Service's Great Falls website. These were our wins on the journey with the Park Service. Signage is now in the Visitor Center's museum space that shares information about Pointer and a part of his letter. A page dedicated to the story of Capt. George Pointer and his life has been added to the National Park Service's Great Falls website, https://www.nps.gov/grfa/learn/historyculture/captain-george-pointer.htm. With the information that we provided and that they had in their archives, the rangers did a wonderful job of telling key aspects of George Pointer's story. I give them my greatest appreciation for their work to make sure his story was told. I still hope that eventually George Pointer is given an exhibit space dedicated to just him.

In the spring of 2018, I revisited the Pointer cabin site after two years. I became alarmed to discover that within that time the public had created bike paths and walking paths through the site. I knew something would have to be done immediately if anything was to be preserved. Dismayed over the abuse of this historic property, Barbara, Tiggy, Tim, and I contacted the Chesapeake and Ohio Canal National Historical Park, which was responsible for the Maryland side of Great Falls. We requested that the area be blocked off to prevent further destruction of the site and asked to meet with the people who could enact change. The Chesapeake and Ohio Canal National Historical Park organization arranged meetings to discuss what to do. After the meeting dates, as well as their participants, changed numerous times, we finally met in August 2018 at Lock House 6, which is near what we believe is the location of Pointer's cabin. Having requested the presence of specific members of the Chesapeake and Ohio Canal group, we had anticipated a large group for the discussion; however, only three of them attended. We shared the maps that

Barbara and Tiggy provided from their research showing two possible Pointer structures, one being the cabin and the other being the powder magazine. I expressed concern for preserving and protecting their remains and the possibility of getting funding to rebuild the cabin or a memorial for where the cabin was. I explained that the site had been overrun by the public and that I feared nothing would be left if another two years passed with no action.

As the meeting progressed, it became apparent that the team from Chesapeake and Ohio Canal National Historical Park was not there to support our efforts but to derail them. This extremely disappointing development took us completely by surprise since we were under the impression that they were aware of the research done to confirm this site. One of the participants, introduced as a park archaeologist, began the meeting by sharing some undated maps that he said were of the area in question. One map showed a large structure labeled "US Mill." As he spoke about the map, he said that Pointer's cabin and the powder magazine could not have been in the location we thought because the mill structure was there. However, I believe his map showed a structure farther down the river and closer to Georgetown. Our research identified the location of the cabin site to be up river, above the entrance to the feeder canal, and across from Snake Island on the Potomac. When the archaeologist finished insisting that his information was correct, I asked if I could have the maps since they were copies and not originals. I wanted to use them for my further research. I was told no. As an afterthought, I remembered reading about and seeing a map earlier of a large mill located farther down river nearer to Georgetown. The map was probably the same one the archaeologist showed us at the meeting.

The group then left the canal house to visit the location in question. When we arrived at the structure's remains, I asked the archaeologist to confirm what we believed was a powder magazine located on the site. He responded that he did not know what the structure was. Since my original request was to protect the remaining artifacts from damage and it was still an open question, I asked another ranger about roping off the area. She replied that roping off the area would interfere with the public's activities in the park. She did offer us the opportunity of being volunteers to protect the area by showing up every so often to observe how the area in question was used, though there was no discussion about what would happen if we reported more damage. That the rangers did not consider the preservation of this area, which we believe is the homestead of George Pointer, an important African American man and historic figure, as a priority due to other ongoing projects was shocking to me. Another "why?" and "why not?" were added to my list of questions.

Meanwhile, after sharing with my larger family my discovery of George Pointer and the Harris family's owning a farm on the land, which is now called

At the Pointer family gathering in 2015, Benjamin Magee and Brittany Jeffries hold the sign proclaiming the reunion. Photograph by Tanya Hardy.

Lafayette Park in Chevy Chase, my family agreed to form a committee to organize a family reunion in honor of those ancestors. Once we arrived at a reunion date—August 15, 2015—I visited the DC Department of Parks and Recreation to reserve the park's space for our event. They asked a couple of times if I was sure I wanted to have the reunion there. I was told the neighborhood was very particular about who used the park. I asked if the Park Service was responsible for distributing park permits, and they replied, yes. I shared that my family members were the original owners of that property before it was taken from them by eminent domain to build a planned park, a school, and an all-white community. Then the office was extremely helpful in making sure the reunion was able to happen at Lafayette Park and was a memorable occasion for everyone.

The day of the reunion proved to be a perfect one at Lafayette Park, with lots of sunshine and blue sky. We set up the chairs, tables, and grills. We posted signs and a large banner across the gazebo at the top of the hill. The families that usually visited the park on Saturdays with their children appeared quite curious about what we were doing. After all, this was considered a neighborhood playground and park, and we were not members of the neighborhood. We greeted the stares with a hello or a wave; slowly, some of the regulars asked what was going on. When they heard that this property used to be owned by our ancestors and this was the first time that we could come together on what used to be family land, the response was very supportive, and many congratulated us on celebrating a 242-year legacy. Barbara and Tiggy joined us for the day, and they spoke to our group about their research and how honored they were to be a part of this special day. Once again pride filled me as I reflected

Families descended from George Pointer gathered in 2015 for a reunion at Lafayette Elementary School Park, site of the farm of his granddaughter, Mary Ann Harris. Photograph by Tanya Hardy.

on the fact that this was the first time we had held a family reunion. I watched family members who had not seen each other in years arrive, give hugs, introduce new family members, and share the excitement of being together. We talked, we ate, we took pictures. The next day we held a family banquet to continue the celebration and to talk about plans for our next reunion. As we said our goodbyes and family members prepared to make their trips back home, I was pleased that the weekend was such a success. I hoped that this gathering would be the beginning of annual reunions and give us the opportunity to rebuild family connections that were lost after our homeplace was taken from us.

Over the past five years, I—along with the assistance of my "George Pointer team members" Tanya, Barbara, Tiggy, and Tim—have worked tirelessly to give George Pointer the notoriety he deserves. We have attended numerous meetings with District of Columbia councilmen and US congresswomen, sharing information and seeking support. I gave a lecture at the African American Civil War Museum about two of my ancestors who had enlisted and served in the US Colored Troops during the Civil War and who were descendants of George Pointer's. I shared my family's story at community meetings where we discussed changing the name of Lafayette Park to George Pointer or Pointer-Harris Park but settled with a change to Lafayette-Pointer Park. (I still question why the park's name could not be fully changed. I recently learned a little about Lafayette and his stand against slavery. He would have probably disallowed his name on a park that had disenfranchised African American families.) I also had the pleasure of sharing my story with elementary and high school audiences at Lafayette Elementary School and Woodrow Wilson High School.

Without Tim's help, consistent support, and encouragement, I would have given up. He was quick to take the lead in ensuring that I was able to speak with persons and organizations that could support my mission to make "Capt. George Pointer" a household name. When Barbara and Tiggy's hard work, persistence, and determination to get this book published was finally rewarded with a yes from Georgetown University Press, we all felt that victory was ours. Had it not been for their placing George Pointer's "hand" in mine, he would have still been unknown to me. Finally, without Tanya, my lifeline crutch and tireless warrior, I would have given up long ago. She was constantly conducting research, arranging meetings, encouraging me when I began to lose hope, and accompanying me to meetings and events. Her constant presence made this journey so much easier to bear.

The skepticism that had been lingering within me for so long is finally dissipating. As I think about the life of George Pointer, my only regret is that I did not know his story when I was younger. He was someone I could have embraced as a role model. I could have learned and applied powerful lessons from his life's story. The more I read and research about him, the more I realize that his is a universal story that must be shared. He was a man who had the fear of God in him. He was humble and patient and had a solid plan for living. George Pointer was also a family man who was confident in himself and brilliant in his execution of his work.

I still have work to do toward my mission. My next goal is to get Capt. George Pointer's amazing letter out of the National Archives and into the National Museum of African American History and Culture, where all can finally learn his story. I am confident that this too will become a reality.

—James Fisher, eighth-generation descendant of Capt. George Pointer, with Tanya Gaskins Hardy

# Foreword

*Between Freedom and Equality: The History of an African American Family in Washington, DC* is a remarkable story about a remarkable family history. It begins with an eleven-page letter written by the family patriarch, George Pointer, when he was fifty-five years old in 1829, to the board of directors of the Chesapeake and Ohio (C&O) Canal Company. Born in 1773 on a tobacco plantation, he was the property of William Wallace, as were eight other Black people. The farm was nine miles north of Georgetown and about twenty-seven miles north of George Washington's Mount Vernon, which was on the Virginia side of the Potomac River.

It was difficult to transport tobacco to the port of Georgetown, with its water "falls," some with a thirty-foot drop, so human chattel and horses were used to roll and pull barrels along land routes to the port. To solve the transport dilemma, George Washington and others in Maryland and Virginia established the Potomac Company as one of the first interstate commerce ventures in 1785. Its first directive was to grant slaveholders the right to rent their slaves to dig a canal near the Little Falls along the Potomac. Wallace rented out his thirteen-year-old slave, George, who wrote that "I at that period occupied the place where my little humble cottage now stands being given to me by the directors and company in 1787." He wrote the letter in 1829 to ask the board of the C&O Canal Company to preserve his home as it was digging the new canal near where the first dam in the Potomac had been built. His letter is preserved in the National Archives, but no answer is recorded.

When Washington was inaugurated in 1789, he gave up his post as president of the Potomac Company's board but kept his Potomac stocks. He had investments to protect.

Three years later, Pointer bought his freedom from Wallace. No manumission papers exist. Not long after he married Betty Townsend, who appears to have been a free woman, although she also had no manumission records; they had no marriage records either. Pointer now had the freedom to sell his labor for wages and even to own property, but lacking his "freedom papers" or "certificate of freedom," he could have been kidnapped back into slavery. The laws in Maryland and Virginia required freed slaves to leave sometimes, and freed Blacks never felt fully free, as kidnapping was a constant fear. George was listed in the 1800 census under the category "All the free Persons." Years later, at the inaugural ground breaking of the C&O Canal Company on July 4, 1828, Pointer was still working for Potomac Company in charge of assembling the company's boats.

The next year, 1829, he asked the company to "compensate . . . an aged and distressed family" and to "give me Some Little place adjacent to the new Canal, that they may upon it support themselves for the few days that they may have to breathe upon this earth—Which is but a few." No records exist of his and Betty's deaths. They may have been victims of the 1832 cholera epidemic.

The next generation of Pointers grew up amid whites who feared slave revolts. The New England Anti-Slavery Society (founded in Boston in 1831, the same year as Nat Turner's rebellion in Southampton, Virginia) proclaimed in 1834 that "the District of Columbia is a great market to which human flesh is duly sent for sale from neighboring states, and then sold again to supply the markets of the South." In Congress the first group of abolitionists elected to the US House of Representatives—Joshua Giddings of Ohio, Seth Gates of New York, William Slade of Vermont, and John Quincy Adams of Massachusetts—submitted several hundred thousand petitions from the residents of their states protesting slavery in the nation's capital. Soon Congress banned all antislavery discussion in its halls, banned abolitionist tracts from congressional mailing, and outlawed the DC Anti-Slavery Society.

The Pointers' elder daughter, Elizabeth, was visited by the sheriff of Montgomery County, Maryland, who was taking a census of those freed people deemed eligible for "the Removal of Colored People" to Africa provision of the American Colonization Society. Founded in 1816 by Robert Finley, John Randolph, Henry Clay, Daniel Webster, and others who signed the organization's constitution in Washington, the American Colonization Society promoted the colonization of free Blacks to Africa. Like Richard Allen and Absalom Jones, Black abolitionists in Philadelphia who knew the society viewed free Blacks as dangerous Blacks, Elizabeth had no interest in joining the exodus.

Her brother, William, and his wife, Ann, lived for a while in Georgetown but moved back to the family home five miles to the north. They felt safer there. But when he tried to follow in his father's footsteps to work at the C&O Canal Company, he was turned down. The fear of a Nat Turner–type

rebellion led the company to lean toward hiring Irish and German workers, some of whom they imported, and Blacks suffered from the racism of
whites who were old and new to America. The 1835 Snow Riots in the city,
although ignited by white Navy Yard workers, also made it difficult for free
Blacks. William was able to survive because he inherited his father's boat,
fishing pots, and garden. By selling fresh fish and vegetables, he would survive—that is, until the Potomac River flooded in 1843. Then he lost both
his father's home and his fishing boat and pots. The family soon moved to
Annapolis, Maryland. Fourteen years later their son William sought a new
freedom and joined the Maryland Thirtieth Regiment of the US Colored
Troops (USCT).

Their niece, Mary Ann, who had been living with the Pointers, did not join
them in Annapolis. She married Thomas Harris, a free Black man. When she
was pregnant with her first child, she wanted to ensure its freedom by obtaining a certificate of her freedom, and for this she had to have whites present
who would testify to her status. Her family settled in the far northwest side
of Washington, DC, in the 1840s on two acres of land called Dry Meadows
off Broad Branch Road in the neighborhood now called Chevy Chase. They
settled there around the time of another momentous event in the city, when
in 1848 abolitionists freed seventy-seven Washington slaves and spirited them
away on a boat named the *Pearl,* only to be stopped and the slaves recaptured.
The following year Congressman Abraham Lincoln of Illinois offered legislation to emancipate DC's slaves. It failed, and he left the matter alone until he
became president.

The Harrises' home off of Broad Branch Road became the center of the
extended Pointer family and for neighboring Blacks for the next three generations. They had eight children (a daughter Mary died when she was about nine
years old in 1850) who were supported by Thomas's work as a skilled laborer,
Mary Ann's as a seamstress, and the entire family's work on the family farm.
When their eldest, John, set out to work, he had to obtain his freedom papers near the time of Abraham Lincoln's first inauguration and the exodus of
Virginia and its southern neighbors from the Union to form the Confederacy.
Soon the Harris home would be surrounded by military forts, such as Fort
Stevens, Fort DeRussy, and Fort Reno, that were connected by Military Road
and were needed to protect the city.

John and his younger brother Joseph desperately wanted to join the Union
Army, but racial prejudice stood in their way. As they watched thousands of
young white men pass through the city on the way south, and others who were
wounded in Southern battlefields come to the city, their yearning to serve

only grew. Even though President Lincoln had emancipated enslaved Africans in the city on April 15, 1862, and the District failed to meet its quota of white recruits, it took Frederick Douglass to convince Lincoln to muster "Colored Regiments." The Harrises, it appears, had a family meeting, and soon John and Joseph went marching on with the District of Columbia's First Regiment USCT. Theirs is the story of Black men fighting for the right to fight and of Black men serving with dignity and honor. Theirs is the story of joining with other Black units to form the "African Brigade." John was wounded in the siege of Petersburg and left disabled, while his brother was still in the trenches in Petersburg. At the same time, their mother, father, and siblings were forced to leave their home in Washington as Gen. Jubal Early's rebel soldiers descended on Tenleytown in the northwestern part of the city. Their cousin William Pointer had joined the Maryland Thirtieth Regiment USCT and was fighting near Richmond, where the Union Army lost four thousand men in one day in what Ulysses S. Grant called one of the saddest days of the war. John, Joseph, and William returned home alive.

After the war, most of the Harris children had left the two-acre farm to raise their own families. Joseph, who was five years younger than John, single, and literate, moved to New York City, where he remained for two decades. John moved back to Georgetown and settled in the Black neighborhood called Herring Hill. Two decades later, his son, Louis, married Mary Estella and took the civil service exam, becoming only one of seventy Blacks working at the US Postal Service in 1893. Mary began work at the US Treasury Department. Both served in a segregated workforce, separated by screens and forced to use separate bathrooms and to sit in the rear of the cafeteria. They bought a house in Georgetown. Some years later after the death of Louis's father, Louis's mother moved in with them.

The family homesteads in Tenleytown, Reno, Georgetown, and Dry Meadows no longer exist. Black families and churches have moved, many due to some form of gentrification, and Black cemeteries have been relocated. But succeeding generations of the family still live in the area.

That is why this story is so important and so remarkable. It tells the story of the Black struggle for freedom and equality, using hard work as the measure of a person. Here also is the story of African Americans' service to the nation. Sons and grandsons went off to war, but while white union soldiers went to preserve their union and their own rights, the descendants of George Pointer went to attain and secure theirs. Like so many African Americans in Washington, succeeding generations of Pointers became public servants and worked for the federal government but still were denied equal rights. Thus, it is also the story of how hard work and patriotism were still not enough. Yet the family endured and maintained their dignity.

Barbara Boyle Torrey and Clara Myrick Green have thoroughly researched generations of Pointers and, by doing so, have documented the history of Black life in Washington over two centuries. This is a history of time at a particular time, of place at a particular place, of family through a particular family. It is the history of the arduous journey from slavery to freedom and the struggle to achieve equality. Torrey and Green provide us with a macro history of Washington through the micro history of generations of descendants of George Pointer. And by doing so, they give us the history of a people, the African American people in Washington, DC. Nothing could be finer.

—Maurice Jackson

# Acknowledgments

Our thanks go to Hope LeGro, our editor, who worked relentlessly on our manuscript; Elizabeth Crowley Webber of Georgetown University Press and Vicki Chamlee for shaping our manuscript; Caroline Green for reformatting the manuscript; Jane Levey, the managing editor of the *Washington History Journal*, who published our second article on George Pointer and recommended that we go to Georgetown University Press; James Fisher who is George Pointer's descendant; Tanya Hardy, who helped us make the connection between the eighteenth century and the twenty-first; and Tim Hannapel, whose enthusiasm kept everyone going.

We are indebted to two archivists, Al Laporta of St. John's Episcopal Church, Georgetown, DC, and Wayne Mori of St. Paul's Episcopal Cathedral, Buffalo, New York. Both were generous in supplying important material relating to George Pointer's great-grandson's work at their respective churches.

Many people helped us in supplying illustrations and in research libraries across the country: Patricia Abelard Anderson, Mike Copperthite, Rev. Sarah Duggin, Carlton Fletcher, C. R. Gibbs, Linda Gross, Laura Brower Hagood, Anne McDonough, JoEllen McKillop Dickie, Chelsea Morris, Kay Peterson, John Rutter, and many others.

For those who gave advice, comments, or forbearance: Carol Beehler, Greg Duncan, D. J. Jaffe, Faith Mitchell, Tim Smeeding, and Kay Toll.

Most important are our husbands, E. Fuller Torrey and Richard C. Green, who read multiple versions of this book, who climbed over rocks and ruins looking for George Pointer, and who encouraged us for years as we slowly pieced his story together.

BETWEEN FREEDOM AND EQUALITY

# Introduction

I was born in the year A.D. 1773. 11th of October in Frederick County Maryland.
I was born a slave and continued one for 19 years.
—CAPT. GEORGE POINTER

Thus begins a remarkable eleven-page letter of a man who spent his life working for George Washington's Potomac Company.[1] The company undertook one of the most ambitious river navigation projects in young America and was eventually bought by the Chesapeake and Ohio Canal Company. In 1829 when George Pointer was fifty-five years old, he wrote a letter to the company's board of directors asking the members to preserve his home during the construction of their new canal. To strengthen his petition, he recounted how he had risen from being an enslaved laborer to becoming a supervisory engineer in his nearly forty-year career with the Potomac Company.

Pointer lived on the banks of the Potomac River five miles north of Georgetown. We first learned about him while writing a local history, and after discovering his letter in the National Archives, we became intrigued about what happened to him. The Potomac Company's own records confirm almost every detail of his long letter, making George Pointer a unique narrator, not only of his own life but also of a compelling period in the history of the new republic.

Pointer's letter begins the story of six generations of his family, spanning almost two hundred years. This story was originally constructed on the scaffolding of the decennial censuses, but we slowly found much more data, including legal documents, newspaper articles, military records, and personal recollections. As we learned more about each generation, we began to recognize several themes that had not been visible at the beginning of the story. These themes have all been well described by researchers on African American history, but we had the advantage of observing them evolve over many generations of a single family.

## The Strength of Families and the Fragility of Their Freedom

An important theme throughout this story was the resilience of the Pointer families in every generation despite racism, wars, deadly epidemics, and economic collapses. The Pointer generations all lived in the shadows of American history, with racism casting the biggest shadow. It made George Pointer's freedom and that of his immediate descendants always fragile because they had no documents to certify their independence. As a result, they faced the dangers of being sold back into slavery at any time or being incarcerated for trivial reasons. The strength and stability of the family was the most important bulwark that all freed people had against natural threats and man-made disasters.

The stability of the Pointer families came in part from living in the same rural neighborhoods for generations. George Pointer's family and then his son's family lived in the same cottage for over fifty-six years and shared many of the same neighbors in an integrated area. After race riots in downtown Washington in 1835, Pointer's granddaughter, Mary Ann, and her husband settled in a rural area of the District as far away as they could get from the slave markets downtown without moving into the slave state of Maryland.

Eventually, the couple bought two acres of farmland in what is now Chevy Chase. Owning property meant that they and their descendants never had to move, and their farm became the center of the family for over eighty years. They were unusual because they bought their land at a time when only 9 percent of Black residents of the District owned property.

The Pointer descendants often had the same Black and white neighbors for many decades, and the stability of their integrated neighborhoods gave them some protection against the random racism of strangers. Their white neighbors were particularly important because many legal documents required white witnesses, so these neighbors guaranteed access to legal protection for the Pointer generations in the courts. In one case, years after George Pointer had died, his granddaughter needed a white witness to verify that she had been born free. Her witness was the son of Pointer's original slave owner who had been born the same year as Pointer, and the two boys had grown up together. Later as adults they had lived within two miles of each other and clearly had remained friends throughout their lives.

## Long Lives and Stable Marriages

The strength of the Pointer families was reinforced by their long lives. Because the rural areas where the Pointer generations lived were sparsely populated, they were less affected by infectious diseases that periodically ravaged the towns. Most of the Pointers in each generation who survived childhood illnesses lived much longer than was expected in the nineteenth century. They also had long and stable marriages: George Pointer was married for almost forty years, and his granddaughter was married for over fifty. Long lives and marriages continued into the later generations, building on their ancestors' strong foundations.

Long lives also mean that grandchildren would know their grandparents and that the lessons of their lives would accumulate over time. Living grandparents are an important source of physical and financial support for their families also. George Pointer raised his granddaughter, and when she became the matriarch of the family, she too helped raise several of her grandchildren. Long life does not guarantee stability and security in families, but longevity makes it more likely than when grandparents are unknown and when young parents die prematurely.

## Education, Work, and Migration

Another major theme of the story of the Pointer generations is the importance of education in their lives and how it affected their options for work. George Pointer's letter proves his literacy, and he had a reputation for being more literate than his supervisor. However, the lack of any schooling for Black children in rural areas before the Civil War meant that the next two Pointer generations could not read and write enough to describe themselves as literate in the censuses.

Following the Civil War, one of Reconstruction's greatest successes was the building of over four thousand schools for Black children in the South, including one near the Pointers' descendants in Chevy Chase. It brought about dramatic improvements in the lives of the fourth and fifth generations of the Pointers. Even though most of the Black schools were flimsy and overcrowded, a few years of schooling made important differences in the children's future.

In the fourth generation, the two unschooled brothers who lived in Georgetown spent their lives as a laborer and a driver, respectively, but the lives of their two literate brothers were transformed. Joseph Harris, who learned to read in the military, moved to New York City and became a Pullman Palace Car Company porter. Lorenzo Harris, who attended the little Reconstruction school near his family's farm, moved to Buffalo, where he was an Episcopal sexton in a major cathedral in western New York State. Not everyone who was literate migrated for better work, but those who did migrate were more likely to be literate.[2]

In the fifth generation of the family, every child was literate. Louis Harris, who grew up in Georgetown, became the first federal civil servant in his extended family, and his cousin William Moten became a prominent funeral director in Washington. William's brother, John A. Moten, was employed by the US National Park Service at Fort Reno Park.

In every generation, however, literacy had more influence on the working lives of the men than on their sisters. The girls had also attended the nearby schools, but with their more limited options, they never moved far away. Like their mothers and most Black women, they worked all their lives as housekeepers, cooks, or laundresses in their neighborhoods.

### The Displacement of Residents and the Segregation of Neighborhoods

Another theme that emerged from the story of the Pointer family is the gradual segregation in the twentieth century of what had been integrated neighborhoods in the eighteenth and nineteenth centuries. Integrated neighborhoods did not mean an absence of racism, of course, but they facilitated more interaction between Black and white families and their children. By the end of the nineteenth century, however, white urban dwellers looked for new housing in less crowded neighborhoods. They took the new streetcar lines out to the rural areas of the District, and the real estate barons of the Gilded Age soon followed them.

The developing neighborhood associations wanted more white schools to attract affluent home buyers and realized that they could solve two problems at once. They could use eminent domain, an English legal principle enshrined in the Constitution, to require families to sell their homes so that new schools could be built on their property. Subsequently, restricted covenants could be put into new housing contracts so that Black families could not buy new homes in their old neighborhood. This process occurred in major cities across the United States.

In Washington the deliberate segregation of neighborhoods affected the fourth, fifth, and sixth Pointer generations. Lafayette Elementary School was built on the ground that George Pointer's descendants had owned for over eighty years. Western High School (now Duke Ellington High School) in Georgetown was built on land where Lewis Harris in the fourth generation had rented. Alice Deal Middle School and Woodrow Wilson High School were built on the land that had belonged to fifth-generation William Moten and where his sister's family had rented a home. This strategy succeeded in replacing Black homes with white schools and gave the District its segregated neighborhoods.

The story of the Pointer generations is not typical of many African American families that had lived through the same tumultuous times of American history. George Pointer and his descendants were free much earlier than most African Americans. When Pointer bought his freedom in Montgomery County, Maryland, less than 2 percent of African Americans were freed, so he and his descendants had more than seventy years to learn the habits of freedom before most Black people were emancipated in 1863. Research suggests that it took two generations for Black Civil War veterans who were born enslaved to gain the same advantages in literacy, jobs, and education as those Black veterans who had been born free.[3]

The Pointer story is also not typical because some of Pointer's descendants had the security of owning their own property when so few Black families living in the District owned their homes. Furthermore, Pointer's descendants lived in Washington, DC, a unique town where racism was tempered by the many residents who came from northern and western states. Although there were lynchings in the surrounding counties, no known lynchings occurred in the District. The advantages of the Pointer generations, however, did not protect them from the relentless residential segregation of the early twentieth century. In that way the lives of later generations were similar to those of most other African Americans in the country.

Fortunately, Ancestry.com helped us make the final leap from the sixth generation to the present. James Fisher, an eighth-generation descendant of George Pointer's, and his partner Tanya Hardy were reaching back in history as we were reaching forward. They were as surprised to find us as we were to meet them. In August 2015, they organized the first reunion of George and Elizabeth Pointer's descendants on the grounds of Lafayette Elementary School in Chevy Chase, land that had once belonged to their ancestors. The following year James, Tanya, and other family members were recognized at a Historical Society of Washington, DC, reception.

This story owes James and Tanya a great deal. They lobbied the National Park Service to recognize George Pointer's role in the building of the Potomac Company's Canal, and they have lobbied to rename the Lafayette School Park after their accomplished ancestor. Most important, they have worked hard to link the present history of the current Pointer descendants to their past, and they are preserving both for the future.

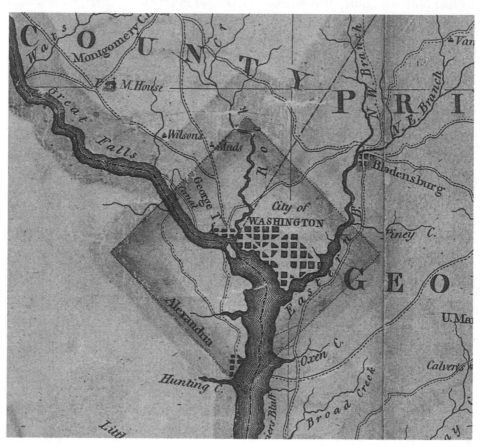

Detail from a map of the Territory of Columbia, 1794. The Potomac Canal around Little Falls is marked "canal" just northwest of Georgetown ("George T" on the map). George Pointer was born near the Presbyterian Meeting House, marked "PM House" on the upper left corner of the map. Courtesy of Library of Congress, Geography and Map Division.

# 1

## From Slavery to Freedom

Three years before the Declaration of Independence, George Pointer was born enslaved on a tobacco plantation owned by William Wallace. The Wallace farm was near the banks of the Potomac River in a rural area that the British called the Lower Potomac Hundred. Only two hundred and twenty families lived in the entire area, which stretched from the little port of Georgetown to a crossroads named Rockville, eighteen miles to the north. William Wallace was typical of prosperous white farmers at the time: he owned nine slaves and had six sons and two daughters of his own. One of his sons was born the same year as Pointer, and the two boys would remain friends for the rest of their lives.[1]

No records of George Pointer's parents or of his early childhood exist. Censuses and tax records asked only how many enslaved people were in a household. Moreover, when slaves were mentioned in family records, usually only a first name was used. Two sources of circumstantial evidence, which are discussed later, tie William Wallace to George Pointer. Since the Wallaces were a prominent family in colonial Maryland's Frederick County, the conditions of Pointer's early childhood can be inferred from what is known about his place of birth.

Before the Revolutionary War, homes of tobacco farmers in this rural area of Maryland were usually not much more than two rooms with a sloped-roof front porch and a sleeping loft where often their white children and the slaves would sleep. The homes were made of logs and had a large stone fireplace at one end that was used for both warmth and cooking. The Wallace land grant was called Brothers' Industry, and its boundaries were between the Potomac River and a dirt road, later called River Road, that ran south to the port of Georgetown.[2]

In the eighteenth century, no formal schools existed in rural Maryland, but families would sometimes hire private tutors for their children. The Wallace family must have arranged for their children's education because they were literate as adults. Pointer also learned to read and write since he was later described as being more literate than his British employer, and the long letter he wrote late in life verified it.[3] He may have learned to read as another Maryland slave did: Frederick Douglass made "friends of all the little white boys" and wrote, "As many of these as I could, I converted into teachers."[4]

On Sundays, enslaved people such as George Pointer often accompanied their owners to church but sat in a segregated gallery. In 1746 the Wallace family had donated the northeast corner of their land to a Presbyterian meetinghouse, which was located at the crossroads now called Potomac. Itinerant ministers preached universal freedom and the abolition of slavery, but they also warned that the process should be slow. Slaves needed to have their souls saved first, and then they needed to learn a trade, both of which could take a lifetime.[5]

When Pointer was born, tobacco was Maryland's major cash crop and most important export; it was even a common currency that could be used to barter or pay debts and taxes. It was a labor-intensive crop, and although Maryland had an abundance of fertile land, it had a shortage of cheap labor. Tobacco growers such as the Wallace family needed all of their slaves to work, both the adults and the children.[6]

As a child George Pointer presumably worked in the tobacco fields. Josiah Henson, an enslaved man who grew up on a Maryland farm about four miles northeast of the Wallace home, described that work: "My earliest employments were, to carry buckets of water to the men at work, to hold a horse-plough, used for weeding, . . . and as I grew older and taller, to take care of master's saddle-horse. . . . In ordinary times we had two regular meals in a day; . . . In harvest season we had three. . . . Our dress for the children, nothing but a shirt . . . and a pair of coarse shoes once a year."[7]

Tobacco dominated the lives of rural farmers and their slaves before the American Revolution. They had to clear patches of land from the dense

View of the port of Georgetown, circa 1795, looking up the Potomac River. Drawing by George Isham Parkyns (1750–1820). Courtesy of Library of Congress, Prints and Photographs Division.

vegetation and then plant tobacco, weed the fields, harvest the crop, and dry the leaves in the barns. They also had to fell trees to build the barrels that held up to a thousand pounds of tobacco and then transport them to the closest port to be shipped to the nicotine-addicted Europeans.[8]

The closest port to the Wallace farm was Georgetown, which was nine miles down the Potomac River. George Washington once called Georgetown "the greatest tobacco market in Maryland if not the Union."[9] Although the Wallaces lived near the Potomac River, they could not use it to transport the harvest to market because the Little Falls of the Potomac area was located between their farm and the port. They were the last falls on the river as it descends to the Chesapeake Bay, and they were a drop of thirty-two feet through a narrow gorge filled with boulders. A year's tobacco harvest could be lost in minutes going through the falls, so tobacco was usually transported overland. Enslaved people and horses would roll the large barrels of dried tobacco on the rutted and dusty "rolling roads" to the port of Georgetown, where they were loaded on oceangoing vessels.[10]

The many falls on the Potomac River frustrated more than just the Wallace family and their farming neighbors. Georgetown merchants considered the falls the major obstacles to expanding trade with the western frontier. Georgetown was the farthest inland seaport in the mid-Atlantic colonies, and if navigation around the falls could be improved, the town's commercial influence would be extended hundreds of miles inland. In the eighteenth century, the thriving port was in competition with Baltimore for the frontier trade, and to compete with Baltimore, which had better roads, the Georgetown merchants needed a more navigable river.[11]

## The Formation of the Potomac Company

The falls on the Potomac also posed a practical challenge to property owners such as George Washington. Although he lived at Mount Vernon, eighteen miles downriver from Georgetown, he also owned property above the falls on the river. In the 1750s, during the French and Indian War, he had acquired land near the headwaters of the Potomac River in what is now West Virginia and Pennsylvania. It was good land for farming but too remote from markets to be profitable unless the river could be improved. In 1770 Washington visited his frontier property, and when he returned to Mount Vernon, he wrote his good friend Thomas Johnson about forming a company to open "the inland navigation of the Potowmack.... That no person concerned in this event wishes to see an undertaking of the sort go forward with more sincerity and ardor than I do, I can truly assure you."[12]

Improving the navigation of the Potomac River would be a passion of Washington's for the rest of his life, and solving the problem would dominate the rest of George Pointer's life. In 1772 Washington persuaded the Virginia House of Burgesses to publicly support improvements to the Potomac River's navigation. However, the Maryland legislature had jurisdiction over the river, and their delegates were preoccupied by the storms of revolution. Washington eventually abandoned the idea of obtaining public support for improving the Potomac and instead invested some of his own money along with that of other private entrepreneurs to build a canal around the Little Falls. Soon afterward, however, he assumed command of the Continental Army, and the American Revolution eclipsed his interest in the Potomac River for the next seven years.[13]

In 1783 after the war ended, Washington returned to his neglected plantation at Mount Vernon, and within months he was again thinking about his frontier property and the challenges of navigation on the Potomac. He took another trip to his property at its headwaters, and when he returned, he wrote a letter to the governor of Virginia, again extolling the advantages of improving the navigation of the Potomac. With the finesse of an experienced lobbyist, he also included a bill he had drafted for the governor's consideration.[14]

The historian Joel Achenbach notes that "Washington's idea about the natural superiority of the Potomac as a highway to the frontier had grown into something like a faith. He was prepared to gamble a great deal on this river—his time, his money, his reputation."[15] Washington also knew that without improving the rivers on the East Coast, eastern merchants would forfeit the frontier trade.

In 1785 Washington invited Virginia and Maryland state delegates to Mount Vernon to discuss improving the navigation of the Potomac River. The resulting Mount Vernon Compact established the Potomac Company, funded by Maryland and Virginia and by private shareholders. It was the first interstate commerce agreement in the new United States and was signed before the new country's Constitution was written. In May 1785, George Washington joined fifty-six shareholders at the company's first meeting, where he was elected president of the five-person board. The other board members were all his good friends, including Thomas Johnson and Thomas Sim Lee (Maryland's first and second governors); and George Gilpin, a well-known surveyor in Virginia. The fifth board member was Col. John Fitzgerald, Washington's aide de camp during the Revolutionary War.[16]

One of the first actions the Potomac Company's board of directors took in October 1785 was to authorize the renting of enslaved people from local slaveholders to begin digging a canal around the Little Falls on the river. Per the recorded notes of a board meeting, "It was ordered that one hundred good and ableworking Negroes should be hired for the use of the Company for each of whom there should be an Allowance of twenty Pounds; Virg[ini]a Currency, also cloath them and pay their Levies and furnish them with Rations . . . and a sufficiency of Bread each Day and also a reasonable quantity of Spirits when Necessary."[17]

The Potomac Company's recruitment of slaveholders willing to rent out their slaves went too slowly that first year. Therefore, at the end of the harvest in October the following year, the board of directors again placed an advertisement for the rental of enslaved laborers at an increased "rent." They offered the slave owners $5.32 a month for an enslaved man without skills and 25 percent more for "experienced" workers. Today, these wages would be worth approximately $100 to $125.[18] George Pointer was thirteen years old when he became one of the first to be rented to the Potomac Company.[19]

There is no record of what Pointer looked like, but historical data provides some clues. At the beginning of the nineteenth century, young male slaves who were born in Maryland were about five feet tall at age thirteen. Those born enslaved in rural areas were a little taller than those born in urban areas because they had more access to food and less exposure to disease. By the time enslaved males were twenty-one years old, they were about five foot seven, within an inch of the height of white men the same age born in rural areas.[20] That is simply an average, however; some people, such as the six-foot-four George Washington, were much taller. Whatever his height, Pointer must have been unusually strong based on his later descriptions of years of cutting and hauling heavy rocks for the Potomac Company.

Maryland's rural economy, which had been primarily based on tobacco before the American Revolution, expanded rapidly after the war into food crops, which were less demanding. As a result, the demand for farm labor became more seasonal, and the rental of slaves once the harvest was completed became more common.[21] Meanwhile, the Maryland government suspected that renting out enslaved people would ultimately undermine the institution of slavery, and in 1787 legislators enacted a new law to curb it. The new law, however, was too weak and unenforceable to make a difference to slave owners such as William Wallace, and many simply ignored it.[22]

The Potomac Company gave thirteen-year-old George Pointer a place to live, which Pointer mentioned in his letter many years later: "I at that period occupied the place where my Little humble cottage now stands it Being given to me by the Directors and Company in 1787."[23] Later company reports refer to his cottage and describe its approximate location. An 1820 report to the Potomac Company mentions "clearing out a considerable portion of

The stone structure in the foreground is what remains of the eighteenth-century US powder magazine, which overlooks the rubble dam that extends into the Potomac River. It is located just north of the lockhouse at Lock 6 of the Chesapeake and Ohio Canal. Photo by Clara Myrick Green.

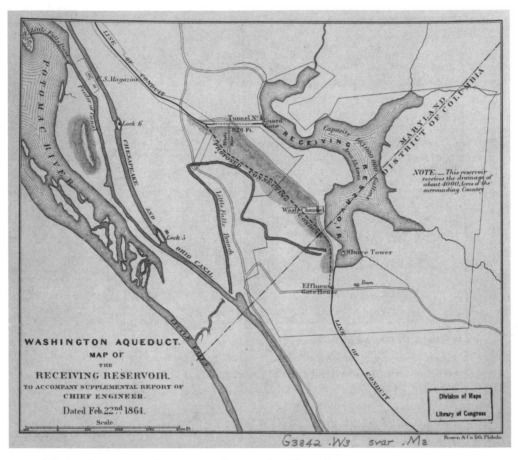

G3842 .W3 svar .Ma

Map of the Washington aqueduct in 1864, showing the US powder
magazine, which is marked on the on the upper left corner of the map.
Courtesy of Library of Congress, Geography and Map Division.

the Canal—rebuilding from the foundation the tumbling dam by Poynters house."[24] The tumbling dam, also called the rubble dam, was the first dam on the Potomac, funneling river water into the mouth of the Little Falls canal. It still exists today near Lock 6 of the Chesapeake & Ohio Canal, whose company succeeded the Potomac Company.

An 1843 flood report by the C&O Canal Company also referred to large breaches near the powder magazine and the dam "near Pointer's."[25] The magazine was a stone structure where the canal company stored gunpowder, which is both dangerous and was then very expensive. On July 3, 1787, a formal report was made that some of it had been stolen; thus, the "humble cottage" that the Potomac Company gave Pointer that same year likely then also served as a guard post for the gunpowder at night.[26] The powder magazine is shown on early nineteenth-century maps overlooking the dam and still exists today.

The building of a canal around the Little Falls was a much bigger challenge than either George Washington or the other board members of the Potomac Company had initially realized. Three canal locks had to be built so that boats could both descend and ascend the thirty-two-foot drop in the river and do so smoothly without losing their cargo. The problem was that no canal locks

Postcard of a painting of George Washington at Great Falls titled *Diorama of George Washington Inspecting Construction of the Potomac River Canal* (published circa 1958). Reprinted with permission of Hagley Museum and Library in Delaware.

had been built in North America. Diagrams of locks drawn by European engineers in England and France had already circulated in America, and on paper they looked straightforward. Perhaps after winning the Revolutionary War against the most powerful nation in the world, everything looked possible to the newly independent Americans.[27]

The Potomac Company's board of directors met regularly in the spring, summer, and fall, and members used the meetings to inspect the progress being made on the construction of the canal.[28] George Pointer described the visits in his letter written over thirty years later: "Yearly in the month of October General Washington would come to view the progress of the work, and well I recollect that at every squad of workmen he passed he would give a dollar to."[29]

In 1787 George Washington went to Philadelphia to attend a convention that was drafting a constitution for the new country. Initially, his election as the president of the convention did not interfere with his presiding at the regular board meetings of the Potomac Company, but his subsequent election as the first president of the United States changed everything. After his inauguration in 1789 in New York City, he stepped down as president of the board, but he kept his Potomac Company stock. His retention of the stock presented a potential financial conflict of interest in his role as president of the United States, but in 1789 the new government had bigger things to worry about.[30]

Survey of the Upper Potomac River

Washington left the Potomac Company's board in the hands of his friends. In July 1789, Colonel Gilpin, the Virginian surveyor and board member, led the first complete survey of the upper Potomac River. The 218-mile trip on the under-charted river would include many rapids and falls. Gilpin was joined by the company's new Scottish chief engineer, and because it was going to be a difficult trip, the engineer presumably ordered those who were his most reliable employees to join them.[31] And that is how sixteen-year-old George Pointer took the longest trip of his young life. "The chief engineer as well as I can recollect was Mr. John Smith from Scotland," Pointer wrote, "whom General Washington as I learnt employed to explore the route of the Potomack Canal, it fell to my Lot to be his servant during the period of the Exploration, as well as I can recollect Col. Gilpen of Alexandria was one of the directors."[32]

The survey began at the headwaters of the Savage River, located in what is now West Virginia. A hundred years earlier, Algonquian people had been living on the shores of the upper river, but by the time the survey team passed, their villages were deserted. Their presence still lingered, however, in the name they had given the river. Roughly translated, the Algonquian word "Potomac" means "trading place" and was spelled as many different ways as there are letters in the name.[33]

The survey team covered about four miles a day, measuring precisely both the distance and the 1,160-foot drop in the river before it reached the tidewater at Georgetown. The team's survey notes recorded the few farms along the banks of the river and the occasional small settlements, such as Fort Cumberland, Maryland. Between the river's headwaters and the Great Falls, the team had carefully written thirty-five entries in the survey notes.[34]

At Great Falls, the survey team might have paused to consider what it was proposing to do. The Great Falls are seventy-six feet high, and the locks would have to be built into the solid rock walls lining the river. The Potomac Company was not only going to build the first major canal locks built in the United States but also going to attempt the largest engineering project in North America.[35] But if there were any doubts about the undertaking, they were not recorded in the survey notes.

Below the Great Falls, the river enters the Potomac Gorge, which stretches eleven miles down to the Little Falls. The gorge has a wide variety of plants and animals that thrive in this boundary between the Piedmont plateau and the coastal plains. The survey team made three more entries before reaching the bottom of the Little Falls, five miles north of Georgetown.[36]

In 1792 the Potomac Company labor force varied from 60 men in the slower winter months to 170 during the summer. Many of the workers were indentured immigrants; enslaved men were less than 20 percent of the company's labor force despite attempts to hire more. Most of the slaves were working at the Little Falls that year, but a few had been shifted upstream to the more formidable challenges at the Great Falls.[37]

The 1792 company payroll for the Great Falls construction site listed the first names of six enslaved men with the names of their owners.[38] Two of them were named George despite that at the time less than half of the slaves in Maryland bore Anglo-American names, and George was not one of the most popular.[39] The two slaves named George were distinguished in the payrolls by the tone of their skin. One was named simply George, and the other one was called Yellow George, which meant that he was of mixed race, a rarity at the time for the enslaved. Though we cannot definitively say which man was George Pointer, it is possible to draw a reasonable conclusion. The 1755 Maryland colonial census distinguished slaves and free Black people by age and whether they were "mulatto" or "Negro"; it described as mulatto 92 percent of young free Black people in Frederick County but only 0.4 percent of the young people who were enslaved. The discrepancy between the two is because enslaved people who were biracial were much more likely to be manumitted than Negro slaves.[40]

According to his letter, Pointer was manumitted at age nineteen sometime between October 1792 and October 1793, and his manumission is strong circumstantial evidence that he was of mixed race. Additional evidence includes the 1820 census, which described George Pointer as white; the 1850 census, which described his granddaughter as mulatto; and Civil War military records, which described his grandson and great-grandson as having light skin tones. Therefore, George Pointer was likely the Yellow George on the Potomac Company's 1792 payroll whose owner was listed as William Wallis (another way to spell Wallace in the eighteenth century).[41] Moreover, years after George Pointer died in the nineteenth century, William Wallace's white son, who was born in the same year as Pointer, played a critical role in the support of Pointer's granddaughter.[42]

Buying Freedom

As he said in the letter that he wrote at the end of his life, George Pointer bought his freedom for $300: "I had the good fortune to get in the good graces of my master the engineer and the Company, having been well recommended by the engineer and directors for the faithful Services rendered them by me, my master Told me, that if I would pay him 300$ In a given time that I should be my Own man, which I did out of the Hard earnings I Received from the company."[43]

Three hundred dollars was the market rate for a young enslaved slave male in Maryland between 1787 and 1809, an amount that would be worth about $7,000 in today's purchasing power.[44] Despite manumitting George Pointer, William Wallace continued to buy and own slaves for the rest of his life.[45] In 1790 he owned nine enslaved people, and ten years later, despite freeing George Pointer, Wallace had fourteen. His wealthy neighbors—the Magruders, the Belts, and the Brookes—were also slave owners; county records show that they occasionally sold slaves, but there are no records of them manumitting any. Thus, the manumission of George Pointer at the age of nineteen was aberrant given the norms of Wallace's neighbors, but it was not uneconomic given the calculus of slavery.[46]

A number of eighteenth- and nineteenth-century observers have suggested that one of the main reasons for permitting manumission was that the owner was related to the freed slave. Maryland law, which was based on the Roman principle of *partus sequitur ventre* (the child follows the mother), decreed that the enslaved status of the mother alone determined the status of her child. Therefore, Pointer's mother was enslaved, and if he was biracial, his father must have been a white man. Pointer was conceived at the end of the 1772–73 winter holiday season, and although proximity may suggest his paternity, visiting male relatives and neighbors during the holidays frustrate the identification of any specific male as his father.[47]

George Pointer was born in Frederick County, Maryland, but in 1776 when the large county was divided into three smaller ones, the Wallace farm became part of the newly created Montgomery County. In 1793 when George Pointer was manumitted, less than 2 percent of the county's population were free Black people. Owners were required to register manumissions in the county courthouse in Rockville, about nine miles northeast of the Wallace farm. After registration, the former slave was issued a legal certificate of freedom with his or her name, age, physical characteristics, and status at birth, as well as the name of his or her former owner. Freed slaves were required to carry the certificate at all times to prove that they had been freed.[48]

Between 1790 and 1795, the Montgomery County Courthouse, which was in the Hungerford Tavern in Rockville, documented the sale of 103 enslaved people. It also issued ninety-one certificates of freedom, but none of them was for George Pointer.[49] Slave owners such as Wallace had two economic incentives to not register a manumission. Maryland required that they post a bond to cover any public costs a freed slave might incur, so the owner saved the cost of bond if he did not document the manumission. In addition, Maryland actively discouraged slave owners from manumitting slaves by allowing any creditor of an owner's to halt the process until the owner repaid his debts. Thus, if Wallace had outstanding debts when he freed George Pointer, he may not have wanted to confront his creditors before his loans came due.[50]

In 1793 the lack of formal documentation of Pointer's manumission, however, would have practical consequences in Montgomery County, where over 98 percent of the Black population was enslaved. In the same year that Pointer was freed, the US Congress passed the first Fugitive Slave Act, which allowed owners to pursue runaway slaves across state lines. This provided an incentive for unscrupulous men to kidnap undocumented freed people and sell them back into slavery. A reasonable assumption of white people meeting a young Black man was that he was enslaved, and if he was unaccompanied and without documentation, they might also assume he was a fugitive. Lacking a certificate of freedom made Pointer especially vulnerable to kidnapping. Although in Maryland the racial laws were not strictly enforced, that they could be applied without warning created a permanent risk for all undocumented freed people in a slave state.[51]

In the eighteenth century, many enslaved people did not have last names, and when they were freed, some simply used the word "free" in front of their names. In fact, in the 1800 census, two neighbors of the Pointer family were named Free Hannah and Free Toby. At the end of the eighteenth century, however, freed slaves in Maryland began to baptize themselves with surnames as they entered their new life of freedom. Although a few newly freed people gave themselves their former owners' names, over 90 percent understandably gave themselves different names.[52]

There is no obvious reason why the young George chose Pointer for his last name at the end of the eighteenth century. The surname was first used in early thirteenth-century England to refer to a person who made cords that fastened clothing, but by the eighteenth century it also referred to indicators of time or place. The few people named Pointer (also spelled Poynter) in the United States were mostly white and living in various parts of the south, including southern Virginia, North Carolina, and Georgia. No Pointers, either Black or white, were recorded as living in Maryland in the eighteenth century.[53]

Shortly after George Pointer bought his freedom, he married a woman named Betty Townsend. There is no evidence of her origins. She probably was free because she already had a last name, but no manumission record for Betty Townsend is in the Montgomery County Courthouse or in other records in Maryland or the District of Columbia. However, as George Pointer had worked the full length of the upper Potomac River by the time he was freed, he could have met his wife almost anywhere. And given that George Pointer was likely biracial, she probably was as well, since at that time over 80 percent of men of mixed race married women who were like them.[54]

No marriage record for the Pointers exists because at the time marriages among Black people, both slave and free, were de facto rather than de jure.[55] George Pointer's wife is referred to as Betty on the Potomac Company payrolls that recorded her wages for boarding Black laborers, and she was named Elizabeth Townsend in an 1838 legal document in the DC Court. By 1793, George and Betty Pointer had their first child and named her Elizabeth.[56]

In the same year that William Wallace gave George Pointer his freedom, he also gave some land to his own son, Charles, who was Pointer's age. The land was about two miles south of the Wallace farm and two miles north of Pointer's cottage; it originally belonged to the Magruders, who had been neighbors of the Wallace family for almost a century. Major Magruder had recently died, and perhaps William Wallace was helping his friend's widow if she needed money. Presumably he gave the land to Charles since being the middle son, he would not inherit his father's farm.[57]

Charles Wallace and George Pointer were two young men of different races and circumstances who had grown up together on the same farm. George Pointer would have three children and at least four grandchildren before he died. Charles Wallace would be a farmer for the rest of his life, and family histories and official censuses showed that he never married.[58] Yet many years later, he would play a seminal role in the life of Pointer's descendants.

George Pointer would spend the rest of his life working for the Potomac Company, building the first major river navigation system in North America. One historian described this project as heroic: "The locks constructed at Great Falls were the engineering feat of the eighteenth century and were described in every scientific publication in the civilized world."[59] George Washington, who was usually quite understated, called it "a business of great magnitude," and for George Pointer, it was the opportunity of a lifetime.[60]

Plan of the city of Washington, Territory of Columbia, 1819, in an engraving by W. H. & D. Lizars, Edin'r. Courtesy of Library of Congress, Geography and Map Division.

# 2

## The Risks of Freedom in a Slave State

George Pointer's new freedom in 1793 expanded the boundaries of his life, but it did not remove them. As a freed man, he could now keep his wages and own property. At the same time, however, his freedom was restricted. He could not own a dog or a gun without a special license. In Montgomery County, Maryland, he was prohibited from attending large meetings that were led by Black people, and after the turn of the century in Washington, DC, he needed a special permit to pick blackberries. Such racial laws created a cramped corner for the lives of free Black people, but at least they did not have to share that corner with an owner.[1]

In the nineteenth century, Maryland was considered a racial "middle ground" between the northern free states and the deep southern slave states.[2] However, in the eighteenth century, when George Pointer bought his freedom, Maryland shared the characteristics of the other states in the Deep South. Enslaved people were a third of its population, but free Black people were less than 2 percent. As the populations of both the enslaved and freed people grew in Maryland in the nineteenth century, the number of racial laws controlling their lives increased there as well as throughout the South.[3]

By the first decades of the nineteenth century, Maryland and the District of Columbia had so many racial laws that some were not enforceable given the limited resources of local governments. One example was an 1832 Maryland law that required former slaves to leave the state after manumission unless white people would testify annually to their good behavior. This law appears to have been enforced only once before the Civil War. Free Black people in Maryland, however, had to live with the constant risk of the random enforcement of obscure laws.[4]

In 1817 Jesse Torrey, a Philadelphia abolitionist, estimated that several thousand free Black people had been kidnapped and resold into slavery in southern states: "They [kidnappers] have lately invented a method of attaining their objects, through the instrumentality of the laws: —Having selected a suitable free coloured person, to make a *pitch* upon, the *conjuring* kidnapper employs a confederate, to ascertain the distinguishing marks of his body, and then claims and obtains him as a slave, before a magistrate, by describing those marks, and proving the truth of his assertions."[5]

The risk of kidnapping meant every free Black person who lived in a slave state had to have white patrons who could vouch for their freedom. Fortunately, Pointer had lived for many years near several white families whose members could testify that he was free. He was also respected by the white men who employed him, and they would presumably have also testified on his behalf.[6]

In 1796 the Potomac Company made twenty-two-year-old George Pointer a supervisor of five boats that transported chiseled stone blocks to Great Falls from the Seneca quarry, eight miles upriver in Montgomery County, Maryland. As he wrote, "I was Directed by him [Captain Meyers, the engineer] to take charge of five Boats that was to run the free stone from Seneca to the great falls From day to day for the use of the locks; which duty it was well known I Executed faithfully and to the Satisfaction of Capt. Meyers and the company."[7]

By 1798 the Potomac Company had not completed the locks, but it had built a temporary machine to lower cargo from boats at the top of the Great Falls to the bottom of the falls, seventy-six feet below. The cargo could then be reloaded into the boats to be shipped downriver to Georgetown. George Pointer described it: "In the meantime a machine was got under way to lower the flour down for the boats to take it down as the Locks was not finished. . . . Other produce came down so profusely, that the company thought it expedient that pilots should be chosen to carry the western boats down, four was chosen and among them was your petitioners humble Servant."[8]

In his first term as president, George Washington could not follow the Potomac Canal Company's business closely no matter how important he thought it was. The demands of governing a new country where every action became a precedent for the future was more than a full-time job. By his second term, however,

View of the locks at Great Falls, Virginia, in the 1790s. Painting by William H. Bond, *National Geographic*, June 1987. Reprinted with permission from National Geographic Society.

Washington resumed writing letters to his friends about the company's business. Perhaps he found the challenges of the Potomac Company more concrete and satisfying than the complex problems of a new democracy.[9]

In 1797, after completing his second presidential term and retiring from politics, Washington again began attending the Potomac Company's shareholders' meetings. The company was not doing well financially, and in May 1798 he gave it a sizable loan of $3,498 (approximately $70,000 in today's dollars).[10] He also updated his will, bequeathing his shares of the company to "the Endowment of a university to be established within the limits of the District of Columbia under the auspices of the general government."[11] The eventual bankruptcy of the Potomac Company meant his bequest was never used, but it was testimony of his continued optimism in the fortunes of the company.

Washington missed the shareholders' meeting in December 1798, and his shares were voted by proxy. On February 22, 1799, he attended a celebration of his birthday at the Union Hotel in Georgetown at Bridge and Twenty-Ninth Streets, Northwest (today Bridge Street is M Street). That December he died at home at the age of sixty-seven.[12] The locks at Great Falls were officially opened three years later. George Pointer was twenty-six when Washington died, and he would continue working for the Potomac Company for another thirty years.

In 1800 George Pointer appeared for the first time in the decennial population census as Geo. Pointer under the category "All the free Persons." The four other people in his household were not listed by age or gender, but they were almost certainly his wife, Betty, and their three children. The Pointer household appeared in the Georgetown section of the District of Columbia census; however, all the evidence suggests that their cottage was really in Maryland, less than a mile from a poorly marked boundary. The census taker's geographical error made little difference legally since the land that had been donated by Maryland and Virginia to create the District continued to be governed by the laws of the donor states.[13]

Since both Maryland and Virginia were concerned about slaves using the Potomac River to run away, they required all free Black people living along the river to have a certificate of freedom. Fortunately for Pointer, who had no certificate, the law was rarely enforced. Although he had worked on the canal for over ten years and must have been well known by the people who lived near the river, he would have been vulnerable to the suspicions of strangers.[14]

## The Pointers' Neighborhood

In 1800 a mix of people lived along the banks of the Potomac River near the Pointers' home, and two of the five nearest households were headed by free Black people. Free Toby was a previously enslaved man without a last name who lived next door. The head of the other household was a woman named Free Hannah, who was the sister of Yarrow Mamout, a well-known freed slave in Georgetown.[15]

Hannah and Yarrow Mamout were Muslims and members of the Fulani people in what is now Guinea, West Africa. When they were in their teens, slave traders kidnapped them in 1752 and brought them to Annapolis, Maryland, on the slave ship *Elijah*. Hannah was sold to the owner of the Hungerford Tavern in Rockville, Maryland, and Yarrow was sold to Samuel Beall, who owned property in both western Maryland and Georgetown. Yarrow eventually gained his freedom and settled in Georgetown, where he was immortalized in 1819 when his portrait was painted by one of America's most famous artists, Charles Willson Peale. The portrait hangs today in the Philadelphia Museum of Art.[16]

Hannah worked for many years at the Hungerford Tavern, which was located about nine miles from the farm where George Pointer was born. When she was manumitted at the age of sixty, she moved near the Pointers' cottage along the Potomac River. Freeing older slaves, especially women, was a common practice when the cost of their upkeep became higher than their value. After Hannah's death, her daughter, who was Yarrow Mamout's next of kin, applied for repayment of a loan her uncle had made before his death in Georgetown. In 1843 she won the lawsuit and so confirmed her mother's relationship to her famous brother.[17]

In addition to the free Black and white households along the Potomac River, a number of slaves also worked on nearby farms. In Maryland free Black people socialized with the enslaved, and the Pointers likely would have known an enslaved man named Nace, who was owned by a white man living a quarter mile east of their cottage.[18] In 1812 Nace was sold to a wealthy farmer in southern Maryland whose farm was next door to the Jesuit plantation St. Thomas Manor.[19] If the farmer had traded Nace to the Jesuits sometime over the next twenty-five years, he may have been one of the enslaved with the same name and approximate age whom the Jesuits sold in 1838 to pay the debts of their college in Georgetown. This is just speculation, but it illustrates how fragile the friendships between the enslaved and free Black people could be.[20]

## Pointer's Work with the Potomac Company

George Pointer's name appears many times in the records of the Potomac Company between 1796 and 1829. Between the fall of 1800 and the summer of 1801, he was regularly paid cash for such work as "boating corn," carrying pork from Little Falls to Great Falls, and the "waggoning of Casks." He was also repeatedly entrusted with money to purchase meat, grain, and work supplies for the Potomac Company's laborers.[21]

In January 1801, the board of directors ordered "Mr. Pointer [to] give notice to the Owners of Boats and Scows now lying at the Basin of the Great Falls . . . [that] the owners immediately remove [them]."[22] The directors obviously were comfortable asking a twenty-eight-year-old former slave to order white boat owners to get out of the company's way. This is the first time the formal reference "Mr. Pointer" was used in the company records. That same year he was also given $3.33 a month for board, presumably for his lodging while he was working away from home.[23] Not only were Pointer's wages the same as those of white laborers but also he and other free Black laborers were provided with the same food and liquor rations.[24]

In 1795, two years after George Pointer had bought his freedom, Leonard Harbaugh, a contractor from Georgetown, became the new superintendent of the Potomac Company. Harbaugh was a slave owner and apparently a difficult man; he constantly quarreled with the board of directors, rarely met his deadlines, and never controlled costs.[25] Presumably George Pointer also found him difficult, because by 1802 Pointer had bought his own riverboat and was contracting himself out to the Potomac Company instead of staying under the direct supervision of Harbaugh.[26] As Pointer later documented: "I went To Boating for myself and continued in that capacity untill new directors were appointed and an engineer also, who was Mr. Josias Thompson."[27] People may have begun calling Pointer "Captain" at the time that he was boating independently, and he used the title years later when he signed his 1829 letter.

Leonard Harbaugh probably did not like Pointer much either because, as historian Robert Kapsch noted, Pointer "could read and write better than some of the engineers and superintendents such as Leonard Harbaugh."[28] When Pointer left the company, Harbaugh likely was the person at the Potomac Company's board meeting on May 11, 1802, who demanded the repossession of the company's cottage where Pointer had been living for fifteen years. The notes from the board meeting show "Poynter's house [to] be taken possession of and set apart for the use of the men while employed in quarrying stone on the banks of the Canal."[29]

That stone quarry was a mile downstream from the Pointers' house, and cut marks on the rock walls are still visible testimony today of the Potomac Company's work. The outcome of the discussion about the Pointers' house was not recorded in the company's *Proceedings*, but soon afterward the company began paying Betty Pointer $7 a month for "cooking and the lodging of six Negro men."[30] The timing of her payments suggests that this may have been the resolution of the board's discussion about the disposition of the Pointer cottage. Subsequent censuses recorded the Pointers living in the same place with the same neighbors for the rest of their lives.

By the end of 1806, the Potomac Company's board of directors had found Harbaugh too difficult to work with and fired him.[31] The board replaced him with a Georgetown engineer, Josiah Thompson, and very soon afterward Thompson rehired George Pointer and gave him considerably greater responsibilities. Pointer described his new responsibilities as challenging and dangerous: "I was chosen by Mr. Thompson to Superintend the hands in removing the obstruction and making a good way For the passage of Boats. . . . I next went with the Directors and engineer to the Shenandoah River. I was left by Mr. Thompson to Superintend the navigation of that river such as removing dams and fish potts and many time run the risk of Loosing my Life by the inhabitants . . . for having removed the Same."[32]

Pointer was working near the confluence of the Shenandoah and Potomac Rivers where the town of Harpers Ferry overlooks both rivers. To make the river more navigable, Pointer was tasked with destroying the dams and the stone fish traps that the farmers used on the Shenandoah River to catch fish but that impeded the flow of the water.[33] It is easy to imagine how angry the local farmers and fishermen would have been at the Potomac Company for destroying their means of fishing, especially since the company did not own the river. Presumably, their anger would have been focused on the company's representative, whom they would have viewed as nothing more than a freed slave.

In 1808 Albert Gallatin, the US secretary of the treasury, gave a lengthy and detailed report to the Senate describing twenty infrastructure projects that were being planned in the United States, including canals and toll roads. Most of the projects, which were described at length, were merely proposals. A few others had begun, but the work on several had been suspended. None of the projects was as ambitious as the Potomac Canal with the huge locks at Great Falls that at that point were open for business. The Gallatin report concluded that "the trade of this [Potomac] canal, especially during the year 1807 has been so great that there appears every prospect of its becoming a productive work."[34]

At the time the Gallatin report was published, the terminus of the Potomac Canal was the thriving port of Georgetown. Raw products, such as tobacco, wheat, and wool, were arriving by canal from the west to be shipped to ports on the Eastern Seaboard and exported abroad. The harbor town had a number of warehouses, taverns, and a college, and it was large enough to support a fire department. In addition, the town had begun to pave several of its main streets with cobblestones, some of which came from the ballast of visiting ships.[35]

The Potomac Company's best year financially was 1811, just before the War of 1812 with Great Britain. By the end of the war in 1815, however, the White House had been burned, and half the trade on the Potomac Canal had been diverted to Philadelphia and Baltimore.[36] By 1816 the company was running major deficits, and Mr. Thompson, who was about to resign, asked George

Pointer to accompany him to meet with the company's board of directors. Pointer later described the meeting in his 1829 letter:

> Mr. Thompson . . . called on me to meet the board that had assembled at the Union tavern [in Georgetown], . . . [Mr. Thompson] then told the board that they thought Inexpedient to employ any engineer on the Potomack, as I had had experience enough to Superintend any work on the Potomack that they might want done, Consequently I was named by Mr. Henry Foxall to Superintend . . . a parcel of hands for the purpose at that time of building a wall to throw the water in the canal at the great falls.[37]

Henry Foxall was a wealthy owner of a munitions factory on the Potomac River just north of Georgetown and was well known for giving his own enslaved workers job training and then their freedom.[38] Making Pointer a formal engineering supervisor was the most practical action the company could take when it was struggling financially. Pointer was more experienced and less expensive than more formally trained engineers who had never worked on the river. Soon afterward Pointer became a supervisor at both Great Falls and upstream at the Seneca Canal.

Work on the canal was dangerous since all the digging and cutting of stone were done by hand and aided by gunpowder. The company's records included payments to disabled workers. After more than thirty years' working on the river, Pointer himself in the spring of 1819 had a major accident, which he described:

> I then commenced running free Stone from Seneca to the Little Locks that were then building; in running the Stone above mentioned on a certain day—there was a parcel of boats fast in Seneca Falls with marble for the Capitol; I could not get by. consequently I had to run Out Side. Unfortunately my boat struck, I was precipitated out of her, and a broken Leg was the issue of it. I Laid in that Situation four days without medical aid, I However Saved the cargo and got it down Safe to the Little Falls its Place of destination.[39]

A broken leg was a serious injury at the beginning of the nineteenth century since there were few doctors available and no anesthetics except alcohol to dull the pain. Most fractures were simply splinted and left to heal if they could. Since Pointer continued working on the river for the next decade, his leg must have mended enough to be functional, although he likely walked with a limp.

On July 25, 1819, the directors of the Potomac Company met in Georgetown with John Mason, the son of a Virginia statesman, presiding. The fortunes of the company had been declining since the War of 1812. In 1819 an economic panic and a severe drought further damaged the Potomac Canal's finances.[40]

View of the port of Georgetown, looking downriver, 1801. Print by T. Cartwright after a work by George Beck. Courtesy of Library of Congress, Prints and Photographs Division.

European demand for raw materials had collapsed at the end of the Napoleonic Wars, and the inflationary policies of American banks led to a severe economic depression. As a result, the number of boats using the Potomac Canal in 1819 was only 60 percent of the number eight years earlier, and the decrease in tonnage was even more alarming.[41] The company's financial problems were surely discussed at the meeting, but the only business recorded that day was to pay the accounts of three men, one of which was George Pointer's "acc't for forty eight dollars and forty two cents."[42] Pointer's payment was almost half his annual wages and is worth approximately $1,000 in today's dollars. Although its purpose was not specified, presumably this payment was compensation for his broken leg.[43]

In 1820 the Pointer household was again erroneously listed in the census of the District of Columbia. It included a woman at least forty-five years old, who was presumably Betty Pointer, and a young woman between the ages of sixteen and twenty-six, who probably was their daughter Elizabeth. The Pointers' two other children had grown up and left home. Curiously, Pointer and the members of his household were categorized as "whites," which was clearly a mistake by the census taker; however, it again indicates that Pointer and his family members may have had a light complexion. A study of the 1860 census of New Orleans suggested that about 5 percent of households were racially misclassified: a third of them were mulatto households classified as white; the rest were European descendants classified as mulatto.[44]

The Potomac Company never recovered from the combination of the national economic collapse in 1819 and the four-year drought that had begun in the same year. Sometime in the early 1820s, Pointer asked the Potomac Company's board for permission to build his own fish traps near the entrance of the Little Falls canal.

> At that Time I asked Leave of the board to build me some fish potts out side of the navigation of the Potomack near the spout of the Little falls, they thought it was wrong to grant me that Liberty in so much as I had been employed by the company to tear down a number that had been established above on the Potomack, but they being informed and Knowing at the same time that if they granted me the Liberty that it could not effect the navigation in no respect; Immediately granted me the Liberty of doing so, which I completed after Eight hard years Labour . . . the fish that was Taken in them was carried to the markets of Geo Town and Washington.[45]

The irony of Pointer's asking to build fish pots when he had destroyed the fish pots of farmers on the Shenandoah River a decade earlier was not lost on Pointer or the board, which gave him permission.

The Decline of the Potomac Company

Despite the vision of George Washington and the dedicated work of men such as George Pointer, the Potomac Company was never financially strong. Its best year had been 1811, but thereafter the finances of the company slowly declined into bankruptcy. An independent report to Congress in 1823 concluded, "The problem was not caused by the ineptitude of the Potomac Company, but by the fact that knowledge of how to create an in-river navigation system did not exist when the company undertook its improvements of the river."[46] The report also concluded that land transportation was twenty times more expensive than water transportation, and an in-ground canal should be built on the banks of the Potomac.[47]

In the early nineteenth century, roads and turnpikes in the United States were inadequate, and a number of canals were being built in other states, such as the Erie Canal in New York. Georgetown merchants were eager not to be left behind, and eventually a new company, the Chesapeake and Ohio Canal Company (C&O Company), was formed to build a still water canal. While waiting for its formal acquisition by the C&O Company, the Potomac Company continued to contract with Pointer for occasional maintenance work. The last payment to Pointer was on July 22, 1828, for "clearing away sand bar from the front of the Lower lock gates at the Little Falls: $13.00."[48] This payment was most likely for work he had done three weeks earlier in preparation for the inaugural ceremony of the new Chesapeake and Ohio Canal Company. It was also one of the final expenditures of the bankrupt Potomac Company.

The inaugural ground breaking of the C&O Canal was scheduled for July 4, 1828, and President John Quincy Adams agreed to preside over the ceremony. The president wrote in his diary that he left the White House the morning of the fourth with his son and headed for the Union Hotel—the same hotel where George Washington had eaten and held numerous meetings over the years—in Georgetown. At the hotel, the directors of the new C&O Company assembled with foreign dignitaries and the mayors of Washington and Georgetown. They were joined by senators, congressmen, and other high government officials as well as the directors of the old Potomac Company.

Many residents of Georgetown and Washington City gathered near the hotel and along the main street of Georgetown to glimpse the procession of carriages and officials on horseback as they headed to the wharf to the sounds of the US Marine Band. Participants boarded two steamships that were accompanied by a number of small vessels following in their wake. Once the steamboats reached a low bridge that crossed the Potomac Canal, officials disembarked to proceed up the Potomac Canal on canal boats "just within the bounds of the State of Maryland."[49]

The Potomac Company provided the canal boats, and as the company's remaining engineer, George Pointer would have been in charge of assembling and organizing them. He was accompanied by his young granddaughter, Mary Ann, who was about eight years old at the time, and her grandfather gave her the chance to steer the canal boat bearing President Adams. It was an unforgettable event for the young girl, who in later years described it to her children and grandchildren.

A hundred years later, as Washington began planning a centennial celebration of the groundbreaking ceremony, Mary Ann's children repeated the story to the *Washington Post*, which published a photograph of her daughter Mary Moten. The caption of the photo appearing on June 2, 1928, read, "Canal Child: Mary Moten, 73-year-old daughter of the Mary [Ann] Harris who piloted President John Quincy Adams and his party up the old Potomac Canal to the ground breaking for the Chesapeake and Ohio Canal 100 years ago."

Ground breaking for the new canal took place near the Potomac Company's old gunpowder magazine and dam, which were within sight of George Pointer's cottage. The president of the Potomac Company opened the ceremony by wishing success for the new canal and then introduced President Adams, who spoke of the nation's history and its promise. John Quincy Adams got a little carried away in his remarks: "The project contemplates a conquest over physical nature, such as has never been achieved by man. The wonders of the ancient world, the Pyramids of Egypt, the Colossus of Rhodes, the Temple of Ephesus, the Mausoleum of Artemisia, the Wall of China, sink into insignificance before it."[50]

The president was given a ceremonial spade to make the first turn of dirt for the construction, and after some effort, he lifted a clump of soil to the sound of celebratory gunfire from a battery of the US Artillery. The salute was repeated along the river by other artilleries stationed at intervals as far south as Alexandria. Mary Ann told her children a "wondrous barbeque . . . followed the ceremonies" and that she had danced with the president. She also told her children that she had met her future husband that day on the banks of the Potomac.[51]

The presidential group re-embarked and returned to the steamships and more celebration and fireworks downtown. Adams wrote in his diary that evening: "I got through awkwardly, but without gross and palpable failure." Later that year, he was defeated by Andrew Jackson for a second term as president.[52]

In August 1829, heavy flooding made the former Potomac Company's Little Falls canal unusable for boat traffic.[53] Rather than repairing the old canal, the C&O Company's new board of directors decided to bypass it and build another one parallel to it. The new construction, however, would have demolished the Pointers' cottage, so George Pointer approached Mr. McCord, the Georgetown contractor who was in charge of building the canal through Pointer's house.[54] Pointer later wrote,

> I spoke to Mr. McCord about [the digging of the new canal] Destroying me . . . and his answer to me was that I was Injured considerably by it but he could not help it, and that the company ought to compensate . . . an aged and distressed Family. . . .
>
> The Chesapeake and Ohio Canal is drawing near my Little Cottage. . . .
>
> I do trust in God, the giver of all things, that if the new Company does Dispossess us from our Little Humble Cottage, that hitherto has not been a detriment to the old Canal Company nor anybody Living, and which was given to me, that they will give me Some Little place . . .[55]

Pointer strengthened his request to the C&O Company's board to spare his cottage by describing in his letter his many accomplishments in the decades he had worked for the Potomac Company. What he did not mention in his letter was that although many employees had worked for the company over the years, Pointer himself was almost certainly the longest employed as he had been originally hired in 1787 and was the last person paid in 1828.[56]

By 1829 George Pointer had already outlived his life expectancy at birth by twenty years, so it is not surprising that his letter reflects a premonition of his own death when asking for "Some Little place adjacent to the new Canal, that they may upon it Support themselves for the few days that they have to breathe upon this earth—Which is but few."[57] He ended his letter:

> God has prospered the old Canal that the father of his . . . Country First brought into existence and may he favour the new one, My well wishes the Company has for its future Prosperity—
>
> Gentlemen, I have the honor to be, with the greatest obligation to you all, your very humble and obedient Servant
>
> Capt. George Pointer
>
> Sept. 5th 1829.[58]

Pointer's letter to the C&O Company's board of directors has been well preserved in the company's files at the National Archives. There is, however, no mention in the company's records that his letter was ever discussed or answered. Nonetheless, the next year the 1830 census again counted the Pointer household with some of the same neighbors reported in 1820, suggesting that the Pointers were still living in their cottage.[59]

By 1830 the new C&O Canal had bypassed the Pointers' home and was headed north toward Harpers Ferry. Their oldest daughter, Elizabeth, who had been living with them in the 1820 census, was living elsewhere in Montgomery County.[60] Their son, William, had married and was likely living near Georgetown because records indicate that the couple buried their first child in a coffin made by a well-known Georgetown cabinetmaker. The Pointers' second daughter, Mary, had not been recorded in either the 1820 census or the 1830 census and may have died. Her early death would explain why her young daughter, Mary Ann, was living with her grandparents.

In 1830 one of the people in the Pointer household was listed in the census as blind, possibly with cataracts, which were not treatable in the nineteenth century. Both Pointers apparently died in the 1830s. No death records for them exist, but an 1838 District of Columbia legal document referred to Betty as deceased. Neither George nor Betty Pointer appeared in the 1840 census.[61]

The most likely cause of death for George and Betty Pointer was the terrible cholera epidemic in 1832. Cholera is caused by contaminated drinking water, and cholera epidemics periodically hit the United States in the eighteenth and nineteenth centuries, disproportionately killing children and the elderly.[62] In the summer of 1832, a national cholera epidemic reached Washington. Between August 29 and October 20, the Jesuits of Holy Trinity Church in Georgetown recorded seventy-one deaths, which was more than four times the number of deaths at the same time the previous year. Cholera caused two-thirds of the deaths in Georgetown in 1832. More than half of the deceased were Black people, and two-thirds of them were freed people.[63]

Although the epidemic hit Georgetown very hard, its heaviest toll was on the people living along the C&O Canal. An engineer for the company reported, "I regret to announce to you, through the Board of Directors the fact that Asiatic Cholera has made its appearance on the line of canal . . . we have had 6 cases within the last 3 days and 5 deaths."[64]

A District physician also noted that the DC cholera epidemic appeared to be especially lethal for the people living along the Potomac near the C&O Canal—more specifically, for the "colored population especially to the free blacks."[65] The Pointers were one of the more prominent free Black families along the canal, and thus the doctor's statement may have been, in effect, their obituary.

Disproportionate deaths among free Black people had been noted for other diseases as well. Epidemics in Baltimore before the Civil War caused an estimated 50 percent higher mortality in free Black people than among the enslaved. One physician speculated that slave owners cared for their enslaved people as they did for other business investments, and they saw epidemics as a threat to their wealth. No one, however, apparently valued the free Black population enough to take care of them in similar circumstances.[66]

By the time the Pointers died in the 1830s, New York's Erie Canal, which stretched from Albany to Buffalo, had triumphantly opened and demonstrated how inexpensive canal transportation could be. The United States had only seventy miles of railroads, and no one anticipated that three decades later there would be thirty thousand railroad miles, transforming the country and eclipsing the canals.[67] The Potomac Company's project, however, had been the first major transportation infrastructure project in North America. It never became the financial success that George Washington had dreamed of, but it was both a magnificent failure and a towering achievement of George Pointer's long life.

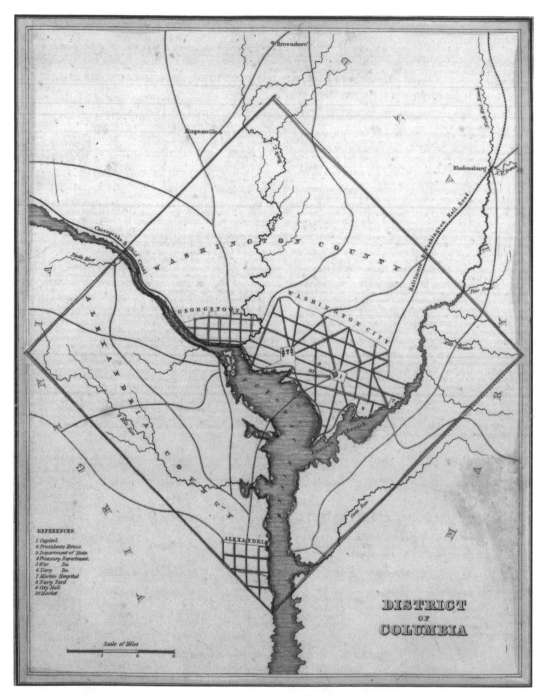

An 1835 map of the District of Columbia showing the city of Washington, Georgetown, Alexandria, and Washington County. Courtesy of Library of Congress, Geography and Map Division.

# 3

## Nat Turner's Long Shadow

When George and Betty Pointer died in the 1830s, they were survived by their daughter, Elizabeth; their son, William; and their granddaughter, Mary Ann. Elizabeth had lived with them until sometime in the 1820s and had then moved into a place of her own in Montgomery County. William was most likely living with his wife near Georgetown because they were customers of a well-known Georgetown cabinetmaker. The Pointers were raising their granddaughter after the apparent death of her mother, Mary, in the 1820s.

All three Pointer children had spent their childhoods on the banks of the Potomac River, five miles upstream from the port of Georgetown. The Pointer children had grown up in a rural neighborhood where the white plantation owners and their slaves worked their farms on the high palisades that overlooked the river. Pointer and his immediate neighbors, both Black and white, lived on the flood plains between the palisades and the river. Their neighborhood was relatively stable with the same neighbors, sometimes of many years. For instance, in the 1800 census, the white Wilson brothers —Lancelot and Normand—lived four households away from the Pointers, and twenty years later in the 1820 census they were still there but by then were five households away. In the 1830 census, 25 percent of the twenty households on both sides of the Pointers were free Black families.

Racial prejudice was pervasive, but it was not rigidly codified in 1830. In 1831, however, everything changed after the biggest slave rebellion in the United States. Slave rebellions were not new in the country. Several had occurred in Maryland in the eighteenth century, with one in Prince George's County in 1738 and another in Annapolis a year later.[1] These rebellions were small and unsuccessful, but at the end of the eighteenth century, a slave insurrection in the French colony of Saint-Domingue, later named Haiti, had a lasting impact in the United States. The uprising was particularly brutal, in part because the slaves outnumbered the French colonists. Its audacity and its success made the Haitian revolution an inspiration to enslaved people everywhere. Historian Henry Louis Gates Jr. said that "the revolution of the slaves in Haiti made real every slave owner's worst nightmare."[2] Slave owners who imported many slaves from the Caribbean became so afraid of importing rebels from Haiti that they supported the prohibition of the international slave trade a few years later.[3]

In 1800, while the Haitian revolution was still making newspaper headlines, thousands of enslaved Virginians, led by a literate blacksmith, organized a protest march in Richmond, Virginia. This protest confirmed the power of literacy, and southern states tightened laws forbidding the education of the enslaved. Within twenty years of the Haitian slaves winning their freedom, at least five major slave revolts occurred, including one in 1822 when a free Black carpenter named Denmark Vesey led a slave rebellion in South Carolina. Vesey made slave owners realize that they were threatened not only by their slaves being literate but also by free Black people organizing their slaves against them.[4]

In 1831 Nat Turner, a literate and religious slave, led an armed rebellion in Southampton, Virginia. The raid was described in lurid detail: "[Nat Turner and his followers] burst into his master's house and murdered every one of the white inmates. . . . [They] most shockingly mangled the bodies of their victims. . . . The head of the youthful maiden was in one part of the room and her mangled body was in another."[5]

In the course of the following two days, fifty-five white men, women, and children were killed, and the white population retaliated by killing more than a hundred enslaved people and two free Black men. This slave rebellion was the largest in American history. Estimates of the total number of slaves killed varied, but no one could deny their decreased number on the Southampton County records the following year.[6]

American historians describe Nat Turner's revolution as having "ripped across the Union"; in the District it was called "cataclysmic."[7] State legislatures

in the South quickly passed new racial laws that included prohibiting litera-
ture "calculated to excite insurrection."[8] Members of the District of Columbia's
Abolition Society, which had been an influential group before the rebellion,
were so frightened that the society stopped meeting. To prevent more free
Black people from moving to Georgetown, the town strengthened its racial
codes and nightly curfew to prevent their movement after dark.[9] The blood-
shed from Nat Turner's rebellion was too graphic to be forgotten, and it became a lasting threat between the white and Black communities throughout
the South. George and Betty Pointer's children and grandchildren would live
the rest of their lives in the long shadow of its backlash.[10]

### Elizabeth Pointer and the Maryland Colonization Society

George and Betty Pointer's eldest child, Elizabeth, was named after her
mother, a tradition in many Black families.[11] As noted previously, Elizabeth
was still living with her parents in the 1820 census when she was in her twen-
ties, but shortly thereafter she moved out on her own in Montgomery County.
In her father's 1829 letter to the C&O Canal Company he lamented, "My Little
Cottage that I have occupied for 43 years, unmolested with an aged Wife and
some offspring but alas none left to assist us."[12]

In the aftermath of the Nat Turner rebellion, many white Maryland slave
owners considered free Black people as the major threat to their system of
slavery.[13] The owners resurrected an old idea of sending as many free Black
people as they could to colonize land in West Africa.[14] The colonization movement had been promoted since the late eighteenth century, and by 1817 Francis
Scott Key had become one of its leaders. He was a slave owner, a well-known
lawyer, and the author of a poem titled "Defence of Fort McHenry," which was
adopted as the national anthem a century later.[15]

Before the Nat Turner insurrection, the American Colonization Society
had neither the resources nor the organization to do much more than talk
about the idea. After the insurrection, however, the Maryland government
made its chapter an official state board and appropriated $200,000 over ten
years to oversee "the Removal of Coloured People" to Africa. Its colonization
program was more aggressively funded than that of any other southern state
at the time.[16]

The Maryland Colonization Society used some of its new funds to take a
census of all free Black people in Maryland who would be eligible for a one-
way passage to Africa. In 1832 William O'Neale Jr., the sheriff of Montgomery
County, was in charge of a special census in his county. It must have been
traumatic when the sheriff appeared at Elizabeth Pointer's door unannounced
to collect information regarding her possible deportation. The sheriff listed

# LETTERS

## ON THE

# COLONIZATION SOCIETY;

### WITH A VIEW OF

## ITS PROBABLE RESULTS,

#### UNDER THE FOLLOWING HEADS:

*The Origin of the Society ; Increase of the Coloured Population ;
Manumission of Slaves in this country ;*

DECLARATIONS OF LEGISLATURES, AND OTHER ASSEMBLED
BODIES, IN FAVOUR OF THE SOCIETY ;

**Situation of the Colonists at Monrovia and other towns; Moral and Religious Character of the Settlers; Soil, Climate, Productions, and Commerce of Liberia;**

Advantages to the free coloured Population, by emigration to Liberia ; Disadvantages of slavery to the white population; Character of the Natives of Africa, before the irruptions of the Barbarians; Effects of Colonization on the Slave Trade, with a slight sketch of that nefarious and accursed traffic.

---

ADDRESSED TO THE HON. CHARLES F. MERCER, M. H. R. U. S.

---

## BY M. CAREY.

---

### THIRD EDITION, ENLARGED AND IMPROVED:

---

"Nearly **2,000** persons have kindled a beacon fire at Monrovia, to cast a broad blaze of light into the dark recesses of that benighted land ; and though much pains have been taken to overrate the cost, and undervalue the results, yet the annals of colonization may be triumphantly challenged for a parallel.

"Five years of preliminary operations were requisite for surveying the coast—propitiating the natives—and selecting the most eligible ·ite. Numerous agents were subsequently employed—ships chartered –the coast cleared—schools, factories, hospitals, churches, government buildings and dwellings erected—and the many expenses requisite here were defrayed ;—and yet, for every fifty dollars expended by the society from its commencement, we have not only a settler to show, but an ample and fertile territory in reserve, where our future emigrants may ' sit down under their own vines and fig trees, with none to make them afraid.' During the last year, an amount, nearly equal to the united expenditures, has been exported by the colonists. *From Philadelphia alone, eleven vessels have sailed*; three of them chartered through the efforts of the Pennsylvania Society, and bearing to the land of their fathers a large number of slaves, manumitted by the benevolence of their late owners."—*Cresson.*

Philadelphia, May 29, 1832.

---

YOUNG, PRINTER.

Cover of an 1832 pamphlet by the Colonization Society. Courtesy of Library of Congress, Prints and Photographs Division.

Elizabeth Pointer as living on her own, and she was the only person named Pointer who was recorded in the special census that year in either Montgomery County or elsewhere in Maryland.[17]

The Maryland Assembly had confidently assumed that a few incentives, such as paid transportation and the accompaniment of a newly trained Black doctor, would be sufficient incentive to convince free Black people to willingly leave the only homes they had ever known and sail to a continent they had never seen. Even though Maryland's efforts to send Black people to Africa were more ambitious and provided more funding for them than other states did at the time, it did not persuade many people to leave.[18] Only 1 percent of Maryland's free Black population, about 627 people, went to Africa between 1832 and 1841.[19]

No one named Pointer was recorded on the ship manifests leaving Maryland, and, in fact, no free Black person from Montgomery County ever went to Africa with the American Colonization Society's program.[20] A Maryland historian writing in 1889 noted, "All plans for removing the blacks with their own consent were destined perhaps to prove illusory, as the negro had showed an invincible indisposition to go."[21] Elizabeth Pointer did not go to Africa, but she was never recorded again in any census or other official documents. She may have either married and changed her name or died before the 1840 census.


William Pointer and the Potomac River Floods of 1843

Elizabeth's brother, William, was also caught in the backlash after Nat Turner's rebellion but in a subtler way than she was. William had been born at the end of the eighteenth century and had married a free Black woman named Ann when they were both very young.[22] Soon afterward they had their first child, but unfortunately the child died in August 1818.

On August 24, 1818, Ann Pointer bought a small coffin made from stained wood for her infant. She chose the cheapest kind of coffin available, but it was still an expensive luxury for the young Black couple. It was built by a well-known Georgetown cabinetmaker who for over sixty years meticulously recorded the names and races of his customers. Because his shop was on Thirty-First Street near the river in Georgetown, William and Ann Pointer were probably living nearby when their infant died. Their infant was the only Pointer descendant found in the cabinetmaker's records.[23]

Georgetown was, at that time, a thriving port of about five thousand residents. Because it had a good harbor, it was the center of commerce for the District of Columbia. It also maintained its identity as a separate town within the District and overshadowed the City of Washington, which was

View of Georgetown steamboat wharf in 1839, drawing by Augustus Kollner (1813–1906). Courtesy of Library of Congress, Prints and Photographs Division.

still being built. In the early 1800s, the Potomac Company's canals (and after 1828 the Chesapeake and Ohio Canal) transported raw materials from the western frontier to the Georgetown mills along the riverbanks, and then the goods were loaded on oceangoing ships in the harbor. The mills and ships in Georgetown provided good jobs for a young free Black man with a family to support.[24]

Although Georgetown was a town that needed William Pointer's labor before Nat Turner's rebellion, it became a hostile place to continue working afterward. Free Black people were refused shop licenses to do business and were forbidden to be on the streets after ten o'clock at night. They also suffered daily harassments. In 1835 street riots against Black people reinforced how dangerous the urban areas had become for them.[25] Sometime in the 1830s, probably after the deaths of George and Betty Pointer, William, Ann, and their children moved back to the safety of his rural childhood home five miles north on the Potomac River.

The Pointer home on the river was safer than the streets of Georgetown because William already knew a number of the white neighbors from his childhood, and they all had known his parents. Zacharia Green's household was three households away from George Pointer's cottage, according to the 1830 census, and was two away from William's family in 1840. John Burrows's family was also a neighbor of both George Pointer in the 1820s and William Pointer in the next decade.

When William and Ann Pointer returned to his childhood home, they had two girls older than ten years of age and a son who likely was born after the move, based on later records.[26] William would have assumed that he could follow in his father's footsteps and work for the C&O Canal Company to support his family; however, after the Nat Turner rebellion, the company abruptly stopped hiring Black laborers.[27] The owners' fear of free Black men led them to rely on Irish and German workers, whom they imported on term contracts. The immigrants were more expensive laborers than free Black Americans and were also harder to manage because they deserted their jobs more often, but at least they posed no threat of insurrection against the white owners of the company.[28]

Vouchers from the C&O Canal Company between 1830 and 1850 recorded the names of many of William Pointer's white neighbors who supplied food, equipment, and construction materials to the canal company.[29] The canal company's records do not mention William Pointer or any other known Black man working either for a salary or being paid on contract.[30] William Pointer was fortunate because he had his childhood home as well as his father's riverboat and fish pots. William likely farmed his father's garden plot and may have used the boat to take surplus fish and produce to markets where he could still sell them without a license.

In addition to inheriting his parents' home and neighbors, William Pointer also inherited his niece, Mary Ann, the daughter of his older sister Mary. His sister had married a man named Plummer, a popular name among free Black people living in Prince George's County, east of Washington City. Pointer's niece was born around 1820, but her mother was never recorded in any records after having given birth. She apparently died, and the 1830 census recorded her young daughter living with her grandparents, George and Betty Pointer. As noted in chapter 2, an article in the *Washington Post* almost a century later on June 2, 1928, described the young Mary Ann's participation in the inauguration of the C&O Canal in 1828. Mary Ann continued living with her uncle after her grandparents died. Their closest Black neighbor in the 1830s was the Williams family, and many years later, Mary Ann rented a room in her home to one of their sons, whom she would have known as a small child.

After Nat Turner's rebellion, the prejudice against free Black people living along the river also hardened. Because so many white laborers were on the C&O Canal and white farmers were working on the river's palisades, the canal's towpath was only occasionally used as a route for escaping slaves. One fugitive slave, however, documented his escape on the towpath in 1837, a time when William Pointer and his family were living there. James Curry, a twenty-two-year-old enslaved man from North Carolina, had escaped from his owner and was trying to reach the Mason-Dixon Line when he lost his way north of Washington. He later recalled,

> I then took the Montgomery road, but, wishing to escape Baltimore, I turned off, . . . and fell back again upon the Potomac river, and travelled on the tow path of the canal from Friday night until Sunday morning, when I lay down and slept a little, . . . I determined to go on until I could find a place of safety. I soon saw a man riding towards me on horse-back. As he came near, he put his eyes upon me, and I felt sure that he intended to question me. I fell to praying to God to protect me, and so begging and praying fervently, I went forward. When he met me, he stopped his horse, leaned forward and looked at me, and then, without speaking, rode on again. I still fully believe it was at first his intention to question me. I soon entered a colored person's house on the side of the canal, where they gave me breakfast and treated me very kindly.[31]

Curry was typical of runaway slaves at the time. A document compiled by a New York City abolitionist in 1855–56 recorded that those fugitive slaves who passed through New York City were on average twenty-five years old, and 75 percent of them were males from Maryland and Virginia.[32]

Curry eventually reached Massachusetts, where he told his story. Although he does not mention where along the river he was sheltered while escaping, it is possible that he was at the Pointers' home. The Pointers may have done something similar for other fugitives at another time.

In April 1843, the Potomac River flooded. As a heavy winter snow in western Maryland melted rapidly, the river swallowed its banks as far south as Georgetown. The cellars of Georgetown waterfront buildings were swamped with several feet of mud, and the harbor was crippled.[33] Five months later, a second flood produced by heavy rains sent the river to "a height unprecedented within the memory of man." According to a damage report prepared for the C&O Company,

> The Georgetown level had suffered two large breaches—one near Pointers and the other opposite the Alexandria Aqueduct quarry. . . . From the Alexandria Aqueduct to Dam No. 1 [the dam at the Pointers' house] the canal banks had been washed considerably, particularly above the Powder Magazine. Near the dam there was another serious breach and the banks were washed badly. About one-third of the Lockhouse at Lock No. 6 had been carried away, and he [Superintendent Young] assumed that it would go entirely.[34]

The house at Lock 6 was a sturdy, square house made of large, whitewashed stone blocks and was within sight of the Pointers' home. If the lockhouse was destroyed, then the rest of the nearby houses, including the Pointer cottage, must have been swept away as well. The destruction of homes was confirmed in the 1850 census when none of the people who had been living around the lockkeeper's house at Lock 6 ten years earlier were still there. The homes of William Pointer's family and all their neighbors must have been destroyed, and the residents had not returned. Only the white households, whose large estates were on much higher ground, remained.[35]

William Pointer surely lost his home as well as his father's boat and fish pots, which were essential for feeding his family. Perhaps he initially sought shelter for his family with his father's white childhood friend, Charles Wallace, who was still living on higher ground about two miles north. In the longer term, however, Pointer needed both a job to support his family and a new place to live. Wallace would have known through his network of Maryland family and friends that at that time the federal government was building the US Naval Academy in Annapolis and was hiring free Black men for manual jobs. Because Maryland law prohibited the hiring of Black laborers from out of state, William would have had an advantage in applying for these jobs.[36]

Although exactly when Pointer moved his family to Annapolis is not clear, subsequent records show that he did, suggesting he may have been hired for one of the many jobs at the Naval Academy. In the 1840s, the forty-mile trip from Washington, DC, to Annapolis was a long two-day ride by horse and cart or a three-hour trip that cost $2.50 on the new train. If William had been hired before he moved his family, he might have been able to afford to take the new train, since the Naval Academy paid federal salaries that were higher and more reliable than wages in the private sector.[37]

When the William Pointer family arrived in Annapolis sometime after the 1843 Potomac floods, they found it was a very different town than Georgetown. It was less than half the size of Georgetown, and 85 percent of the Black people in Annapolis were enslaved compared to only 33 percent in Georgetown.[38] An 1844 government map of Annapolis shows approximately four hundred households clustered around three streets that ran from State House and Church Circles down to the harbor. Behind these houses were fields and small houses where some of the Black families lived. On a high hill behind the State House was an eighteenth-century windmill towering over an inlet inauspiciously named Graveyard Creek. The old Fort Severn, jutting out into the Annapolis Harbor, was surrounded by the new buildings of the Naval Academy.[39]

The white culture in Annapolis was dominated by many angry slave owners. After the Nat Turner rebellion, the Maryland legislature had taken a number of measures to get rid of as many free Black residents as possible. But despite this hostility, the number of free Black people continued to increase relative to the white population. African colonization had been an expensive failure, and the refusal to give residency permits to free Black people from other states had also failed to stem their growth.[40]

Southern white people in general worried they would soon become a minority in their own towns if they could not limit the number of free Black residents.[41] In 1842 Maryland slave owners had held their first convention in Annapolis "to take measures to protect the interests of the slave system." The slave owners' convention proposed a prohibition on all further manumissions and the removal of all free Black children from their parents and then from the state once they became adults. The Maryland legislature adopted none of these proposals, but the hostile environment for free Black people in Annapolis would surely have discouraged most of them, especially those with children, from moving there without the prospect of a good job.[42]

Annapolis was a regular international port of entry for infectious diseases. Smallpox had been a yearly scourge there in the eighteenth century, and it continued to kill people in the nineteenth century. In 1849 smallpox and scarlet fever were the most prevalent causes of death in Annapolis; one-third of the Black adults older than forty years of age who died that year had smallpox.[43]

At that time William and Ann Pointer would have been close to fifty years old. Since they never appeared in the 1850 decennial census or in any other public records, they apparently died in the meantime, but we don't know the cause or year of their deaths. If they died in one of the epidemics at the end of the 1840s, their young son, William, who would have been only about ten years old, would have been presumably cared for by his older sisters. We do know that fourteen years later, the younger William was living and working in Annapolis when he enlisted in the Thirtieth Maryland US Colored Troops.[44]

Mary Ann Harris, the Panic of 1837, and Her Certificate of Freedom

William Pointer's niece, Mary Ann, did not accompany his family members when they moved to Annapolis, even though she had been living with them after her grandparents died. In 1837, six years before the Potomac floods of 1843 when she was about seventeen years old, she had left her uncle's family to marry Thomas Harris. He was a free Black man who was eight years older than she was, and she later told her children that they had met at the inauguration of the C&O Canal celebration. Raised in Montgomery County, Maryland, he described himself in the census as a laborer.

Mary Ann and Thomas Harris had married six years after Nat Turner's rebellion when racial tensions had worsened considerably, aggravated by the rapid growth in the population of free Black people in the District. In 1800 there had been only 783 free Black people in the newly created District of Columbia, but by the time they married, there were close to 8,000. These free people were concentrated in the urban areas of Washington City and Georgetown, where their growth was most obvious and least welcome.[45]

After the rebellion in 1831, the increasing Black population in the District became a powder keg with a long fuse. After four years passed, a major race riot broke out in the August heat of 1835. When a respected white widow mistakenly accused a young male slave of attempting to murder her, white men rampaged every night for two weeks in downtown Washington, destroying Black people's tenements, workplaces, schools, and a church. One well-known Black restaurant owner fled town as his property burned. At night the city was lit by the fires of white mobs, forcing the mayor to call for military protection to put down the riots. The 1835 riots were followed two years later by another horrifying incident.[46]

At about the time that Mary Ann and Thomas Harris married, the American economy collapsed. The Panic of 1837 was partly caused by inadequate banking regulations, causing the supply of money to plummet and many people's savings to disappear. The worst financial disaster in the young history of the United States lasted for seven years. Even the long-established Georgetown College (later a university) became so indebted that the Jesuits chose to stave off bankruptcy by selling their enslaved workers to plantation owners in the South. Suddenly unable to pay their bills, many other white people also needed funds.[47]

In 1837 Dorcas Allen was an undocumented free Black woman working in Georgetown; she had been treated as a free Black woman by her Methodist mistress and had married a freeman. The economic collapse, however, made her mistress's family desperate for money. Without a certificate of freedom, Allen and her four children were defenseless. A slave trader named James H. Birch bought her and her children and put them in a slave pen in Alexandria, planning to resell them as quickly as possible. During the first night, Dorcas Allen killed two of her children rather than letting them be sold into slavery. The public was horrified. The *Alexandria Gazette* screamed, "HORRIBLE BARBARITY . . . a most barbarous and unnatural murder . . . strangling her two infants . . . attempt to murder her other two children."[48]

The Alexandria authorities demanded that the city's prosecutor, Francis Scott Key, try Allen for murder. The Allen case was legally complicated: if she were found guilty of murder, the slave trader would lose the value of his property because he could not resell her. Commerce in slavery won the verdict in the case. The court found Dorcas Allen not guilty by reason of insanity and thus preserved the value of Birch's commercial property.

Allen's husband frantically raised money to buy the freedom of his wife and remaining children before they could be sold. One of the contributors was John Quincy Adams, who had returned to the capital as a congressman after his defeat for a second presidential term. Dorcas Allen's husband paid the slave trader for his family's freedom, and they immediately moved north and out of the reach of the racial laws of the District.

Four years later in Washington, the same slave trader kidnapped his most famous victim, Solomon Northrop, a well-educated free Black man from New York State who had been lured to Washington with the promise of work. Northrup was enslaved in Louisiana for twelve years before being rescued by white friends. After he returned home to New York, he wrote a book titled *Twelve Years a Slave* about his experiences as a slave. One hundred and sixty years later, his story was made into an award-winning movie that graphically showed the risks of being a free Black man in the District and the horrors of slavery in the South.[49]

At the time of Dorcas Allen's murder trial, Mary Ann was about seventeen years old and newly married. She would certainly have been aware of the sensational trial because it was widely reported and discussed in Washington. Like Dorcas, Mary Ann was a married free Black woman who also did not have a certificate documenting her freedom. She was also likely pregnant with her first child, who was born the following year.

As previously noted, freedom for Black people in Maryland and the District was inherited through the mother, not the father, in a standard that had been adopted from Roman law.[50] Mary Ann's lack of documentation suggests that Mary Ann's mother and her grandmother, Betty Pointer, had lacked legal documents that they could have passed down to their children and grandchildren. To get a certificate of freedom to guarantee her free status and that of her future children, Mary Ann had to identify two white people who could verify that her mother had been free. Furthermore, her witnesses had to come to the Washington District Court to testify for her. Such arrangements would have been a major logistical challenge at a time when both communications and transportation were frustratingly slow.[51]

In the 1830s, the new District Courthouse was in a neoclassical building a few blocks northwest of the unfinished Capitol building. In addition to the courts, the courthouse included the District's city hall and administrative offices. It was built to be deliberately imposing with large marble columns and sweeping stairs, so it must have been especially intimidating for a young Black woman who presumably had never visited the courthouse before.[52] Mary Ann's fear of not having a certificate of freedom, however, overcame any trepidation about going into this formidable court. On November 24, 1838, she walked out with the certificate she needed to ensure the freedom of herself and of her future children.

### CERTIFICATE OF FREEDOM
*Mary Ann Plummer Harris*

> Charles Wallace states that the bearer, Marian Plummer, has asked if he knew anything of her grandmother, Elizabeth Townsend, alias Pointer, and her mother, Mary Plummer the daughter of Elizabeth Pointer. Wallace certifies that he knew them when the old Potomack Company began its operations at the Little Falls of the Potomac River and was acquainted with them until they died. They always passed as free persons. Maria Brown swears that Mary Ann Harris is a free woman and was born of free parents.[53]

Mary Ann's name was spelled two different ways in this short legal document, but that did not seem to bother the court. One witness was Mrs. Mary (Maria) Brown, a white midwife who may have assisted at Mary Ann's birth. She had testified in other certificate of freedom cases before she provided the supporting evidence for Mary Ann.[54]

Mary Ann's other witness, Charles Wallace, was the son of her grandfather's owner. As noted previously, he was born the same year as George Pointer, and they had grown up together on the Wallace farm in Montgomery County. By the time Charles Wallace testified for George Pointer's granddaughter, he was a sixty-five-year-old man and still lived on his farm along the Potomac River, two miles north of George Pointer's cottage. The twenty-two-mile round trip to the District Courthouse would have taken him the better part of a day; the trip also would have taken considerable stamina for the elderly man on the rutted dirt roads of the early nineteenth century.

Charles Wallace said on the certificate that he knew Mary Ann's mother and grandmother "when the old Potomack Company began its operations at the Little Falls of the Potomac." He implied that he did not know Elizabeth (Betty) before the work began on the Potomac Canal and her marriage to George Pointer. Therefore, she probably did not come from either the Wallace farm or the farms of any of their close neighbors. Wallace also confirmed that neither Betty Pointer nor Mary Ann's mother were alive in 1838.

Wallace's appearance in court on behalf of Mary Ann was a critical kindness. He was probably the only white person who had known three generations of Pointer women and was willing to make a long round trip to acknowledge it. If Charles Wallace and George Pointer were half-brothers, as was suggested in chapter 1, then Mary Ann Harris would have been Charles's grandniece, which could explain his efforts on her behalf. At the very least, the testimony of Charles Wallace for George Pointer's granddaughter is proof of the men's long friendship and the obligations that such a childhood friendship created more than a half century later, even years after Pointer's death.

Two years later, the 1840 census registered sixty-seven-year-old Charles Wallace as living by himself on his farm with no slaves, but he did have another Wallace family next door and long-term family friends, the Magruders, just down the road. Ten years later he was seventy-seven and had moved back to the old Wallace family home, where he was living with the widow of his much younger brother on the farm where he and George Pointer had been born.[55] By 1860 Charles Wallace had apparently died, since his name is not found in either the census or subsequent Wallace family records.[56]

Soon after Mary Ann received her certificate of freedom, her first son, John, was born, and his freedom was guaranteed by her certificate. He was born in the aftermath of the Panic of 1837, when bankruptcies, unemployment, and poverty were still increasing. In the middle of the economic depression, Mary Ann and Thomas Harris settled in the rural area of the District known as Washington County, which was still dominated by large tobacco plantations with many enslaved people. The 1840 census registered Mary Ann and Thomas Harris as living on a "country road." At the time Abner Pierce had just built the three-mile road to connect his mill on the Rock Creek to the roads heading north. Today the road is called Broad Branch.[57]

Most free Black people preferred to live in urban centers, where there was more work and a larger free Black community, than in the rural areas of Washington County. Mary Ann and Thomas Harris, however, had retreated to a more isolated area, presumably to escape the recent racial violence downtown. Ironically, in less than twenty-five years, violence would envelop their rural home when they would be caught in deadly cross fire between the Union army and the invading Confederate troops.

Detail from a topographical map of the District of Columbia in 1856–59 showing rural Washington County. The Belt farm is visible in the upper left quadrant of the map; the Harris farm was just east of the Belt household. Map by Albert Boschke with D. McClelland, Blanchard & Mohun, Hugh B. Sweeny, and Thos. Blagden and published in 1861. Courtesy of Library of Congress, Geography and Map Division.

# 4

## The Gathering Storm

George Pointer's granddaughter, Mary Ann, married well. Her husband, Thomas Harris, often described himself as a laborer or gardener in the censuses, meaning that they would never be rich, but because they both lived long and worked hard, they were always financially secure. Soon after Mary Ann received her certificate of freedom in 1838, she and Thomas settled in the most remote, northwest corner of the District within what was called Washington County. It was less than a quarter mile from the Maryland border and about as far as they could get from the slave pens of Georgetown without moving into the slave state of Maryland.

Washington County was part of the land that Maryland had donated in 1799 to establish the new capital of the United States. The donated land included the small Potomac River port of Georgetown and a marshy area nearby that would be designated the city of Washington. The rest of the land gift was simply called Washington County, an area that was much larger than Washington City and Georgetown combined. It was a forested, sparsely populated land that dominated maps of the early District. Much of the land consisted of old plantations interspersed with small settlements of both

Black and white people. Its forests were sliced by dirt roads leading out of the capital city and by creeks running down to the Potomac. When Mary Ann and Thomas Harris moved to the county, its population was only slightly more than three thousand people, of whom more than a quarter were enslaved.[1]

The Harrises may have chosen the rural area to get away from the restrictive Black codes in Washington City and Georgetown, but they also may have wanted to avoid the increasing crime downtown. In the 1840s, crime was much higher in Washington City than in Washington County. Moreover, Black people were disproportionately targeted by the inadequate city police force, and as a result they made up half of the prison inmates.[2] Washington County did not have its own police force, so the District's Black codes were not as strictly enforced as they were in the city.

The sparsely populated countryside of Washington County also had the advantage that life there was healthier than in the densely packed alleys and streets of the city. Charles Dickens visited the District in 1842 and wrote, "It is very unhealthy. Few people would live in Washington, I take it, who are not obliged to reside there."[3] The author of the mortality report based on the 1850 census for Washington County also noted that the county was healthier than the city, and he suggested that the low mortality rate in the county was because of the "abundance of clean water and good soil and plentiful herring in the river."[4]

One benefit of Mary Ann and Thomas Harris's move to the far reaches of Washington County was that they were less visible. In 1840 the 288 free Black people made up less than 10 percent of the county's population in the sprawling rural area, and since the county was so large, their presence would attract little attention. Of course, the Harrises were unlikely to have moved to Washington County unless Thomas had work and unless a white friend or a Black community could offer some protection. Given that Thomas had described himself in the 1840 census as a laborer, he may have been employed by one of the nearby farms. The presence of several free Black households nearby would also have given them some sense of security.[5]

By 1850 the Harris family had five children. There was no school for them, but growing up free in a rural area would have allowed the children to become both independent and resourceful, useful qualities for their later lives. Rural life, however, could occasionally be as dangerous as life in Washington City. In 1850 the oldest Harris daughter, nine-year-old Mary, was severely burned, and within twenty-four hours, she died. Although the cause of her burns is not recorded, Mary would have been old enough to help with the cooking, which might have led to her traumatic death. By the end of the decade, the Harrises had three more children. Their last child, born in 1858, was a daughter whom they also named Mary, probably after her sister.[6]

The small community of free Black and white households in which the Harrises settled eventually became known as the Broad Branch settlement.[7] The 1850 census listed a total of 176 households located in the western half of Washington County, "west of the Seventh Street turnpike," between Georgia Avenue and the Potomac River. Nine of the 176 were free Black households, and five of them were near the settlement where the Harrises lived. Four of those five Black families owned their farms, and sometime in the 1850s Thomas and Mary Ann Harris had saved enough money to buy their two acres from one of their Black neighbors.[8]

A few free Black people had begun buying property in the District as early as 1806. In some cases, land could be bought from a former master, or sometimes it was an inheritance from a master's will.[9] Still, land ownership by free Black residents was not widespread. By the 1850s, the Harrises and their neighbors were among only 9 percent of free Black people who owned property in the District of Columbia.[10] The purchase of their farm represented a long-term investment in their future and meant that Mary Ann and Thomas Harris became a permanent part of an integrated settlement where their descendants would live for over eighty years.[11]

### The Harris Farm of Dry Meadows

The triangular two-acre Harris farm was in a favorable location: it was on top of a small hill that sloped down to the Broad Branch Road, and a tributary of the Rock Creek was not far away. In later legal documents, their farm was called Dry Meadows, a term used for land that had no natural body of water on it and therefore they had to rely on rain for their crops and themselves.

The land where the farm was located had apparently appealed to even earlier settlers. Archaeological digs on the property done in 2014 discovered bits of stone and shatter rocks that were evidence of early Algonquian toolmaking.[12] In the seventeenth century, most of the Native American villages in the area were near rivers or marshlands and were usually built on a hill so that both animals and people could be seen from a safe distance. For a time, a group of these Native Americans must have found the place a suitable site for settlement. The Algonquians were part of a larger chiefdom of the Conoys, which included five groups east of the Potomac River. After British colonialists arrived and settled the area, the Algonquians retreated to the north and west, leaving only a few remnants of their lives behind.[13]

Subsequently, the land became part of a land grant given by the British crown in 1725 to one of the early Maryland colonists, Col. Joseph Belt and his family. They were from Scotland and named their land grant Cheivy Chace after a famous Scottish military battle against the English. When the boundaries of the District of Columbia were established, most of the Belt plantation lay on the Maryland side of the border, but their house was on the District side.[14]

By the 1850s, when Mary Ann and Thomas had bought their two acres, the plantation had descended to Charles Belt, a bachelor who ran it with the help of an enslaved family who had grown up on the property. The Belt house was made of imported bricks that, though expensive, made it a more fireproof building than the usual wooden homes. The plantation was across a dirt road that ran alongside the Harrises' land.[15]

The proximity of white owners, their slaves, and free Black people in rural Washington County was similar to George Pointer's integrated neighborhood on the banks of the Potomac fifty years earlier. Racial integration was a necessity in the eighteenth and early nineteenth centuries because both groups were dependent on each other for labor and jobs, and the work required employers and workers to live near one another. The scholars Douglas Massey and Nancy Denton observed that the integration of nineteenth-century communities meant that "the two racial groups moved in a common social world,

The Belt house in Chevy Chase near the Harris property on what is present-day Oliver Street. It was razed in 1907. General photograph collection, Historical Society of Washington, DC. Reprinted with permission.

spoke a common language, shared a common culture and interacted personally on a regular basis."[16]

The Harrises' farm became the physical center of their family over the next three generations. It was large enough to grow much of their food, and likely the family, as did the other farmers, acquired a few animals. Eventually they grew enough produce to sell the surplus at markets. Although Broad Branch Road was not paved until the twentieth century, it would have been a good route south to the Rock Creek and the markets in Georgetown. Farther east, the Seventh Street Turnpike provided another route to the city, but it was in such bad condition from overuse that it was often impassable. Farmers avoided it until improvements began after the Civil War.[17]

The 1850 census recorded Mary Ann Harris as mulatto, while her husband, Thomas, and their children were listed as Negro. Although Mary Ann was always listed as mulatto, racial distinctions were applied inconsistently in the censuses and were at the discretion of the census taker. In later years, the Harrises' second son, Joseph, was usually recorded as mulatto, but occasionally he was categorized as Negro and once as white. Although the racial designations were imprecise, the social outcomes were not. In the early nineteenth century, African Americans who were described as mulatto were four times more likely to be free than those who were not, and they also were more likely to marry each other and to own property.[18]

The Growth of Racial Tensions

The racial violence that the Harrises had escaped by moving into rural Washington County continued to increase in the city. In 1848, when seventy-five District slaves attempted to escape on a ship named the *Pearl*, white residents of Washington City rioted for several days. In the meantime, some people were beginning to seriously consider the abolition of slavery in the nation's capital because it was so disruptive, destabilizing, and unprofitable.[19] A year later a new congressman named Abraham Lincoln proposed to emancipate the District's slaves and pay compensation to their owners. The idea, however, was considered too radical at the time, and it was ignored, as was he.[20]

The 1850s were among the "most tumultuous" decades in American history.[21] The storms over slavery swept across the national stage and engulfed the US Congress. Between 1845 and 1859, five territories and the Republic of Texas applied for statehood, and each application reignited fierce fights about whether they would be slave or free states. In 1850 Congress forced a compromise between the slave and free states by adopting provisions that allowed each of the competing regions of the country to win and lose something simultaneously. For instance, California would become a free state, but the Fugitive Slave Act was made much stronger. The compromise also abolished slave trading in Washington, DC.

The Compromise of 1850, however, was a failure from its beginning. Northerners found the requirement to return fugitive slaves unacceptable, and most Southerners found the North's refusal to recognize their property rights unconstitutional. Southerners began to seriously consider seceding from a Union that refused to recognize their interests.[22] Although the Compromise of 1850 was short lived, in retrospect it likely helped to delay the Civil War for ten years. It also defined the rhetorical battlefields on which the eventual war would be fought.[23]

In 1857 the Supreme Court ruled that Dred Scott, an enslaved man who had been brought to a free state, did not have any right to sue for his freedom in court. The ruling was written broadly to apply to all Black people, not just those in bondage, and meant that neither the Harrises nor any other Black person would have the fundamental right of American citizens to legal protections in the courts of the country. Although the Supreme Court expected the Dred Scott decision to resolve the status of Black people everywhere in the country, it had the opposite effect by enflaming opposition in free states. In 1859 a raid by the abolitionist John Brown against the US Army's armory in nearby Harpers Ferry in western Virginia fractured the Union further.[24]

By 1860 the population of the District of Columbia had increased to seventy-five thousand residents. Rural Washington County gained some two thousand people, mostly white. Free people of color continued to gravitate to the urban areas, where there were more jobs. Small settlements of Black residents, such as that on Broad Branch Road, also grew, but much of the growth came from the families' increasing number of children.[25] By 1860 Thomas and Mary Ann had seven children at home, ranging in age from two to twenty-one.[26] Mary Ann was working as a seamstress, presumably for white women in the neighborhood, and their two eldest sons had become laborers, almost certainly farm laborers like their father. The Harris farm in 1860 was valued at $100, which would be worth just over $3,000 today, and they had other property, perhaps animals or farm equipment, valued at $40.[27]

The Harris household also had a boarder, thirty-three-year-old Charles Williams, who was listed as a laborer and probably worked for the family in exchange for room and board. According to the 1840 census, Charles Williams's father was a free Black man who lived along the Potomac River next to Mary Ann's uncle, William Pointer. Mary Ann, who was seven years older than Charles Williams, likely would have known him when he was a young child. Although most of the Williams family moved to north Georgetown after the 1843 Potomac floods, they clearly had remained family friends. It was common that one family's growing prosperity benefited its neighbors and friends by spreading both the work and the income.[28]

The white neighbors of the Harrises had also remained in the area throughout the 1850s. John Chappell, who lived with his six children on Grant Road, during the winter ran a private school for boys about a mile south of the Harris farm.[29] The Black children of the area, who had no school, presumably watched the white boys walking past their homes to school every day. A few new families had also moved into the area including two stonecutters from the British Isles who by 1860 had settled nearby with their families. Thus, at the brink of the Civil War, the neighborhood continued to be integrated with Black farmers, white immigrants, and white owners on small farms, as well as large plantations with enslaved people. Neighbors knew and interacted with one another despite the growing tensions in the city and the nation, and one white neighbor would come to the aid of John, the eldest of the Harris children.[30]

John Harris turned twenty-one in 1860 and presumably wanted to take advantage of the growing number of jobs in more urban areas. Given the risks of being identified by white strangers as a fugitive slave, however, he needed proof that he was indeed a free Black man. As was the case when his mother obtained her certificate of freedom in 1838, he needed the testimony of a white witness, and John appealed to a white neighbor whom he had known all his life. In September 1860, Martha Parker met him at a local county courthouse to testify on his behalf before a judge.

Martha Parker was living with her mother and siblings close to the Dry Meadows farm, but her friendship with Mary Ann Harris may have gone back many years before. When Mary Ann was living with her grandparents George and Betty Pointer in their cottage by the Potomac River, one of their white neighbors was David C. Parker. The Parkers had a daughter named Martha who was approximately the same age as Mary Ann, so the friendship between Martha Parker and Mary Ann may have possibly preceded the Harrises' move to Broad Branch Road.

In court Martha Parker said that she had known John as an infant because she had been a neighbor of the Harris family for twenty years.[31] She also swore that John's mother, Mary Ann, was a free Black woman. Thus, on September 17, 1860, John Harris left the Washington County Courthouse with a certificate of freedom that would allow him to safely look for work beyond his immediate neighborhood. Soon afterward he began working in Georgetown as a servant.[32]

No matter how integrated the District was, the capital was still a Southern city. Seventy-five percent of the residents who had not been born there came from Southern states. That is why when Abraham Lincoln, who opposed the expansion of slavery, won the presidency in 1860, many District citizens were furious. Tensions in the area were so high, especially in Baltimore, that Lincoln arrived in the capital by train under the cover of darkness. Before his inauguration, seven Southern states had seceded from the Union. Four more slave states, including Virginia, which was within sight of the District when looking across the river, soon joined the Confederacy.[33]

After Virginia joined the Confederacy, Maryland's loyalties became a critical issue for everyone in the District. Slave-holding Maryland surrounded the District on three sides, and Maryland's state capital at Annapolis was only forty miles away. Most of the eligible white voters in Annapolis had supported Stephen Douglas. Only one man had voted for Abraham Lincoln, so the residents of Annapolis had to confront the election of a president that virtually none of them wanted.[34]

## Civil War in Washington

In April 1861, six days after Fort Sumter in South Carolina had fallen to rebel soldiers, Lincoln's government sent seven hundred Union troops by ship to protect the US Naval Academy in Annapolis. The Maryland governor ordered the troops to remain aboard ship for fear of violence in the streets; however, the irascible general Benjamin F. Butler from Massachusetts retorted that the Naval Academy was federal property and ordered his troops to occupy the town. The Maryland General Assembly hastily retreated to Frederick, where the members eventually decided that they did not have the authority to make a decision about secession. Thus, Maryland unenthusiastically stayed in the Union. It was fortunate because if Maryland had seceded, the District of Columbia would have been trapped behind the enemy lines of two Confederate states, and the capital of the Union would have had to move north, leaving its Black residents unprotected from Southern armies.[35]

Like its legislature, the sympathies of Maryland's residents were deeply divided. Of the eighty-five thousand Maryland citizens who joined the military, one-third went to fight for the Confederacy, as did one-third of the Naval Academy's midshipmen. The border between Maryland and Washington County, DC, was a quarter mile from the Harris farm and was unmarked. Large properties, such as that of Charles Belt, straddled both sides. That Maryland did not secede from the Union must have been a relief to the Harrises' Broad Branch neighbors, but within months their land would become the front line of defense for the District of Columbia.

In preparation for a likely Confederate attack on Washington, army engineers immediately began constructing a ring of sixty-eight forts that would encircle the District. The Harris home was just outside the ring of forts, so it was exposed to any Confederate attack from the north. Military Road, which was built to connect the forts, was a quarter mile south of the Harris farm. Fort Kearny was located less than a mile to the southeast; Fort Pennsylvania, later renamed Fort Reno, was two miles to the southwest; Fort DeRussy was a half mile to the east; and Fort Stevens was two and a half miles due east. To create sight lines for the troops in the forts, the military cleared all trees in a mile-wide swath both in front of and between the forts, and the clearing would have included the Harris property. By autumn the small Broad Branch settlement must have been bare of large vegetation, and the families therefore would have seen clearly the preparations for war all around them.[36]

Union soldiers from many states occupied the new forts. State regiments arrived from Pennsylvania, Rhode Island, and as far west as Indiana. An elite regiment of soldiers who had originally been firemen in New York were called Zouaves and were an exotic sight in their French-Algerian red-trimmed uniforms and with their long swords.[37] The new forts immediately attracted Black people fleeing slavery and searching for food and work. The influx of both soldiers and former slaves around the forts was a mixed blessing for the long-time residents like the Harrises. As one local historian recalled, the local population "had a ready market for their milk and produce . . . but apples and chickens often vanished, tombstones became oven walls and fences fed campfires."[38]

With the beginning of the Civil War, Washington City changed even more than Washington County did. Since neighboring Virginia had joined the Confederacy, the District was immediately placed on a wartime footing, and soldiers from Northern states along with new government workers and fugitive slaves began to flood the city. General Butler had declared the fugitives to be "contraband"; therefore, they did not have to be returned to their owners as the prewar laws had required. Many of the fugitives were concentrated in downtown Washington, where they looked for jobs and security, but their rapidly growing presence also fanned the racial tensions in the city. Strict enforcement of the racial codes increased, and any Black person on the streets appearing to have no occupation or documentation could be arrested. Once arrested, presumably for violating some law, a Black person had little chance to prove his or her innocence.[39]

The most important change for Black people in the District came on April 16, 1862, when President Lincoln signed a bill emancipating the slaves in the District of Columbia and authorizing compensation of their owners. When the bill was first presented to Congress in early April, the District's City Council protested and wrote up a resolution expressing the members' distaste of the idea. The council members urged Congress to be careful "to provide Just and proper safe-guards against converting this city, located as it is between two

Photo of Civil War–era guards checking identification at the ferry landing on Mason's Island in the Potomac River. Georgetown is visible across the river. Photo by George N. Barnard (1819–1902). Courtesy of Library of Congress, Prints and Photographs Division.

Slaveholding States, into an asylum for free negros, a population undesirable in every American community." Despite their opposition to the bill, as well as that of most white residents, two-thirds of the senators voted in favor of it, and a week later it passed in the House.[40]

After the emancipation of the District's slaves, the city's Black codes were repealed, thus making both Washington City and Georgetown less restrictive places for Black residents to live and work. Under the DC emancipation law, slaveholders within the District were required to release their slaves but were allowed to petition the government for compensation if they swore loyalty to the federal government. This approach was similar to that of Lincoln's proposed bill when he was a congressman. A Baltimore slave dealer reviewed the petitions for compensation and determined each slave's worth based on a current theoretical price in a slave market. Not surprisingly, slave owners estimated the worth of their slaves much higher than they could have realistically received in the market. Owners generally received compensation that was on average about 40 percent of the value they had requested in their petitions.[41]

At Georgetown's Visitation Convent and School, located close to where John Harris was living, the nuns requested compensation for eleven enslaved people including the entire Tilghman family, whose six children had been born and grown up enslaved at the convent and school. Since the establishment of Visitation Convent in 1800, the nuns had owned over a hundred slaves, who were often received as gifts or part of an estate. Just as Georgetown College had done, when the nuns were under economic constraints, they sold some of their enslaved people through a slave dealer in southern Maryland, sometimes separating family members. Ignatius Tilghman, the father of the family, had an agreement with the nuns to buy his and his family's freedom over time for a total of $500. Because he had already paid them almost $300, he appealed to the government for reimbursement for this partial payment, but the nuns disputed his claim. Eventually the government deducted the amount he had paid from the compensation made to the Visitation Convent, but no record exists showing that Tilghman himself received any of it.[42]

Beyond Georgetown and Washington City, the 1860 census had counted 834 enslaved people living in Washington County, seven of whom lived across Broad Branch Road at the Belt farm. Charles Belt had inherited the Bowie family of slaves thirteen years earlier after the death of his father, and within a month of the passage of the new emancipation law, he petitioned for compensation.[43] He asked $5,600 for the family, which included Lethea Bowie, her younger brother Henry, and her five children. The children ranged in age from thirteen to thirty-one, and all had been born and raised on the Belt property.[44]

Since the Belt property was so close to the Harris farm, the two Black families, one enslaved and one free, likely would have known one another well, and their children, close in age, then would have grown up as friends. In his petition, Belt described Eliza Bowie, one of the daughters, as "good-natured, good-faced, pleasant" who "stoops a little when walking"; she was about the same age as Ann Harris. Andrew Bowie—who was described as "polite," with "a hesitation in answering," and praised as a "valuable servant, farmhand and cobbler"—was the same age as Lewis Harris. And Hamilton Bowie—whom Belt described as reticent, possessing peculiarly colored eyes that gave him a "green look, [and] quite ingenious," who also handled "carpenter tools very well" and was a "good farm hand"—was in between the ages of Ann and Lewis Harris. Belt's petition to the District commissioners described his former slaves in glowing terms, but his effusive praise clearly also emphasized their worth so that he might receive as much compensation as the slave trader thought appropriate. Belt's petition was accepted, as were most of the 966 petitions by the District's slave owners.[45]

The majority of the District's emancipated slaves, including the freed Visitation Convent slaves in Georgetown and the Bowie family, did not stay with their owners.[46] The two eldest Bowie children eventually moved to Georgetown for work. In 1863 George Bowie ("a valuable servant . . . strong, active, healthy, skillful, sincere") was recorded in his draft registration as having recently worked as a servant in Georgetown. By the time of the 1870 census, his nineteen-year-old sister, Harriet ("a good seamstress and able servant, faithful and honest"), was also working in Georgetown as a servant.

During the Civil War, Washington's public infrastructure was overwhelmed as the city's population exploded; fifty thousand men were in the twenty-five military hospitals alone. The District suffered epidemics of smallpox and cholera as well as recurring episodes of typhus, scarlet fever, and yellow fever, which were spread by the soldiers and freed people who were clustered around the forts.[47] In the hot summer of 1862, a smallpox epidemic hit Washington, DC, and in an August heat wave, typhoid fever broke out at Fort DeRussy and spread to Fort Pennsylvania (Fort Reno). The Harris farm was located near Fort Pennsylvania, where twenty-two soldiers fell ill, and quite possibly this typhus outbreak or others that followed also infected Harris family members.[48] Sometime between 1860 and 1870, two of the Harris children, Ann and Theodore, disappeared from any records, and it is possible that they died in one of these epidemics.

By 1862 John Harris, the eldest of the Harris children, was married to a woman named Mildred. The couple had settled near the campuses of Georgetown University and Visitation Convent, about five miles south of his family's home.[49] John was soon joined in Georgetown by his younger brother Joseph and ten thousand fugitive slaves from neighboring slave-holding states,

View of Georgetown and the Aqueduct Bridge from Virginia in the 1860s. Photo by William Morris Smith. Civil war photographs, 1861–1865, Library of Congress, Prints and Photographs Division.

and they were all looking for work. By the end of the war, an estimated forty thousand more of them had arrived.[50] Fortunately, despite the growing number of job seekers, both Harris brothers found work in Georgetown—John as a house servant and seventeen-year-old Joseph as a waiter in a saloon.[51]

What many young Black men such as John and Joseph really wanted was to join the Union army and fight against the Confederacy, but the federal government would not consider it. Everyone initially assumed the war was going to be short; thus, there was no need for more troops. In addition, many people also thought that Black men would be undisciplined soldiers and untrainable. The Harris brothers and the other Black men in Washington could only watch as the city became flooded with arriving white troops from Northern states as well as the wounded from Southern battlefields.

Within months of the beginning of the war in 1861, Union troops were defeated at the Battles of Bull Run and Ball's Bluff in nearby Virginia, both within forty miles of Georgetown. People began to realize that the war might be longer and deadlier than they had initially assumed. In 1862 the war didn't go much better. In August the Second Battle of Bull Run was another defeat for the Union, and a month later the Union suffered ten thousand casualties in the bloodiest battle of the war in Antietam, Maryland.

## Enlisting in the Union Army

Although the Union still resisted enlisting Black men, individual states began rethinking their racial enlistment policies. In the summer of 1862, the District was beginning to have trouble filling its own subscription of white men willing to risk their lives fighting the Confederacy. Six months later, Lincoln's Emancipation Proclamation specifically declared that the emancipated slaves could be recruited into the armed services of the United States. They "will be received into the armed service of the United States to garrison forts, positions, stations, and other places, and to man vessels of all sorts in said service." The War Department authorized three Northern states—Massachusetts, Connecticut, and Rhode Island—to form Black regiments under state direction. But still the District did not move to enlist Black men.

In the spring of 1863, Frederick Douglass, the best-known Black abolitionist in the country, personally lobbied Lincoln to allow Black men in all Northern states to join the military. Two former army hospital chaplains enlisted the support of influential people in Washington, writing letters to numerous government officials. Aided by a charismatic Black pastor named Henry McNeal Turner, they began to lobby hard at recruitment meetings for the formation of a District regiment.[52] Lincoln hesitated because he was concerned about the resistance from slave-holding states that were fighting for the Union; he could not afford to lose those states if they resisted the formation of Black regiments.

In the first week of May 1863, local organizers circulated notices throughout the District announcing a "Meeting for the Organization of a Colored Regiment in the District of Columbia." Several recruitment meetings at local churches ensued within a few weeks, enraging local Confederate sympathizers. At one early meeting, a regiment of white Massachusetts troops had to be called in to protect the Black attendees inside the church. Despite the hostility against them, many emancipated slaves without jobs or shelter signed up, and since the federal government had not yet committed any support for the recruits, they camped out in Black churches. John and Joseph Harris, who were living in Georgetown, likely also attended the recruitment meetings.[53]

Finally, on May 22, the US War Department established the Bureau of Colored Troops to begin the official recruitment of Black men to serve in the Union army. The Harris brothers must have returned to their family farm to discuss their possible enlistment with their parents. Enlistment was a major gamble for Black men given both the hostility of Southerners in Washington to Black enlistments and the staggering fatality rate of Union soldiers on the battlefields. In addition, John and his wife, Mildred, were expecting their first child. But the Harris brothers must have felt strongly about joining the army because in the next month the two brothers made the biggest decision of their young lives: they enlisted in the District's First Regiment US Colored Troops.

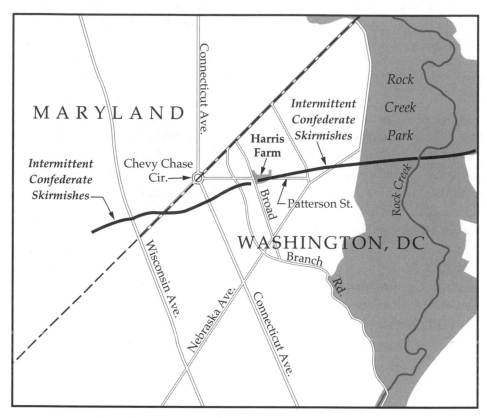

During the Confederate invasion of the District in 1864, a skirmish line
went through the area where the Harris farm was located.

# 5

## The First Regiment of US Colored Troops at War

On July 10, 1863, John and Joseph Harris walked over the Aqueduct Bridge from Georgetown to Virginia and then crossed a causeway to Analostan Island in the middle of the Potomac River. The island had once belonged to George Mason, a Virginia founding father, and nineteenth-century maps often referred to it as Mason's Island. At the end of the eighteenth century, upon George's death, his son John Mason inherited the island and had enslaved workers build him a home on it; it was still standing when the Harris brothers arrived for their training as recruits of the First Regiment of US Colored Troops (USCT) infantry.[1]

The army chose Analostan Island for the training site of the Black soldiers because it was secluded enough to protect them from angry Confederate sympathizers. Its location was unpublicized, and even white officers not involved in the training were initially barred from the camp.[2] The concern about violence against the Black recruits was not just theoretical. Three days after the Harris brothers arrived on the island, draft riots broke out in New York City. During five bloody days of riots, recent immigrants who had initially rioted against the military draft turned their anger against Black people, killing more than a hundred men and destroying their property. In the District, the people's reaction to the draft law was tempered by the overwhelming presence of Union troops already in the city as well as the seclusion of the Black soldiers on an island in the middle of the Potomac.[3]

In the same month the Harris brothers enlisted, poet Walt Whitman visited the USCT training camp:

> After reaching the Island, we get presently in the midst of the camp of the 1st Regiment U.S.C.T. The tents look clean and good; indeed, altogether, in locality especially, the pleasantest camp I have yet seen. The spot is umbrageous, high and dry, with distant sounds of the city. . . . A hundred rods across is Georgetown. The river between is swelled and muddy from the late rains up country. So quiet here, yet full of vitality, all around in the far distance glimpses, as I sweep my eye, of hills, verdure-clad, and with plenteous trees.[4]

In the 1930s, Analostan Island was renamed Roosevelt Island, after President Teddy Roosevelt.

## Boot Camp for Black Soldiers

John Harris was described in his enlistment papers as twenty-one years old and five foot eleven, three inches taller than the average white Union soldier. He had a black complexion, black eyes and hair, and a scar on his right shin. His previous occupation was listed as laborer, a job he had performed for several years on the Harris farm before his employment as a servant in Georgetown. He was assigned to be a cook for his regiment. His brother Joseph was described as a mulatto, seventeen years old, and five feet three with gray eyes, brown hair, and a scar on his arm. His previous occupation was that of waiter in a Georgetown saloon.[5] The two brothers were apparently healthy, but an estimated 25 percent of Black recruits were rejected for medical reasons.[6]

The day John and Joseph Harris enlisted they were accompanied by another young man named William Harris, who was the same age as John and had also been living in Georgetown while working as a waiter. He was probably a cousin on their father's side of the family.[7] William was assigned to Company E, and the Harris brothers were assigned to Company G. Many of Company G's recruits had already enrolled, and by the end of July, the company had its full complement of a hundred men. The regiment, which included ten companies, numbered a thousand soldiers.

The twenty officers of the First Regiment were all white men who had volunteered to lead Black troops, and by doing so, they earned immediate promotions and increased pay. The commanding officer of the regiment was Col.

John H. Holman, an abolitionist originally from Maine who had fought with the Union army in Missouri. Having a commander who was an abolitionist was an advantage for the Black enlistees because they were more likely to get some education than those troops who were led by officers who were indifferent to their needs.[8]

Most of the recruits were given the rank of private, but a few of the men, probably those who were literate, were made sergeants. One of them was George Hatton, who had been born into slavery in rural Maryland. His father had purchased his freedom, and he had come to the District and found work as a porter. Hatton had spoken powerfully and eloquently at early recruitment meetings. He was only twenty-one, the same age as John Harris, but his strong speaking style and personality eventually would draw him into politics after the war.[9]

All of the men received the standard Union uniform consisting of a blue wool coat with brass buttons imprinted with an eagle, a flannel shirt, light blue trousers, an outer coat, underwear, socks, and boots. Much of the clothing was heavy and uncomfortable, and its cost was deducted from the soldiers' pay. Each man was also issued a set of equipment that included a musket, but the first muskets the regiment received were outdated and unwieldly. Only after the officers complained to their superiors did the regiment receive better ones a year later. The combination of clothing, equipment, and gun weighed about fifty pounds.[10]

When Walt Whitman visited the camp, he observed the new recruits queueing up in their companies before the paymaster, with a clerk calling out their names and giving them their wages in cash. He noted specifically the good appearance of the Harris brothers' unit: "Company G in full dress with brass scales on shoulders look'd, perhaps, as well as any of the companies— the men had an unusually alert look."[11]

According to Whitman's description, most companies were paid $10.03, and for reasons unclear to him, a few were paid less. "One company, by the rigid rules of official computation, gets only 23 cents each man. The company (K) is indignant, and after two or three are paid, the refusal to take the paltry sum is universal, and the company marches off to quarters unpaid. . . . Another company (I) gets only 70 cents. The sullen, lowering, disappointed look is general. Half refuse it in this case."[12]

In 1863 the monthly pay for Black recruits was $10 with $3 deducted for their clothing. White soldiers received $3 more each month, plus a clothing allowance. In September a freeborn Black corporal from Massachusetts who had already been in battle wrote a letter to President Lincoln, protesting the unequal pay: "The patient Trusting Descendants of Africa's Clime have dyed the ground with blood, in Defense of the Union. . . . All we lack, is a paler hue,

The First Regiment of the US Colored Troops of the District of Columbia standing in formation. Photo by Mathew Brady (1823–96). Courtesy of Library of Congress, Prints and Photographs Division.

and a better acquaintance with the Alphabet. Now Your Excellency, We have done a Soldiers Duty. Why cant we have a Soldiers pay?"[13]

It would be another year before Congress would provide all soldiers equal pay regardless of color. Even then Congress made a distinction between Black soldiers who had been freemen before the war and those who were freed after the war began. For former slaves, it stipulated that the pay increase was retroactive to January 1, 1864, but for the 20 percent of the men in the First Regiment who had been born free, such as the Harris brothers, it was retroactive to their enlistment.[14]

The distinction between Black soldiers who were born free and those born enslaved created another form of unequal pay, and some officers regarded this as unfair. A colonel in the Fifty-Fourth Massachusetts Regiment contrived a special oath for all Black soldiers to take, one that eliminated the distinction between the formerly enslaved and the freemen, thus ensuring equal pay for all. For the same reason, Colonel Holman had each man in his regiment swear that he "owed no man unrequited labor on or before the nineteenth day of April, 1861." Like all the other men, the Harris brothers swore the oath, and their records were marked "Free April 19, 1861."[15]

The army's pay was never generous, and it had to cover needed supplies as well as contributions to the soldiers' families. A civilian merchant known as a sutler was assigned to the regiment to furnish supplemental provisions, including food such as canned vegetables and items such as tobacco and razors. The sutler followed the regiment after the training finished and often extended credit until the next payday. Both Harris brothers' official records showed that at some point they owed money to their regimental sutler.[16] USCT muster sheets for John Harris from the summer of 1864 listed items for which he owed money: "1 canteen, 41 cts., 1 cartg box belt plate 7 cts." The next month his debt increased thirty-three cents for a haversack, which was a square bag with a strap that could carry four days of rations for meals.[17]

The training of the Black recruits was intense, filled with numerous drills and instruction, since the officers had little time to turn the enlistees into fighting men. Each day began with "Reveille" at five o'clock in the morning, and the men's only free time was two hours in the evening before "Taps" sounded at 9:30 p.m. The men used what little free time they had for instruction in reading and writing.[18] A journalist from Minnesota visited the camp while the Harris brothers were training and was impressed:

Their officers appear to have been very carefully chosen and are men who are anxious they should succeed. In addition to military tactics they [the Black soldiers] are learning to read and may be seen in the intervals between their drills, in little groups with primers and spelling books conning over their lessons. People here are becoming accustomed to see them in United States uniform, and they are more frequently hailed with signs of approbation than with sneers of scorn.[19]

In late July, a general who inspected the First Regiment before the men shipped out noted that they "looked as well" as any white soldiers with the same amount of training.[20] The Harris brothers, however, had reasons to be apprehensive: they had had only one month of training, and the guns they had were outmoded. They surely had also heard of the official policy of the Confederate government that any captured Black soldiers would be sold into slavery or executed. One mother of a Black soldier from Massachusetts wrote to Lincoln about it that same month: "A colored man ought to run no greater risques than a white." She implored him to put rebel prisoners to work in prisons until the practice was stopped and added emphatically, "You ought to do this, and do it at once. Not let the thing run along meet it quickly and manfully, and stop this mean, cowardly cruelty."[21]

At the end of July, President Lincoln issued an order demanding equal protection for both Black and white troops, "for every soldier of the United States, killed in violation of the laws of war, a rebel soldier shall be executed; and for every one enslaved by the enemy, or sold into slavery, a rebel soldier shall be placed at hard labor on the public works and continued at such labor until the other shall be released."[22] This order was thin protection in what had become a savage war. John and Joseph Harris left Washington not knowing that it would be almost two years before they would return. They could not anticipate how much they and their hometown would change in the interim.

## The Battlegrounds of Virginia

The Harris brothers had enlisted at a turning point in the Civil War.[23] The Union victory at Gettysburg on July 4, 1863, forced the Confederate army to retreat into Virginia, and the victory the same day at Vicksburg, Mississippi, ensured the Union's control of the Mississippi River. Nevertheless, some of the fiercest battles of the war lay ahead, and the Harris brothers were sailing into the middle of them. Their ship landed at Elizabeth City, North Carolina, a deepwater port south of Norfolk, Virginia, that the Union troops had captured the previous year.[24]

The men of the First Regiment were initially given either guard duty or "fatigue duty," which involved the backbreaking construction of forts, roads, and defenses. Black troops were more likely than white soldiers to be assigned fatigue duty, and some commanders, including the First Regiment's Colonel Holman, complained to the War Department that the practice was bad for morale. One commander complained to Gen. Edward A. Wild, who at the end of the year would command several USCT regiments including the First Regiment. Describing the excessive fatigue duty as "incessant and trying," the commander reported the adverse physical effects on the troops: "My sick leave has increased from 4 or 5 to nearly 200 in a little over a month."[25] Eventually the army ordered a more equitable distribution of fatigue duty, but it was not rigidly enforced.[26]

Colonel Holman had to confront discrimination among some of his white officers, and he discharged several of them. He also actively recruited a medical officer for the regiment because the one assigned to the troops had deserted. One doctor was fired, and another man with little medical training was also fired for drinking the medicinal alcohol.[27] Since there were few Black doctors, and most white ones did not want to serve with Black troops, finding a replacement was impossible. The lack of a regimental doctor continued to be a problem throughout the war.[28]

One source of support for the men was a newly appointed Black chaplain named Rev. Henry McNeal Turner, who had earlier helped lead the unofficial recruitment effort for the First Regiment USCT in Washington. He was a strong leader who risked his life to accompany the troops onto the battlefield, where he provided help and comfort. Just as important was his determination to educate the men of the regiment, most of whom were illiterate, and he gave them books and tutoring.[29]

In December 1863, the First Regiment joined other Black regiments to form what was called the African Brigade under the command of General Wild. Their first engagement with the enemy came in South Mills, North Carolina, about fifteen miles north of Elizabeth City. The Confederates had sent out parties of guerrillas to attack Union forces, but the African Brigade not only held its ground but also burned Confederate homes and barns, captured horses and boats, and freed as many as twenty-five hundred slaves.[30] In a report on January 3, 1864, Colonel Holman described the men's performance: "When this regiment was formed, it was confidently asserted that it was not possible for a colored man to make a soldier. Many obstacles were put in their way; but by their attention to duty, and by soldierly bearing, the men of this command have overcome these obstacles, [and] have received the commendations of the Commanding general."[31]

In the spring of 1864, the First Regiment was sent up the James River to Wilson's Wharf in Virginia, some thirty miles southeast of Richmond.[32] While the men were there, they would have heard about the cold-blooded slaughter of hundreds of Black soldiers at Fort Pillow, Tennessee, on April 25, 1864. After the Union troops surrendered at Fort Pillow, the Confederate soldiers became enraged because half of the six hundred Union soldiers were Black men whom the Confederates saw as traitors to the South. Although the description of events and the estimates of the number killed at Fort Pillow varied, few Black soldiers survived.[33] The newspapers reported the incident in most major cities. An angry Black New York resident immediately wrote to the secretary of war and demanded that the Union retaliate against the Rebel troops. He suggested that after an equal number of rebel prisoners were executed by Black troops, then "the rebels will learn that the U.S. Govt. is not to be trifled with and the black men will feel not a spirit of revenge."[34]

The lesson of Fort Pillow was clear to every Black Union soldier: the Confederates were more likely to kill Black Union soldiers than take them as prisoners of war. Surrendering would be tantamount to death. Two years after the war ended, the Confederate commanding officer who had ordered the Fort Pillow massacre became the first grand wizard of the Ku Klux Klan.[35]

On May 24, a Confederate force of twenty-five hundred cavalry attacked the First Regiment at Wilson's Wharf. The outnumbered Black troops held their position, and after six hours of fighting, the Confederate forces retreated.[36] The Confederates suffered an estimated one hundred casualties, while the Union force had suffered only two men killed and fourteen wounded. It was an important moral victory for the Black soldiers whose abilities so many people had doubted. Sgt. George Hatton wrote of his comrades in the regiment: "The heroism displayed by the gallent boys of the 1st needs no comment for they have won for themselves unfading laurels, to be stamped on the pages of history."[37] After the war, the Confederate general Fitzhugh Lee, nephew of Robert E. Lee, remarked that the Black troops he and his men had faced at Wilson's Wharf were "a foe worth their steel."[38]

In June, the First Regiment was assigned to join other USCT infantry regiments and two Black cavalry units to form a brigade commanded by Colonel Holman. The Union strategy was to cut Richmond's supply lines and capture the city. The brigade advanced just outside the city of Petersburg, an essential rail and supply center for the Confederacy's capital. Early on the morning of June 15, the battle for Petersburg began on the outskirts of town. The Harris brothers' regiment overcame the first Confederate troops they met and advanced toward the city's defenses under heavy fire. Near sundown and still under fire, the men attacked the enemy's fortifications and, within twenty minutes, captured two batteries. At nine o'clock in the evening, operations were suspended because of darkness.

The initial Union assault on Petersburg's defenses had been successful, and the commanding general praised the Black troops in his official report of the battle: "The gallant and soldierly deportment of the troops . . . the celerity with which they moved to the charge; the steadiness and coolness exhibited by them under heavy and long-continued fire; the impetuosity with which they sprang to the assault; the patient endurance of wounds."[39]

Unfortunately, over 10 percent of the soldiers in the First Regiment were wounded or killed in the three-day battle for Petersburg. On the first day of the fighting, Sergeant Hatton was wounded, and three days later so was John Harris. On June 18, 1864, the last day of the Petersburg attack, John suffered a severe wound to his left hand. Because no physician was assigned to the regiment, any medical assistance for his wound would have been performed by men with no medical training. Meanwhile, as Confederate reinforcements arrived in Petersburg, the Union troops clearly saw that another direct assault would fail; therefore, they set up a siege of the city.

The injured were taken to field hospitals by wagons over bad roads, and usually the men went without medical attendants or pain relievers. John and the other wounded soldiers, a total of 114 men, were eventually transported to the Balfour US General Hospital in Portsmouth, Virginia, which was seventy-six miles away.[40] Eleven days after being wounded, Harris underwent surgery

View of the US Army Hospital complex at Fort Monroe, Virginia, where John Harris recuperated. Reprinted with permission of the Casemate Museum.

to remove his middle finger and "a portion of 3rd metacarpal bone" in the palm of his hand; the operation left his hand permanently disabled. In August he was transferred from Balfour Hospital to the large US General Hospital at Fort Monroe in Hampton, Virginia.[41]

In the chaos of war, and probably due to confusion with a man of the same name in Company E, John's hospital transfer was not properly recorded, and he was briefly listed as having deserted. A court-martial order was issued but then canceled after the mistake was discovered. In fact, the desertion rate of Black soldiers was about 7 percent, which was lower than the 9 percent desertion rate of white soldiers throughout the war.[42] Eventually John rejoined the First Regiment on Christmas Eve of 1864, six months after being injured.[43] The Union Army was sufficiently desperate for men by that time that it brought back to the battlefield even soldiers with permanent disabilities.

## The Invasion of Washington

While John Harris was recuperating in the hospital and his brother Joseph was dug in at the siege of Petersburg, the Harris family's farm in rural Washington was under attack. On July 11, 1864, a corps of eleven thousand Confederate troops, led by Gen. Jubal Early, advanced to the outskirts of the District of Columbia. Early planned to penetrate the northern fortifications of the District, divert Union troops from the siege of Petersburg, and terrorize the District's citizens. He accomplished all three.

Union soldiers had already cleared the land between the forts circling the northern perimeter of the District. With Early's imminent attack, Union troops hurriedly massed on this first line of defense, and a few moved north into the countryside. By the afternoon, some of Early's men were advancing down the Rockville Turnpike and Seventh Street Turnpike (now Georgia Avenue), heading toward Fort Reno and Fort Stevens.[44] Fort Reno was a mile and a half west of the Harris farm, while Fort Stevens was two and a half miles to the east. The family could probably see the forts in the distance and hear the advancing troops.

Unfortunately, the Harris farm was caught between the Union soldiers moving north and Early's troops riding south. When residents saw that the surrounding countryside clearly would become a battlefield, they fled toward town, taking with them whatever possessions they could pile into a wagon.[45] Mary Ann and Thomas Harris and their children likely escaped south to safety via the nearby Rockville Pike.[46] A New York war reporter described the scene as he ventured out onto the pike: "Down the hill thundered a great wagon loaded with household goods of a refugee and a little after I met cattle and negroes fleeing from the enemy."[47]

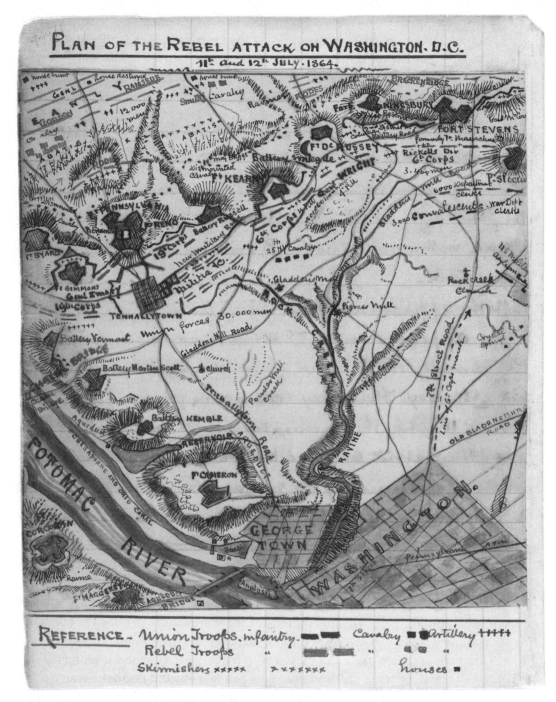

Plan of the Rebel attack on Washington, DC, in 1864. The Harris farm was in the path of
the advancing Confederate troops, a mile northwest of Fort Kearny. Map by Robert Sneden.
Courtesy of Library of Congress, Geography and Map Division.

On July 12, the *Washington Star* published an extra edition with a headline in large letters: "THE INVASION! . . . The farmers in the vicinity lost most of their stock owing, as they said, to our pickets refusing to let the drivers pass through the lines without a permit. [The] stock fell into the hands of the enemy."[48]

Rebel sharpshooters used abandoned barns and outbuildings to fire on Union troops until the Union artillery destroyed the buildings.[49] A number of houses were also burned. A hundred-pound Parrott gun at Fort Reno fired a shell that exploded more than three miles north along the Rockville Pike. The explosion killed four Confederate soldiers but otherwise did little damage.[50] The skirmishes continued into the following day, and at one point, Lincoln himself, accompanied by his wife and several officials, mounted a parapet at Fort Stevens to view the fighting.

By sunset on July 12, the futility of the Confederate troops' position was obvious, and they retreated. The *Washington Star* reported that they drove with them two thousand head of cattle they had stolen from local farmers.[51] Washington had been spared, although the countryside around the forts was scarred. Fields were ruined, and the land was littered with the remains of burned houses and barns and a few bodies of Confederate soldiers.[52] Presumably, the Harris family returned to their farm after the Confederate retreat and calculated their losses in livestock and crops and perhaps their home.

## The Battle for Richmond

Two weeks after the Confederate retreat from Washington, Union troops made another attempt to penetrate the outer defenses of Richmond and to try to take the city. John Harris was still in the hospital recovering from his hand surgery, and Joseph was on picket duty in an outpost in front of the main body of soldiers.

By coincidence, their Annapolis cousin William Pointer, who was in the Maryland Thirtieth Regiment USCT, also was on the front line of the battle for Richmond.[53] Cpl. William Pointer was three years old when the 1843 floods on the Potomac had forced his family to abandon their home and move to Annapolis. William likely had played with his cousins John and Joseph Harris when they were small children, but they probably would not have seen each other after William's family moved away. It is unknown whether they were aware that they were together twenty years later on the battlefields of Virginia. William Pointer's commanding officer was not as good as the one John and Joseph had. Brig. Gen. Edward Ferrero had been a leading dance instructor in

New York City before the Civil War and had even written a book about dancing before teaching at the US Military Academy at West Point, New York.[54]
Unfortunately, his first career was poor preparation for his second, and it is
not surprising that his troops would prove to be better soldiers than he was.

The Thirtieth Regiment was selected as the first Union troops to charge
the Confederate positions at Petersburg. Alas, the assault would be one of the
biggest Union disasters of the war. Mining engineers from Pennsylvania had
dug a tunnel under the Confederate positions on a hill and planned to blow
them up from below.[55] At the last minute both Gen. Ulysses S. Grant and Maj.
Gen. George Meade ordered the inexperienced Thirtieth Regiment to follow
rather than lead a regiment of more seasoned white soldiers.

Grant's decision may have saved William Pointer's life. The initial explosion
on July 30 at 5 a.m. created a large crater that took the Confederates by surprise. They quickly recovered, however, and decimated the poorly positioned
Union troops in the crater. An eyewitness account said, "Ferrero's Negro division . . . burst from the advanced lines, cheering vehemently . . . over a crest
under a heavy fire, . . . over the heads of the white troops in the crater and
captured more than two hundred prisoners and one stand of colors."[56]

However, no amount of experience or patriotism could have prepared
the Union soldiers for their impossible battlefield position. The Confederate
troops held the high ground, shooting the Union troops in the crater below
them. General Ferrero, their dancing school commander, sat out the action
and was reportedly at the rear of the battlefield, drinking rum. An inquiry into
his behavior after the war ridiculed him.

The Union army suffered four thousand casualties on that single day, but
fortunately William Pointer survived. Grant said later, "It was the saddest af-
fair I have witnessed in this war."[57] The Union asked for a four-hour truce to
collect the dead and wounded, but there were so many that the grim task took
eight hours. Given their status in the army, it is reasonable to assume that
both William Pointer and Joseph Harris were among the troops assigned to
bury the dead.

In September 1864, Joseph Harris's First Regiment USCT was ordered
north along the James River to attack Richmond from the east. On October
27, the First Regiment was part of a larger force of both white and Black troops
that attacked the outer defenses at Fair Oaks, five miles east of the city. They
encountered heavy fighting as they penetrated the enemy's defenses, and although exposed to fire in an open field, the First Regiment captured both guns
and prisoners.

A report on the Fair Oaks battle in the *Philadelphia Press* written by Thomas
M. Chester, the only Black war correspondent at the time, described the

performance of the First Regiment in the battle: "The colored troops are the only ones that entered the enemy's works and made any captures that day. . . . The 1st USCT is a fighting regiment, and when Colonel Holman urges them forward, they have never been known to falter or fail." The fighting was heavy, but in the end the Union troops were forced to retreat again. The regiment suffered 124 men killed, wounded, and sickened that day; among them was Colonel Holman, who was wounded, and Joseph Harris, who fell ill.[58]

Clara Barton's Patient

Joseph was evacuated the following day to the field hospital at Point of Rocks, Virginia.[59] The field hospital was a collection of tents and cots that the men took down and set up again as it followed the army. It served primarily as a convalescent ward for the sick but also received the wounded before they were transported to a larger facility for better care. Clara Barton, the celebrated nurse and eventual founder of the American Red Cross, was stationed at the Point of Rocks field hospital when Joseph was admitted. She was in charge of nursing and directly tended to patients, so it is possible that they met. Indeed, at the time of Joseph's admission, she had just returned from checking on her own home in the District of Columbia after General Early's attack on Washington.[60] She surely would have shared what she saw with her patients from the District.

Barton admired the Black soldiers and wrote, "They are ever the objects of my deep commiseration and care, so patient and cheerful, so uniformly polite and soldierly. They are brave men and make no complaints." Joseph Harris spent November and December at the field hospital, long enough to get to know Barton. She often wrote letters for her patients, and if she did so for Joseph, it would have been the first word his parents had heard from their son.[61]

Illness took a much heavier toll than war wounds on both Black and white troops in the Civil War. The hard labor of fatigue duty, the constant exposure to the weather, and an inadequate diet weakened soldiers and compromised their resistance to diseases on the battlefield. In the summer of 1864, one soldier in a USCT regiment in New Orleans was moved to write President Lincoln about the bad conditions leading to illness: "Men are Call to thes fatiuges [fatigue duty] wen sum of them are scarc Able to get Along the Day Before on the Sick List And Prehaps weeks. . . . Hardly have enough Bread to Keep us From starving."[62]

General Wild, a doctor in civilian life, wrote that Black troops, such as the Harris brothers, who had previously lived in the country and who thus had

View of the field hospital in Point of Rocks, Virginia, where Clara Barton worked. Joseph Harris was first admitted here before being moved to the Union hospital at Fort Monroe. Courtesy of Library of Congress, Prints and Photographs Division.

Interior of a Fort Monroe hospital tent, a scene staged by the photographer George Stacy in 1861. Courtesy of Library of Congress, Prints and Photographs Division.

had access to fresh fruits and vegetables, suffered the most from the poor nu-
trition of the Union army's rations.[63] Pneumonia and dysentery were the most
common illnesses among Black soldiers, who were four times more likely than
white soldiers to contract them. Black soldiers were also 25 percent more likely
to die of illnesses than their white counterparts with the same diseases.[64]

Joseph's illness must have been serious because his convalescence was long.
At the end of December 1864, he was transferred to the five-thousand-bed
US General Hospital at Fort Monroe, across the bay from Norfolk. It was the
second-largest Union hospital at the time, with a large garden that supplied
fresh fruit and vegetables for patients' meals, and it offered the best treat-
ments available. The enlisted men were quartered in tents, and the officers
were housed in wooden structures.[65] Joseph's brother John had himself spent
part of the summer and fall of 1864 recuperating from his hand surgery at the
same hospital. Joseph arrived at the hospital just as John was returning to his
regiment for the last nine months of the war. Joseph remained at the hospital
for seven months before he was discharged from the army.[66]

## The End of the War

In January 1865, John Harris and his comrades in the First Regiment sailed in
stormy weather to a staging area near Fort Fisher, one of three Confederate
forts that protected the port of Wilmington, North Carolina. Wilmington
was near the intersection of three railroad lines and the Cape Fear River, and
it was the last major supply route for the Confederate troops still defending
Richmond. By February 22, the Union forces had captured Wilmington, and
the supply chain for the remaining rebel army collapsed. Six weeks later, Gen.
Robert E. Lee surrendered at Appomattox, Virginia.

When General Lee surrendered on April 9, the First Regiment celebrated
with volleys of gunfire in the air. John Harris's brigade marched into the city
of Raleigh without a fight. Just a week later, on April 16, the men received the
shocking news of Lincoln's assassination the previous day, and they put on
badges of mourning to honor the president who had seen them through the
devastating war. Ten days after Lincoln's assassination, Confederate general
Joseph E. Johnston, who still had enough men to continue fighting in North
Carolina, surrendered, and the war in the eastern United States effectively
came to an end. In May Colonel Holman rejoined the First Regiment from
his convalescence, and the men were sent to the Outer Banks of the Carolina
coast and performed guard duty during their last few months of service.[67]

The men now had more time to spend on their studies. Their chaplain,
Henry McNeal Turner, was determined to make every man in the regiment

literate, and he continued to provide the men with books and tutoring. Near the end of the war, his books were destroyed when a boat carrying them sank in the Cape Fear River. Reverend Turner appealed to his superiors for more books, but his repeated requests went unanswered. He was well aware that the valor and sacrifice of Black soldiers would bring them no promotions, so in a final request he sarcastically suggested that perhaps the army could have the men turn in their medals in exchange for books.[68] Whether the soldiers ever received more books is not known. At the beginning of the war, only a hundred out of the more than one thousand men in the First Regiment could read; by the end of the war, there were three hundred.[69]

According to the District newspaper the *National Republican*, of the original 1,000 soldiers of the First Regiment USCT who had left the District in the summer of 1863, only 220 returned to the capital in the fall of 1865. Also returning were 480 additional soldiers who had joined the regiment later in the war. Some of the regiment's original men remained in North Carolina, where they had been discharged, and some migrated to other states.[70] On Sunday, October 8, the steamer carrying John Harris and his remaining comrades returned to Washington, DC, and landed at the Sixth Street wharf, at what today is the District's Southwest waterfront. Cheering crowds of mostly Black Washingtonians welcomed them, and in the afternoon, the men disembarked and marched up Seventh Street to Campbell Hospital, which was located on what is now Florida Avenue.[71]

Two days after the First Regiment arrived at Campbell Hospital, Colonel Holman assembled his men, who shouldered their muskets and in full uniform marched in formation through the city's streets to the White House. President Andrew Johnson reviewed the troops, and as they stood in front of the White House, he addressed them for thirty minutes, thanking them for their service. He also lectured these seasoned combat soldiers about good habits, self-control, and a virtuous life.

At the end of President Johnson's speech, the men marched back to the hospital dining hall, which had been elaborately decorated.[72] Almost eight hundred people attended the banquet. Although Joseph had been discharged from the army directly from the hospital in early May, he likely would have attended the banquet with his brother and fellow soldiers and perhaps their parents as well. There were speeches, singing, and the presentation of bouquets, including a special wreath given to Colonel Holman by Sgt. George Hatton. After dinner, the celebration spread throughout the hospital.[73]

Two days after the banquet, the soldiers of the First Regiment who had returned to the District received their final pay and were formally discharged. Colonel Holman promised he would give written recommendations to any

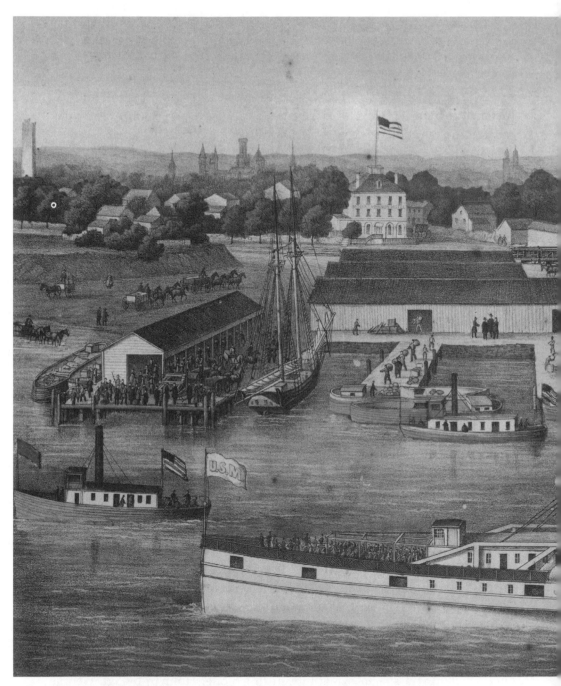

View of the Sixth Street Wharf in Southeast Washington during the Civil War. The First Regiment of the US Colored Troops landed here at the end of the war. Print by Charles Magnus, circa 1863. Courtesy of Library of Congress, Prints and Photographs Division.

man who sought one; he also told them that by defeating the Confederacy, they had earned the right to citizenship and urged them to become leaders in their communities. He presciently warned them about continuing resistance to their voting rights among Southern whites. As an abolitionist, he had been a good commander, fighting for the fair treatment of his troops as well as promoting their training and education. At the end of the war, Holman was made a brigadier general before moving to Missouri. At age fifty-two, he applied for a military pension and died seven years later.[74]

Holman's solicitude toward his troops may have been one of the reasons the First Regiment US Colored Troops experienced fewer deaths than the other Black regiments. Of the twelve hundred men whose names appeared on the regiment's rolls during the war, 15 percent had died, but more than half of those deaths had been due to diseases rather than battle wounds.[75] The First Regiment's mortality rate was only slightly higher than that of white soldiers and lower than the average mortality rate of all Black regiments during the war. By the war's end, approximately thirty-seven thousand Black soldiers had lost their lives, and many more had been wounded or had fallen victim to disease.[76]

### The Immediate Aftermath of the War

The war changed more than society with the abolition of slavery; it also changed the men who had fought in it. Many soldiers in the First Regiment could read and write by the time they mustered out.[77] Most of them had traveled farther than anyone else in their families ever had, and they had matured on the battlefields where they had lost some friends but had made new ones, often from different states. Just as important, many had also acquired new skills. Before the war, 90 percent of the Black soldiers had been farmers or laborers; only 10 percent had a trade. Thirty-five years later, a quarter of the survivors had a trade or were working in stores and factories.[78] Late in the war, one Black soldier expressed the optimism that many of his Black comrades felt at the time: "I think that, under God, this will yet be a pleasant land for the colored man to dwell in."[79]

The Harris brothers returned to the District and were reunited with their families, but neither stayed on the family farm. John rejoined his wife, Mildred, and their young son in Georgetown, where he would work and live for the rest of his life. He and his family were eventually joined there by his two youngest brothers.

Joseph traveled much farther, moving to New York City, the home of some of his fellow soldiers from the First Regiment. In New York, he found work, married, and raised a family, and he would remain there for more than twenty years.[80] Soldiers like Joseph who migrated to cities in the North were more likely to migrate to states where other soldiers in their unit originated.[81] The Harris brothers' First Regiment was primarily made up of soldiers from Maryland and Virginia, but seven soldiers came from Canada and several from the Caribbean. From the mid-Atlantic states, sixteen came from Delaware, fifteen from Pennsylvania, and five from New York. Of the five New Yorkers in the First Regiment, three were from the New York City area, and one man, Charles Brown, was in Company G with Joseph Harris. Brown was three years older than Joseph and a blacksmith from Staten Island. Joseph and Charles had trained together on Mason Island, drilled together in the field, and fought next to each other in Virginia and North Carolina. Charles may have persuaded Joseph to come to New York at the end of the war, although that is just speculation.[82]

William Pointer also survived the war and returned to Annapolis, where he would live for the rest of his life. He worked for the US Navy as a cook aboard training ships, and eventually his three sons worked for the US Naval Academy. In 1949 his grandson was working there when Wesley Brown, the first African American to attend the academy, graduated from the school.

John and Joseph's chaplain, Henry McNeal Turner, who had advocated for the education of the men of the First Regiment, returned to Washington and worked for the Freedmen's Bureau. He dedicated himself to the cause of unifying people of African descent and became an advocate of their emigration to Africa. He also became a bishop in the African Methodist Episcopal Church in Georgia, and almost thirty years later Frederick Douglass would introduce him to a large convocation at the Chicago World's Fair.[83] Henry Louis Gates called Reverend Turner "one of the lions of the race, still roaring at the turn of the century."[84]

Sgt. George Hatton, the sergeant major of the First Regiment, went into politics and in 1869 won a seat on the Washington City Council.[85] It was a time when the world had opened to all of the returning veterans of the First Regiment USCT, and everything seemed possible.

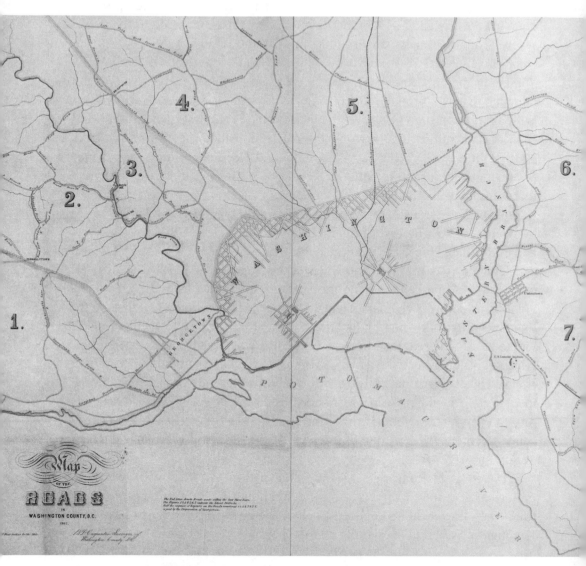

This 1867 map features the roads of rural Washington County, DC. The unmarked farm is on Broad Branch Road in section 2. Map by B. D. Carpenter from the District of Columbia Office of the Surveyor. Courtesy of Library of Congress, Geography and Map Division.

# 6

## Reconstruction and Retreat

When John and Joseph Harris returned home at the end of the war, they were changed men. One observer said that Black soldiers were "completely metamorphosed, not only in appearance and dress, but also in character and relations."[1] John and Joseph were almost two years older, but that was the least of their changes. For the first time, they had traveled beyond the District to other states, and they had experienced the bloody violence of war, seeing men injured and killed. John had lost a finger, and Joseph had been hospitalized for months. Most important, the brothers had fought on the victorious side of the bloodiest war in American history.

An estimated quarter million Union soldiers marched through Washington City on their way home to new lives. Washington, DC, had been a modest government town of seventy-five thousand people at the beginning of the war, but the population had grown 80 percent by 1864. Its growth, however, was uneven. Georgetown had grown by only a third, partly because the university enrollment had declined as the young male students went to war.[2]

As a result of the Emancipation Proclamation, the number of free Black people in the District had grown from 15 percent of the population to a third during the war. A Black educator from New York was so impressed that he commented with pride, "Washington seems to be a kind of a Mecca for sable gentlemen."[3] By the end of the war, Black people had formed small businesses, others filled new jobs in the federal government, and Frederick Douglass had established a local newspaper to give Black residents a public voice.

When the Harris brothers returned to their parents' Dry Meadows farm, they could see how much the area around it had changed. Rural Washington County's population had grown faster than the District's as a whole, and within the county the African American population had increased twice as fast the white population.[4] Many of the fugitive slaves who had clustered around the Union forts during the war had moved into the soldiers' barracks after the troops left. Some of them built homes for themselves from the scraps of wood and metal left behind. Soon a developer bought some property near Fort Reno and subdivided the property into inexpensive small lots, calling it Reno City.[5]

Even the population of the little Broad Branch settlement where the Harrises lived had grown. The number of households between the Harris farm and Charles Belt's large farm had increased considerably.[6] Of course, life on Belt's farm and the homes of other white plantation owners had changed fundamentally with the abolition of slavery. By 1870 Belt was in his seventies, and the old bachelor needed the help of his nephew to run the ancestral property after his former enslaved workers were emancipated and left him.[7]

New Black residents in the Harrises' neighborhood were not necessarily newcomers; indeed, some of them were old family friends. The parents of Charles Williams, the young man who had boarded with the Harris family in the 1850s, moved their family near the Harrises in the 1860s. As noted in chapter 4, the Williamses originally lived near the Pointer cottage on the Potomac River; thus, they had known Mary Ann Harris before she married Thomas. Some of the other new arrivals, such as Marshel Frasier, a formerly enslaved brickmaker from South Carolina, would become lifelong neighbors. The 1870 census showed that most of the new arrivals were not property owners. Despite the brief but destructive Confederate skirmish in the area the previous year, property values had risen, and by 1870 the two-acre Harris farm had doubled in value to $600.[8]

## The Freedmen's Bureau

At the beginning of the war, Frederick Douglass correctly predicted, "Once let the black man get upon his person the brass letter, U.S.; let him get an eagle on his button, . . . and there is no power on earth that can deny that he has earned the right to citizenship."[9] John, Joseph, and the 186,000 other Black soldiers who had fought for the Union and proved that they were as good soldiers as white men assumed at the end of the war that they would be treated accordingly. Lincoln knew that freed people would expect a better life and that the end of the war would just be the beginning of a long process of reconstruction "to bind up the nation's wounds; . . . to do all which may achieve and cherish a just and lasting peace."[10] Preparations for Reconstruction had begun before the end of the war; its goals were to politically reintegrate the southern states back into the polity of the nation and to socially integrate the freedmen into its broader society.

Establishing the Bureau of Refugees, Freedmen, and Abandoned Lands, or the Freedmen's Bureau, was the last major piece of legislation Lincoln signed before his assassination, and he appointed Maj. Gen. Oliver Howard to head the bureau. W. E. B. Du Bois, a critic of Reconstruction, was sympathetic to Howard: "The most fortunate thing that Lincoln gave the Bureau was its head, Oliver Howard. Howard was neither a great administrator nor a great man, but he was a good man. He was sympathetic and humane and tried with endless application and desperate sacrifice to do a hard, thankless duty."[11] Under Howard's direction, the Freedmen's Bureau immediately set up Freedmen's Bureau Courts and boards of arbitration in southern towns to adjudicate the claims of former slaves and their owners. It also established a Freedmen's Savings and Trust Company, or Freedmen's Bank, in New York City and opened branches in Washington and other southern cities a few months later.

The bureau also wanted Black men in the South to be able to vote and run for political office. The white voters in the District were not ready for Black suffrage at the end of the war, but in December 1865 when a referendum on the issue was being organized, twenty-five hundred Black residents of the District signed a petition to Congress asking for the right to vote in local elections. They noted that numerous Black residents of the District were property owners who "pay no inconsiderable amount of taxes; but are nevertheless as slaves to its distribution, unlike other tax-payers they see the proceeds of their labor taken and disposed of without a single voice."[12] The District held the referendum on the contentious issue, and it was overwhelmingly voted down. In Georgetown, only one white man out of 713 voted in favor of giving Black men the vote. Of course, only white men were allowed to vote in the referendum, and the Republicans boycotted it, but the lopsided vote among white male voters was not encouraging.[13]

Despite the overwhelming rejection of Black suffrage by white voters, in January 1867 Congress made it the law in the District over a veto by President

Johnson, and a month later the Black men of the District voted in a local election for the first time. On election day, June 4, 1867, Black buglers began marching and playing around the streets of Washington City at 2 a.m. to ensure that Black men voted. The District was the first place in the country that gave freedmen the right to vote, and they turned out in numbers. Black men were 30 percent of the population in Washington City, but they made up 50 percent of the voters because their participation was so high.[14] Their vote was responsible for the defeat of an unpopular racist mayor. The white residents of Washington realized they were losing control of the city, especially once Ulysses S. Grant, a strong supporter of Reconstruction, was elected president.[15] In the municipal election of 1868, several Black men were elected to the District government, and by the end of the decade, Black men were serving on the District's juries.[16]

For the first time, John and Joseph Harris had a personal friend on the Washington City Council. In 1870 Sgt. George W. Hatton, their comrade in the First Regiment, won a council seat. He had actively recruited Black men for the First Regiment as it was being formed, and he had been wounded at the Battle of Petersburg three days before John was. At the end of the war, Hatton immediately entered Republican politics in the District, first joining a Republican Club to register to vote as many Black men as possible. John and Joseph likely knew him well, and his election to the city council must have made them proud to have served with him in the war.[17]

Between 1869 and 1901, twenty African American men from around the country served in the House of Representatives, and two served in the Senate.[18] During Reconstruction, over six hundred Black men became legislators in southern states. One briefly served as the governor in Louisiana, six were lieutenant governors, and two became state treasurers. Four Black men became superintendents of education, and eight became secretaries of their state. Historian Eric Foner described the changes as "a stunning departure in American politics," but such representation did not last long.[19]

Because the headquarters of the Freedmen's Bureau was located in Washington, the city became a laboratory for the implementation of its reforms. The bureau converted an existing District facility into the Freedmen's Hospital, and although it changed location several times, it continued to serve Washington's Black residents for over a hundred years before becoming a part of Howard University. At the war's end, as many as thirty thousand former slaves in the District of Columbia needed work and shelter. To meet the need, the bureau established housing camps such as the Freedmen's Village in Arlington where the Pentagon now stands. In 1870 Congress appropriated some relief money for coal and food rations for many of the freedmen, and it became the country's first transfer program.[20] Du Bois said that the bureau was "the most extraordinary and far-reaching institution of social uplift that America has ever attempted."[21]

## Public Education for Black Children

The most important permanent change that the Freedmen's Bureau made in its brief life was establishing public schools for Black students for the first time in American history. In Washington County, a few free schools for white children had existed before the war, but the only schools for Black children were private and run by benevolent groups in Washington City. Only a small fraction of Black children in the District received any education at all. The architects of Reconstruction, however, knew that universal public education was essential for the social integration of Black people into the larger society and took important steps toward that goal.[22]

In the seven years following the end of the war, the bureau had established 4,329 schools throughout the South, including in the District of Columbia. A quarter-million Black children attended school by 1870. Some of the pupils would eventually attend the handful of new Black colleges, the most prestigious of which was the District's Howard University, named after the director of the Freedmen's Bureau.[23]

The pace of construction of schools for the District's Black children was initially quite slow, and as a result a government survey of the District's Black residents taken two years after the war found that only one-third of Washington County's 951 Black school-age children were enrolled in school.[24] Fortunately for the two youngest Harris children, one of the first schools established in Washington County was near their farm. The Grant Road Colored School opened in 1866 about a mile south of the family's Broad Branch home. It was near the already existing Grant Road School, which was for white children and whose principal was the Harris family's neighbor John Chappell.[25] The two Harris children still living at home, eleven-year-old Lorenzo and eight-year-old Mary, were among the first students at the new school and were the first Harris generation to have a formal education.[26]

The government did not spend much money on the new school building. It was a basic frame structure costing $960 and measuring only twenty-six by thirty-four feet. The Grant Road Colored School opened in March. If Lorenzo and Mary attended that first spring, they would have joined only seven other classmates, but by the next year, twenty-six students enrolled.[27] Like the other schools in the county, it did not go beyond the first few grades, so the Harris children were enrolled at the school for only a short time.

An 1891 Hopkins Real Estate Map that shows the Grant Road School (the small triangle labeled "school" just east of the Reno neighborhood) and the Harrises' Dry Meadows farm (small triangle in the top right corner of the map labeled "T. Harris"). Created by G. M. Hopkins, C.E. Courtesy of Library of Congress, Geography and Map Division.

The Grant Road School in Tenleytown was initially a school for white children, but in 1882 the building became the school for the area's African American children, replacing their Reconstruction-era school. Public school photograph collection, Historical Society of Washington, DC. Reprinted with permission.

The little school building for Black children was not built to last. In 1882 when a new school for white children opened in Tenleytown, the District government moved the area's Black children into the former white school. Even though the Grant Road School for white children was dilapidated, it was better than the Reconstruction-era structure that had been built for the Black students. The Black community continued to be underserved, however, because the school was used not only by the Broad Branch settlement but also by all of the Black children from Tenleytown and Reno. By the 1890s, 150 children were in a two-room building with a capacity for 74, and some grades were limited to half-day sessions.[28] But despite its inadequacies, two generations of the Pointers' descendants would attend the school and become literate there.

The total cost of the national Freedmen's Bureau's educational programs was about $5 million, a small price to pay to achieve literacy for so many students but a large sum for taxpayers in the North and the South. Each southern state had to bear most of the costs of Reconstruction within its borders, causing a "dramatic" rise in state expenditures. In addition to the costs of Reconstruction, the Freedmen's Bureau was easily corruptible because of the money and contracts that it controlled at a local level. Faced with these problems and the South's continuing opposition to Reconstruction, Congress discontinued future funding for the Freedmen's Bureau in 1872.[29]

The bureau's obituary was written by many historians in the twentieth century. Eric Foner said, "Perhaps the remarkable thing about reconstruction was not that it failed, but that it was attempted at all and survived as long as it did. Its collapse was a tragedy."[30] John Hope Franklin and Alfred A. Moss Jr. compared it with major social experiments in the twentieth century such as the New Deal in the Great Depression and the Marshall Plan in Europe after World War II.[31] W. E. B. Du Bois said, "The attempt to make black men American citizens was in a certain sense all a failure, but a splendid failure."[32] The creation of thousands of public schools was Reconstruction's most enduring legacy, and it survived the bureau's death.

Dry Meadows Farm after the Civil War

Although the Harrises' small farming community gained access to education, the residents still had few other amenities. Public utilities such as running water and sewer systems were not yet available. The family may have had a well, but otherwise water had to be carried from a creek. Oil lamps provided light, while wood and coal were used for heating and cooking. Farms such as theirs usually had a springhouse for keeping items cool in the summer, and produce was preserved in glass jars for winter. Perhaps in later years, when improved roads allowed ice delivery, the family might have bought a new and popular invention, the icebox.[33] Despite their simple living situation, the Harris family enjoyed the advantages of stability that their farm provided.

Changes for the family came inevitably after the war as the children reached adulthood. The Harrises' two-acre property had been big enough for Mary Ann and Thomas to raise their children when they were young, but it was not large enough to support their adult children's own families. As a result, the Harris parents saw their three older sons leave the farm to find work and housing elsewhere. Initially, their two veteran sons were undoubtedly best equipped to be independent. As noted in chapter 5, John, the eldest, returned to Georgetown, where he had worked before the war and where his wife and young son were living. Joseph, who was five years younger than John, had become literate while in the army and did not have a wife or child waiting for him. Free to look for work elsewhere, soon after the war he went to New York City, where he would live for more than two decades.

The third Harris son, Lewis, had remained on the farm during the war, as he was only fifteen years old when his two older brothers enlisted in the Union army. His parents presumably had believed that sending two sons to war was enough, and in any case, they had needed Lewis's help with the farmwork. His only taste of war had come when the Confederate soldiers skirmished near the Harris farm in 1864 and quickly retreated. Lewis's impatience with life on the farm is suggested by his rapid departure when the war was over. By the end of 1865, Lewis had married a woman named Hester O'Neil, and within a year he and his wife had moved to Arlington, Virginia, just across the Potomac River from Georgetown. He became a cart driver, and soon afterward their first child was born. The departure of the three oldest brothers from the Harris farm thus left Thomas and Mary Ann with only their two youngest children at home, and within five years, young Lorenzo too would leave Dry Meadows to work in Georgetown.

In the District, former slaves flooded the job markets after the war, but the Harris brothers had major advantages in competing for jobs. The most important advantage was that they had been free from the time they were born, a status that would have given them a basic confidence and sense of self-sufficiency. They had been well aware of the lives of their enslaved neighbors who worked on the Belt farm across the road. The Harrises had certainly experienced discrimination, which affected all Black people, such as the white neighborhood school that had denied entry to Black students; yet the Harris children never had a slave master to control their lives nor had they ever seen a slave owner abuse their parents. A study of Civil War veterans found that it took two generations for Black men who had been born as slaves to gain the same advantages in literacy, jobs, and education as Black men who had been born free.[34]

The Harris children also had the advantage of having been raised on land that their parents owned. As late as 1890, only 15 percent of Black families living in the District owned their homes; curiously, most of the Black homeowners owned their homes without debt.[35] The Harris family's two-acre farm had given the children a stable environment throughout their formative years, and it provided refuge from the meaner world in Washington City's crowded alleyways.

Since the Harrises could raise their own food, their farm was also a partial refuge from the periodic economic crises that plagued the nineteenth century. The Panic of 1873 was the worst financial disaster since 1837 as many railroads went bankrupt and the stock market closed for ten days. The ensuing depression was so severe that it lasted for five years and caused considerable harm to people who had neither jobs nor land. Both farmers and laborers suffered, of course, but land ownership gave the Harris family food from their gardens and income from any surplus.[36]

Growing up in their Broad Branch settlement meant that the Harris family also enjoyed the stability of having the same neighbors, both Black and white, for many years. During their childhood, the Harris children had interacted with white adults and played with their children. Such familiarity between the races meant that neighbors helped each other regardless of race, as demonstrated when their white neighbor became a witness for John Harris's certificate of freedom in 1862.

The Harris children were also fortunate to have had two parents throughout their childhood, foreshadowing their own stable and long marriages. Children who were born in slavery lived under the constant threat of family separation caused by the sale of a parent. Those enslaved children whose parents worked on a large plantation were more likely to have both parents during their childhood. But most enslaved children were raised on small farms and were more often raised in single-parent families because their parents were more likely to be sold. Even after emancipation, the enslaved children who had been raised by only one parent were more likely themselves to become single parents. By the second generation, however, the lingering effect of slavery on families disappeared.[37]

That the Harris children had both of their parents throughout their childhood was in part due to their parents' good health and longevity. When Thomas Harris became a father at age twenty-seven in 1839, Black men his age were expected to live only another twenty-eight years.[38] Given that, he likely would have died when his last two children were young, and they would have grown up without the benefits of a father figure and his income. Early death was so common in the nineteenth century that many children grew up in single-parent households; thus, the Harris children had a critical advantage in terms of both income and security.[39]

The family patriarch Thomas Harris remained a good provider for the family members who were still on the farm. He listed himself as a gardener in the 1870 census, and although the Harris farm was small, Thomas grew enough produce to feed his family with enough excess to sell at a market in downtown Washington. Like Thomas, most people in rural Washington County were farmers, and their main markets were in the city. If they wanted to sell their produce downtown, they had to be sure it could withstand the long rides on bad roads that were often dusty in the hot summer and muddy in the rainy season.[40] The difficult ten-mile round trip led many farmers to stay in town when they went to market. This was true of Thomas: in the summer of 1880 the census listed Thomas Harris as renting a room at the Washington City home of a former Broad Branch neighbor named John Milbern. In that year's census, in fact, Thomas described himself as a huckster rather than a gardener.

The Harrises had known the Milberns since the 1850s when Thomas Harris purchased the Dry Meadows land from them. By 1880 John Milbern had become a widower and had moved into the city with his young daughter. His apartment near Georgetown was big enough to rent rooms to Thomas and two other families. It was a convenient arrangement for sixty-eight-year-old Thomas, who then could spend time with an old friend and avoid a daily round trip home from the market.

## The Harrises' Daughter Mary Moten

The Harrises' daughter Mary was the youngest of their children and the only surviving girl of the family. She attended the little school near the Dry Meadows farm for several years, and every subsequent census described her as literate. Once Mary finished her limited education at the Grant Road Colored School, she continued living at home, perhaps because she had fewer job opportunities than her brothers did. After the Civil War, more Black women than white women worked in formal jobs out of necessity, but they worked disproportionately in menial jobs. That would be true for Mary as well.[41] Like her mother, Mary Ann, Mary remained at the farm her entire life.

In December 1877, Mary married a widower named Armstead Moten, a shoe and bootmaker from Alexandria, Virginia. She was nineteen years old, and he was thirty-two. Armstead went to live with Mary on the Harris farm, where they built a home for themselves, and the next year they had their first child. The arrangement was almost certainly mutually beneficial for the Motens and Mary's parents. Not only could the two families share farm chores and the care of the young children but also it was undoubtedly financially advantageous for the younger family. Free Black people had commonly shared a home with family members and friends, and those who owned property often took in young family members who might be struggling to support themselves.[42]

Thomas and Mary Ann Harris were fortunate to own two full acres with room enough for the Moten family and their grandchildren to settle. After the war, property values had increased everywhere, making it difficult for many Black people in the District to find affordable housing.[43] Dry Meadows sheltered the younger generation from some of the harsh housing realities that most Black people in the District had to face. In fact, Harris family members—both those living in the Broad Branch settlement and elsewhere—were better off than many Black residents in the city because they all had steady work, decent housing, and a large extended family for financial support.

Although the Harris farm would always be Mary Moten's home, Armstead Moten presumably could not make much money as a shoemaker in the sparsely populated settlement on Broad Branch Road. He worked instead in Georgetown, where there were more people and a higher demand for a cobbler. Unfortunately, he had only two ways to travel the five miles between the Harris farm and Georgetown: by foot, which would be time-consuming and exhausting every day, or by stagecoach, which cost fifty cents round trip.[44]

Probably Armstead Moten boarded with friends or his brothers-in-law in Georgetown during the week. But he certainly returned to the farm regularly because over the next ten years, Mary Moten had four children.

"Deconstruction"

During the 1880s, white residents of Georgetown and Washington City began to take horse-drawn streetcars out to the countryside of Washington County, and they discovered how appealing the rural areas of the District were. A few wealthy Washingtonians, including President Grover Cleveland, built summer homes in the area about three miles south of the Harris farm. By 1884, in response to increasing demand, the value of land in Washington County for the first time exceeded the value of Georgetown property, and by the end of the decade, a streetcar line ran from Georgetown to the District's border with Maryland.[45] Transportation to and from rural Washington County was then much easier for visitors and sightseers who first came out to enjoy the countryside and eventually returned to look for property to build homes.[46] The population of rural communities in the District had also grown enough that Armstead Moten eventually was able to move his cobbler business from Georgetown to Tenleytown, much nearer to his growing family.

An 1890 photo of an electric trolley car that ran along Rockville Pike (Wisconsin Avenue today) from Georgetown to the District's boundary with Maryland, north of Tenleytown. Courtesy of Michael Copperthite and the Copperthite Sellers Family Collection.

The burgeoning population and prosperity of the area, however, brought some of the problems of city life, and with them came the effects of Washington's political landscape. Over the last two decades of the nineteenth century, the initial promises of Reconstruction had faded in the District as they had more generally in the country, and the quality of life for the majority of Black residents diminished. The Washington historian Constance McLaughlin Green wrote of a "withering of hope," partly because of the aftereffects of the economic depression of 1873 but more broadly because of the systematic and progressive disenfranchisement of the Black population in the District.[47]

Unlike other southern cities, the District did not have Jim Crow laws, yet segregation and discrimination grew without formal rules. The relationship between Black and white people in both Washington City and Georgetown gradually eroded as their social interactions diminished. Convenient, affordable housing, always scarce, became more difficult to find, and Black renters were pushed out of centrally located areas as development grew.[48]

Despite the unraveling of many of the improvements under Reconstruction, 1890 was a good year for the Harrises as the Dry Meadows farm continued to be a haven for the family. That year Thomas celebrated his seventy-eighth birthday, and he was still farming and taking some of his produce to market. Mary Ann Harris was seventy years old and the matriarch of an increasing number of grandchildren. The couple had been married for fifty-two years, a notable achievement in an era when death cut many marriages short. They had raised five children to adulthood: their four sons were all married and self-supporting, and their daughter and son-in-law were raising their own four children on the farm.

In 1891 a tectonic shift in the center of the family occurred when Thomas Harris died, and his widow became the head of their family. Fortunately, Mary Ann must have been in good health because, as it turned out, she lived into the twentieth century. She also had considerable support from her daughter's family on the farm and the families of her three sons in Georgetown, which had afforded her sons good jobs and good schools for her grandchildren. But within two years, her eldest son would die, and her youngest would leave for a prestigious job far away.

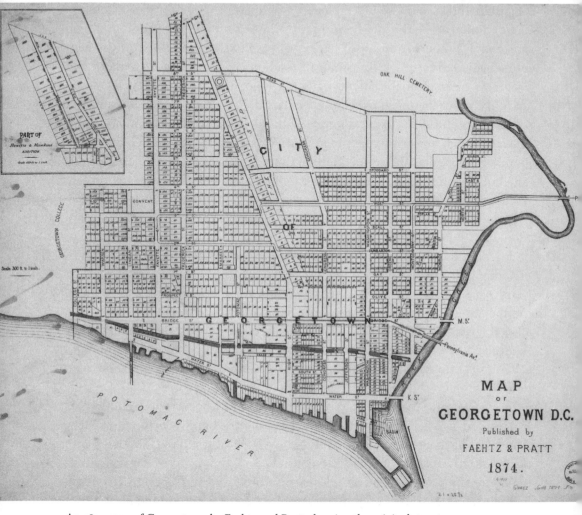

An 1874 map of Georgetown by Faehtz and Pratt showing the original street names.
Courtesy of Library of Congress, Geography and Map Division.

# 7

## At Home in Georgetown

At the end of the Civil War, John Harris returned to his family in Georgetown and remained there, working as a laborer for the rest of his life. Within a few years, two of his younger brothers settled near him, one becoming a driver and the other a church sexton. The families of these three Harris brothers would live near one another in Georgetown for almost two decades, long enough to see the town and their families transformed.

Before the Revolutionary War, Georgetown had been one of the major colonial ports in the mid-Atlantic because of its deep harbor. In the nineteenth century, it had become the terminus first of the Potomac Canal and then of its 1828 successor, the Chesapeake and Ohio Canal. Canal boats brought wheat, flour, and corn to Georgetown from the rural farmlands of Maryland's interior. Flour, wool, and paper mills used the water power of the Potomac River to turn the raw materials into finished goods. Henry Foxall's foundry, well known for its production of cannons used in the War of 1812, had been sold and by 1849 had ceased producing arms, but one of its buildings had been transformed into a flour mill and another into an ice warehouse.[1] Canal boats then returned upriver carrying finished products such as salted fish, bricks, and lumber.[2] In 1835 three thousand oceangoing ships docked in Georgetown harbor and transported 200,000 tons of freight to ports on the East Coast and in Europe.[3]

In 1862 during the Civil War, a horse-drawn streetcar began running between Washington City and Georgetown, making it possible for more people to live in one place and work in another. Many new households needed domestic servants and carriage men, and the increased number of residents in Georgetown led to a need for more taverns. Georgetown's reputation for good taverns had been established long before the Revolutionary War with the regular attendance of founding fathers, such as George Washington. At the end of the Civil War, Georgetown was both the District's center of commerce and a growing suburb for government workers. For the Harris brothers, Georgetown offered a thriving job market and a Black community only five miles from their family home.

## John Harris and Herring Hill

At the end of the Civil War, John Harris was twenty-six years old with a wife and a little son, Louis. They settled in a small, predominantly Black neighborhood called Herring Hill, named after the plentiful fish in nearby Rock Creek. The settlement was on the eastern side of Georgetown and separated from Washington City by the creek and a ravine where the Rock Creek Parkway is now located.[4] A local historian described Herring Hill in the prewar years:

> Free Negroes had developed a stable and self-sustaining community of 951 persons by 1860. Wisps of smoke from little cook fires in narrow backyards, pigpens, cowsheds, small two-story frame dwellings, barking dogs. . . . In antebellum days, working hard within the strict regulation of the Black Code, a free Negro would set up a shanty, buy a horse and cart, and a year later would have a holding worth $100 to $300. Perhaps he had a wharf on Rock Creek and a shed where he would sell fish caught in the creek.[5]

By 1870 Black residents made up 30 percent of Georgetown's population, with Herring Hill as its largest Black neighborhood. More than two hundred families lived in a fifteen-block area.[6] It was so crowded that much of the housing was substandard. An 1879 survey of housing conditions found that none of the Black homes were rated any higher than "fair," and only 5 percent of the houses were connected to the sewer line at that time.[7] Although Black residents lacked basic amenities, for the first time their children had access to a new school.

In 1866 the Chamberlain School for the Colored had opened about five blocks from the Harris home, and by 1869, John and Mildred's son, Louis,

View of Georgetown port from Mason's Island (now Roosevelt Island) in 1868. Photo by William Morris Smith. Courtesy of Library of Congress, Prints and Photographs Division.

was old enough to attend.[8] Unfortunately, the new school building was not large enough to accommodate the number of children in Georgetown, and the next year another survey ordered by Congress found that less than half of the almost nine hundred Black school-age children in Georgetown were enrolled. Yet Chamberlain remained the only school to serve Georgetown's Black residents for ten years, during which time the population of the area's Black children continued to increase.[9]

Louis must have been a good student, judging from his handwriting. In October 1871, his parents opened a bank account for him in the Freedmen's Bank, which had begun operations in downtown Washington City four years earlier. Located in a "handsome new building" on Pennsylvania Avenue across from the US Treasury Department, it was staffed by Black cashiers and tellers. Louis, who was then seven years old, carefully wrote his own name in cursive on the account application. Unfortunately, the bank went bankrupt three years later during the economic Panic of 1873, and many depositors, presumably including Louis, lost most of their savings.[10]

In 1871 Georgetown as a distinct and separate jurisdiction of the District would disappear. That year Congress passed a law combining the three political entities of the District of Columbia—Washington City, Washington County, and Georgetown—into a single administrative unit that would be headed by a governor appointed by the president. The first and the only governor of the District was Alexander "Boss" Shepherd.[11] Having previously been the head of the DC Board of Public Works, he had made substantial improvements to Washington's public infrastructure, supervising the construction of 150 miles of new roads, 120 miles of sewer lines, and the planting of sixty thousand trees in Washington City and Georgetown. Unfortunately, as the head of the Board of Public Works and during his brief stint as the appointed governor, Shepherd also mismanaged the District's finances, and the District government went bankrupt in the midst of the Panic of 1873. In 1874 Congress replaced both Boss Shepherd and the entire territorial government with a board of commissioners appointed by the president. All elective offices disappeared, and District inhabitants, both white and Black, lost any direct say in the management of their affairs. Soon afterward Shepherd also went into personal bankruptcy and moved to Mexico, where he continued his passion for building roads and other public works until his death.[12]

In spite of his mismanagement, Shepherd left behind a much-improved Georgetown. Because the town had been built on hills, many of its streets had been narrow and steep, making it hard to maneuver horse-drawn wagons. Beginning in 1871 many roads were leveled, straightened, and paved. In the Herring Hill neighborhood, huge piles of excavated rubble buried some of the existing streets, and on other streets the entrances of houses were high above the street level.[13] Yet the work also created a number of new public works jobs for Black laborers, who would have included men such as John Harris.

Even with the political upheaval in the city governance and the physical disruption in the streets, John and Mildred continued to live in Georgetown's Herring Hill neighborhood. By 1878 they had added three girls to their family. The structure of their family, with a gap between the older child and the younger ones, was typical of many of Black residents' families in the District because of the absence of the fathers during the war. Recently arrived families of newly freed slaves often had an older child born in a southern state and several much younger ones born in the District.[14]

The war wound to John Harris's hand had caused permanent damage that surely limited his work options, yet in the censuses he always described his work as a laborer. In the 1870s and 1880s, Mildred supplemented John's income by working as a seamstress and taking in laundry, both of which were common jobs for Black women in towns. By 1880 their son, Louis, was sixteen and spending summers with his grandparents at the Dry Meadows farm on Broad Branch Road. Presumably, he was helping his grandfather, who at the time was selling the farm's produce at a city market. In fact, the census that year counted Louis twice, once at his Georgetown home and at his grandparents' farm. He might have found working on the farm a relief from having to take care of his three younger sisters at home.

Within the next decade, two of Louis's three sisters would die. In November 1888, Ada died at age fourteen, and sixteen months later, her sister Ella died at age nineteen. Yellow fever, cholera, smallpox, and malaria arrived by ships docking at the Georgetown port, "causing widespread death, particularly among children."[15] In the 1870s, both smallpox and yellow fever had increased death rates in Washington, and in 1889–91 the nation had also experienced an influenza epidemic. One report described a Black family living in a District slum that had one dead infant and five adults and six children suffering from the flu.[16] After the Civil War, the DC Board of Health had effectively fought for better public health measures and reported a reduction in the number of annual deaths, but epidemics still periodically visited the town through the end of the nineteenth century.

John and Mildred buried their daughters near their home in the Mount Zion Cemetery, which still exists today. The oldest legible gravestone bears the date of 1804, making it one of the oldest known burial grounds in the District. One section of the cemetery was used by the Montgomery Street Methodist Church, which served both white and free Black residents. Although many of the white graves were transferred to another cemetery in the mid-nineteenth century, Mount Zion continued to be one of the few integrated cemeteries in the District at the end of the century. Over the years, it was increasingly neglected, and burials ended in the middle of the twentieth century. Still, it is the burial site of many prominent Black Washingtonians as well as that of Louis Harris's sisters.[17]

## Louis Harris and the US Postal Service

In 1890 the Harrises' grandson Louis married a woman named Mary Estella. The new couple moved in with his parents, who had just suffered the loss of two of their daughters. Within a year of his marriage, Louis took an exam to become a clerk for the US Postal Service. Civil service reforms adopted in 1883 required that the hiring of civil servants be based on merit rather than political patronage. The requirement of a written exam applied first to the jobs that had suffered the most patronage, such as the clerk positions in Washington and all federal jobs outside the District. Thus, Louis Harris had to take a written exam to get his new job, competing against both Black and white men. That year of the people taking the exam, 42 percent passed, their average age was twenty-six, and 59 percent had been educated in a "common school," a nineteenth-century term for a local public school. Apparently, Louis did well on the exam and became the first of the Pointer descendants to become a civil servant.[18]

In 1893 when Louis was hired, only seventy Black men were working for the postal service, and the majority of them were repairing mailbags. Louis became one of the twenty-eight Black employees working as clerks that year. His annual wage was $1,109, more than double the $400 annual salary of the mailbag repairmen. Louis's salary was also almost double the average wages of all Black federal civil servants at the time.[19]

Although Louis's government salary was good, he still had to endure segregation in the postal service. He was required to use a separate locker from those of white workers; in the cafeteria, he took his food from separate steam trays and ate his lunch at segregated tables. But despite its exclusionary practices, the post office provided good jobs for Black men, and by 1923 twenty thousand Black people were working for the postal service throughout the country, representing 40 percent of the entire Black federal workforce.[20]

In 1892 Mary Estella Harris also began working for the federal government at the Bureau of Printing and Engraving, which is part of the US Treasury Department.[21] Women were hired at that time to cut the paper money as it came off the printing presses. Just like the Black employees of the postal service, the bureau's 146 Black employees were segregated from white workers and given separate lockers and bathrooms. They also ate at separate tables at the rear of the cafeteria, although they stood in the same food line with white employees.[22]

In 1894, about two years after Mary Estella began working at the bureau, a new chief was appointed. Shortly afterward a number of Black women employees were dismissed without cause, and their jobs were given to white women who had lower exam scores than those of the dismissed Black women. Some Black women complained to the Civil Service Commission that they had been fired because of their race. After a review, the commission agreed and wrote to the secretary of the treasury, saying that it was unlikely that "the line of cleavage between efficiency and inefficiency could . . . so closely follow the color line."[23] The letter was signed by the Civil Service commissioner and future president Theodore Roosevelt; however, nothing changed in response to the review. By 1894 Mary Estella was no longer working for the bureau.

In 1893 Louis's father, John, died at the age of fifty-four. John Harris had lived twenty-nine years after being wounded in the Civil War and long enough to see his only son obtain a coveted government job that he himself could not have qualified for. John and Mildred had been married thirty years and had rented their home in the Herring Hill neighborhood in Georgetown throughout their marriage.

After John's death, Mildred continued living in the Herring Hill home where they had raised their children. By 1900 she was one of the residents in Georgetown of either race who had lived there the longest.[24] Just after the turn of the century, her son, Louis, and his wife had saved enough money to buy a recently constructed brick house only a five-minute walk from where she lived, and eventually she moved into their new home with them. The handsome brick building where they lived still stands at 2453 P Street, Northwest.

Louis thus had worked his way into Georgetown's Black middle class by the twentieth century, and he continued working as a postal clerk into the 1930s when he was more than seventy years old. Part of his success undoubtedly could be attributed to his education and his parents' stable home life in Herring Hill. He also had two of his uncles—Lorenzo and Lewis—living within a mile of his home for most of his childhood, and surely the proximity of extended family provided him additional stability.

## Lewis Harris in Georgetown

When John and Joseph Harris had enlisted in the Union army, they had left their fifteen-year-old brother, Lewis, at home to help their parents with the farmwork at Dry Meadows. As soon as the war was over, however,

Lewis married Hester and moved to Arlington, Virginia, just across the Potomac River from Georgetown. Arlington had never been as prosperous as Georgetown mainly because it lacked a good harbor. Before the war, the most prominent resident of Arlington had been Robert E. Lee, whose imposing home, Arlington House, overlooked the Potomac River and the capital. During the war, twenty Union forts had been erected to protect Arlington and the western perimeter of the capital, and a thousand former slaves grew hay and vegetables on the Lee estate for the Union army. Eventually, the government resettled an additional three thousand former slaves there, and the Union army turned Mrs. Lee's rose garden into the beginnings of the Arlington National Cemetery.[25]

In the 1870 census, Lewis Harris was described as a cart driver in Arlington and as owning property, perhaps a cart and horse. He may have been hauling crops and people from Arlington to Georgetown, probably crossing the improved Aqueduct Bridge to reach the ships anchored in Georgetown's harbor. He may also have been supplying the freedmen's camps in Arlington with products from Georgetown.

Although Georgetown thrived after the Civil War, the town of Arlington did not. An 1876 map shows only a few streets in a village called Rosslyn, which was surrounded by farms, and a few roads leading west to the surrounding countryside. Perhaps wanting more work nearer his brothers, Lewis and his family moved back across the Potomac River in the mid-1870s. They settled in the northwestern part of Georgetown not far from where his older brothers, John and Joseph, had first lived before the war.[26] Lewis's new neighborhood in Georgetown was a settlement called Brinetown or Bryantown, which was composed primarily of Black residents.[27] Fugitive slaves from Virginia or Maryland had initially settled the area and made their homes on the northern edge of Georgetown, a half mile from the campus of Georgetown College.[28]

Georgetown College, like the nearby Visitation Convent and School, once had numerous enslaved people working there over the years. Before the Civil War, the Jesuits of Georgetown College had owned hundreds of slaves who worked mostly on its plantations in southern Maryland, but, as described earlier, in 1838 the Jesuits had sold most of their slaves to stave off bankruptcy.[29] Ironically, thirty-six years later, and about a year before Lewis's family moved to Georgetown, the college selected as its new president the Reverend Patrick F. Healy, who thus became the first Black leader of a predominantly white American college.

Father Patrick Healy had been born enslaved in Georgia in 1834. His mother was mulatto, and his Irish father was her common-law husband. The Healys raised their nine children as Catholic and sent them north for their education.

Patrick Healy became the first Black Jesuit priest and received his doctorate in Belgium before returning as a professor at Georgetown College. During his presidency of the school, an imposing new building was constructed that was designed by the same architects who had designed the Library of Congress. It housed classrooms and a dormitory for what was then a small college; today it is the school's main administration building and bears Healy's name. In the 1970s, it was designated a National Historic Landmark. Healy Hall is two hundred feet high, so it would have been easily visible from Lewis and Hester's Brinetown neighborhood.[30]

The Brinetown neighborhood was surrounded by woods with open countryside nearby. The land was part of an old estate that included a large house called The Cedars and a spring named Bear Wallow Spring. The Chamberlain School for the Colored, which their nephew Louis attended, was just a ten-minute walk for their own son. Directly across the street from their home was the Methodist Episcopal Church of West Georgetown, a modest mission church built in 1865 to serve the Black community of Brinetown. The church thrived for over forty years, sharing preachers with other Black churches, but as the area became more developed, the church was eventually sold. New housing was built in its place.[31]

On first arriving in Georgetown, Lewis worked as a boatman in the port but then resumed his work as a cart driver. He likely worked for himself, as did many other Black residents of Georgetown who took passengers around town or transported cargo to and from the port. On the first day of May every year, they had a parade. As described by a local historian, "On May Day there was a parade of the negro drivers; many drove carts, drays and wagons, for on that day they had holiday, and paraded with wagons and horses adorned with ribbons, flowers and bright papers, the drivers wearing long white aprons, and headed by a band. They would then go to the woods and feast, dance and sing."[32]

Once the roads heading north out of Georgetown into Washington County were improved, Lewis occasionally might have provided transportation between Georgetown and the Dry Meadows farm for his brothers' families.[33] His work as a driver also may have allowed him to keep in touch with his father's extended family, who presumably lived outside the city. In 1879 Lewis and his wife had a boarder living with them named William Harris, who was probably Lewis's cousin on his father's side who had enlisted in the Union army the same day as Lewis's older brothers, John and Joseph.[34]

Georgetown's commerce was thriving. Large three- and four-masted ships built in Maine arrived in Georgetown with blocks of ice, supplying the modern iceboxes that were becoming common in Washington; they also supplied ice to local businesses, such as ice cream parlors and fishmongers. Once the ships unloaded their frozen cargo, they often made the return trip to New England loaded with coal that had arrived in Georgetown via the C&O Canal on boats from Cumberland, Maryland. Drivers such as Lewis could make a decent living transporting ice and other goods to and from warehouses at the port.[35]

Despite the economic prosperity in the 1880s, the economy of Georgetown slowed in the 1890s as the harbor began to silt over, and fewer ships were able to dock. The C&O Canal Company also struggled to keep the canal functioning in spite of destructive storms and growing competition from the railroads. Railroad investments had stalled during the Civil War, but in the following decade, the miles of railroad tracks had doubled, and the canals could not compete. Georgetown's economy had depended heavily on the C&O Canal for deliveries of raw materials to its numerous mills, but by the end of the century, the canal was headed toward bankruptcy.[36]

The mill closings during the last years of the nineteenth century put Black people in particular out of work. Although skilled laborers found employment, such jobs were reserved primarily for white workers.[37] One new industry was the Hollerith Tabulating Machine Company, the predecessor of IBM, whose device made the data processing of the 1890 census much faster than that of the 1880 census. It moved into a warehouse at 1054 Thirty-First Street that had previously housed a factory that made hogsheads, or barrels. A contemporary photograph of the key punch operators, however, showed only white women at work and white men supervising them.[38]

Beginning in the 1880s, properties in Brinetown and elsewhere in Georgetown were increasingly acquired by small-scale developers who built clusters of three or four row houses that almost invariably were destined for white families.[39] With the increased number of white households came the need for more white schools, and by 1889 the local government had purchased several acres in Brinetown on which to build a school.[40] The Black residents of the neighborhood were forced to move, and before long the area called Brinetown disappeared entirely. The property where Lewis and Hester had first settled became part of the campus of a white school named Western High School. Almost a hundred years later, it became the renowned Duke Ellington School for the Arts, whose outstanding Black graduates include opera singer Denyce Graves and comedian Dave Chappelle.[41]

Lewis Harris and his wife continued to live in Georgetown because he could still earn a living as an experienced driver and had two brothers living nearby. Conditions for Georgetown's Black residents were better than in Washington City. Nonetheless, as the couple had always been renters, the Harrises' lives were repeatedly disrupted by having to change homes. Real estate speculation in the District by land developers had increased dramatically with the growth in population, and over the next twenty years, Lewis's family in Georgetown had to move at least three times as their homes were bought and sold for redevelopment.[42]

By 1899 Lewis may have been experiencing firsthand the decline in independent shipping that was afflicting Georgetown. When he was in his fifties, Lewis began working for a national freight transport company named Adams Express. Although discrimination in hiring was prevalent in the District, Adams Express was unusual in hiring Black employees. The company had started in New England as a small delivery service in the 1830s, and later abolitionists used it to deliver antislavery papers to states in the South. In 1849, in what became a famous case, an enslaved man named Henry Brown escaped from Richmond, Virginia, by successfully shipping himself in a box to Quakers in Philadelphia using Adams Express.[43] By 1854 the company was officially incorporated, and despite its association with abolitionism, its business in the South grew. By the time Lewis joined Adams Express at the end of the nineteenth century, it was the dominant freight transport company in New England and the mid-Atlantic states and had offices across the West.[44]

Lewis's son, Joseph, followed in his father's footsteps as a driver, working as a coachman for a family near Dupont Circle.[45] During their lifetimes, Lewis and his son saw their professions change dramatically from horse-drawn carriages to the horseless buggies. They also saw Georgetown being transformed from a center of commerce to what would eventually become a white suburb of the District.

## Lorenzo Harris and St. John's Episcopal Church

The third Harris brother to move to Georgetown had in fact arrived five years before Lewis did. The youngest of the Harris brothers, Lorenzo was fifteen years old—and only nine years older than his nephew Louis—in 1870 when he moved to Georgetown to find work. Lorenzo had spent several years attending the one-room schoolhouse near the family farm, and by 1870 he had probably learned everything the overcrowded school could offer. The census that year counted Lorenzo twice, once at Dry Meadows and also in a home in Georgetown. He was working as a house servant for Caroline Risque, an affluent widow in her forties who lived with her mother, children, and several servants near Georgetown University's campus. The Risque home was only a mile west of Herring Hill, where Lorenzo's brother John and his family lived. In June 1875, at the age of twenty, Lorenzo married, but within a few years his wife disappeared from official records, presumably having died.[46]

The Risque home was close to St. John's Episcopal Church in Georgetown, and the family may have been members of the congregation. That might explain why, in November 1882, after St. John's longtime sexton died, the church hired Lorenzo to replace him. He was twenty-seven years old when he assumed the responsibilities of the care and upkeep of both the church's building and its property. In the Episcopal Church, the sexton is also a church officer, a job with substantial responsibility but unfortunately without commensurate pay.

St. John's Episcopal Church had been established in 1796 in central Georgetown, and over time many distinguished families had been members.[47] The original church was designed by William Thornton, the architect of the Capitol, and Thomas Jefferson had been one of its financial supporters while he was president of the United States. In 1807 the church's prominent governing board included John Mason, the son of George Mason, one of the colonial leaders in Virginia. Despite its prestigious membership, the church struggled to survive financially. In 1831 the building was sold to pay the church's taxes, but church members repurchased it in 1838.[48] The church accepted Black parishioners, although they were required to use a special exterior stairway to enter the building and had to worship separated from white parishioners.[49]

The archived minutes of the church's governing board (the vestry) contain occasional references to Lorenzo and his work. For the year beginning on Easter in 1884, the vestry approved a yearly salary for Lorenzo of $275. It must have been insufficient for his needs, however, because in December 1886 the church board admonished Lorenzo: "The Vestry requires him [Lorenzo] to be more careful in future in cleaning and dusting all parts of the Church. . . . His outside business must give way."[50] Apparently Lorenzo had taken on some other work to supplement his inadequate salary. Soon afterward the vestry increased his compensation by allowing him to charge a $5 fee for opening the church for weddings. For the year beginning in April 1887, Lorenzo's annual salary was raised by $25.

Six months after he became the church's sexton, Lorenzo married a woman named Celia Marshall, and their marriage, like that of his parents, would last more than fifty years. By 1884 Lorenzo and Celia had settled in a house around the corner from the church, and two years later the couple moved again to another house nearby.[51] Considering his small salary, the church may have owned the properties or at least helped him with the rent. That their home was in a stable, older section of Georgetown meant they were less likely to be threatened by the development projects that were already affecting the predominantly Black neighborhood in the northwestern corner of Georgetown and that had caused his brother Lewis to move so often.

In 1887 the senior priest at Georgetown's St. John's Episcopal Church was replaced by a new rector named John Regester. In his first few years, he must have relied heavily on Lorenzo, who by then had already been working at the church for a number of years. The Reverend Regester must have been quite successful at St. John's because in 1892 he was offered a major promotion: he was selected to be the new rector of St. Paul's Episcopal Cathedral in Buffalo, New York.

The Buffalo cathedral, as it turned out, also needed a sexton, and Regester recommended Lorenzo for the prestigious job. Such a move must have been the biggest decision in Lorenzo and Celia's lives. On the one hand, they had never been to Buffalo and presumably knew no one there except the rector. Moreover, by that time Lorenzo was well known in the congregation of St. John's and likely also in the broader Georgetown community. On the other hand, the fact that Lorenzo's older brother Joseph had ventured to New York City many years earlier must have given Lorenzo confidence to consider such a challenging move. Whatever their reasoning, Lorenzo and Celia accepted the job offer and moved to a city in the north where winters were long and harsh and where the Black community was almost invisible. St. John's Episcopal Church in Georgetown survived the double loss of its rector and sexton, and it still continues to thrive today.

## The Increasing Segregation in Georgetown

An advantage of living in Georgetown for the three Harris brothers was that no matter how often they moved, they were always near each other. Yet in the 1890s, within the space of a few years, Georgetown must have begun to feel like a very different place to them. With the dismantlement of Reconstruction, Georgetown as well as the surrounding area experienced steadily increasing segregation. Even though the District had no formal Jim Crow laws, the civil rights laws outlawing discrimination that had been enacted during Reconstruction were ignored both in Washington City and in Georgetown. Although these Reconstruction statutes were never formally repealed, they effectively became "Lost Laws," forgotten until they were finally eliminated when the city codes were rewritten at the turn of the century.[52]

As segregation and discrimination tightened over the years, social interactions between Black and white people in Washington gradually faded. Even within the Black community, class distinctions widened, and the social importance of having a light skin tone increased. Many well-educated people had a light complexion, and they often became part of the Black upper class. They increasingly separated themselves from those who had worked their

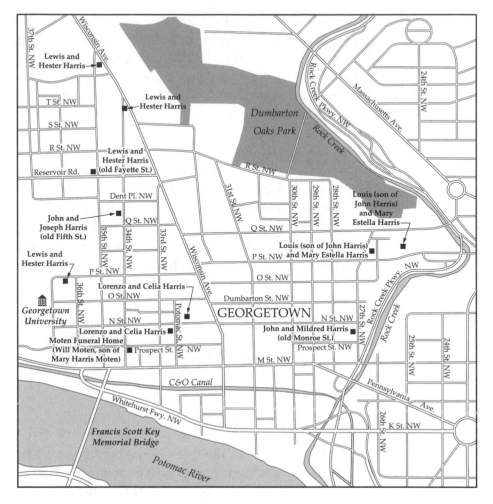

Map of Georgetown marked with residences of Pointer's descendants, 1862–1954. These addresses come from decennial censuses, city directories and plat maps.

John and Mildred Harris and Joseph Harris: 1862–63, 20 Fifth Street (Q Street today)

John and Mildred Harris: 1866–93, 26 Monroe Street (presumably 1337 Twenty-Seventh Street)

Lorenzo Harris: 1870, 22 West First Street (N Street today); Lorenzo and Celia Harris: 1884–85, 1242 Potomac Street; 1886–93, 3241 N Street

Lewis and Hester Harris: 1876+, 204 Fayette Street (Thirty-Fifth Street today); 1882–83, 2025 Thirty-Fifth Street; 1885–93, 2040 Thirty-Fourth Street; 1893–99+, 3241 N Street; 1902–10+, 3618 P Street

Louis and Mary Estella Harris: 1892–98, 1508 Twenty-Sixth Street; 1898–1930+, 2453 P Street

Moten Funeral Home of Will Moten (son of Mary Harris Moten): 1954, 3354 Prospect Street way into the middle class but who had darker skin. In turn, people in the middle class distanced themselves from the poor and less educated. Meanwhile, most white people refused to accept Black people of any shade into their society.[53]

The Harris brothers had the solace of family as the three shared seventeen years in Georgetown and were never far from one another. Their children went to the same school, and as roads improved, the five-mile drive to their parents' Dry Meadows farm made it seem closer. They could also see their father regularly when he came to the District to sell the farm's produce. But the brothers were aging, and in the early 1890s, three major changes occurred in the family. In 1891 the Harris family lost their father, Thomas. His death may not have been a surprise since by then he was in his late seventies. However, the death of John two years later at the age of fifty-four was almost certainly unexpected.

John Harris had survived the war, had been married for thirty years, and had settled with his wife, Mildred, in Georgetown permanently. He had lived long enough to see his son, Louis, graduate from school and be hired by the federal government in a prestigious job for Black workers. John's death so soon after their father's death must have unsettled the family. As a result, Joseph became the oldest surviving Harris son, and soon after the two deaths, he returned to the family farm after many years of living in New York. He remained at Dry Meadows for the rest of his life.

The third major change for the family was Lorenzo and Celia's decision to move to Buffalo. The three Harris brothers had been neighbors for years, but with John's death and Lorenzo's departure in 1893, Lewis was the only Harris brother left in Georgetown. He was still living in the area of Brinetown, which was being gradually gentrified. By 1893 the property where he and Hester had first rented a home was replaced by the new high school, and the Black church that once had been across the street had already been razed. Lorenzo was looking out for his brother, however; before leaving, he apparently arranged an agreement with his landlord and Lewis. By the following year, the city directory recorded Lewis and his wife as living in the home that Lorenzo and Celia had occupied for the previous ten years. Located in central Georgetown, it was relatively protected from the development around the edges of the town, and they lived there for the rest of the decade.[54] Lewis and his family lived in the town for forty years before he died in 1917 at the age of seventy-one.

As senior white government workers moved into the large older homes in the town, the Black population of Georgetown began to dwindle. Nineteenth-century Georgetown had been an important and sustaining community for the three Harris brothers and their families as well as for many other Black families. But later in the twentieth century, the town would become largely white, with exclusive schools and traditional churches. The memories of the Black residents persist, however, as described by the authors of *Black Georgetown Remembered*: "Distinguished by initiative and perseverance in the face of discrimination and economic adversity, Georgetown's African Americans drew strength from the stability of their families, their profound belief in a loving God, and their pride in their own achievements."[55]

# 8

## Migrating North

Soon after returning home at the end of the Civil War, Joseph Harris left the family farm and moved to New York City, already the largest city in the country and one of the commercial capitals of the world. Several years after his move, he began working as a Pullman railroad car porter, a job he would hold for the rest of his life. More than twenty years later, his youngest brother, Lorenzo, would also migrate to the state of New York to become the sexton of Buffalo's Episcopal cathedral. Both brothers were part of a small but steady migration of African Americans out of the South after the Civil War.

The nineteenth-century migrations were precursors of the twentieth-century northern migration, one of the major population movements in American history. The motivation of these migrants undoubtedly varied by person and over time, but most Black migrants from the South were clearly looking for better work. The Civil War had devastated the southern economy, which offered few jobs for the recently freed men. By contrast, the war had strengthened the economy of the North and attracted both the poor and the ambitious of both races. Some migrants might have sought new experiences, especially after the war that had given them their first taste of different cultures and peoples. For Black migrants, a move north was also an escape from the racism and discrimination in the South.[1]

The nineteenth-century northern migration was a movement from rural to urban areas, and the key destinations of southern migrants were the cities of New York, Philadelphia, and Chicago.[2] Of the migrants who went to the state of New York, such as Joseph and Lorenzo, three-quarters settled in New York City.[3] In 1870, 16 percent of the state's Black population comprised migrants who had been born in the South. By the time Lorenzo moved to Buffalo in the 1890s, the number of Black southerners living in the whole state had almost tripled, and they had become over 30 percent of the total Black population.[4]

Black southerners who moved north after the Civil War were not a random selection of the population. In general, those who migrated were more likely to have skills that they could use in urban jobs, such as construction. They also tended to be more literate than the people who stayed behind because their education made them more employable and better able to negotiate with strangers. People who could not read were at risk in a large and unknown city because people could easily take advantage of them. It was probably not coincidental that the two Harris brothers who did migrate were the two brothers who had become literate.[5]

## Joseph Harris in New York City

Joseph Harris was twenty-one years old at the end of the Civil War, and unlike his older brother, John, he was unmarried and less constrained by family responsibilities. He had served in the military and had survived a serious illness, and he had educated himself and acquired a broader view of the world on the battlefields of Virginia. Moreover, in choosing New York, he was rejoining several other members of his regiment.[6] Five members of the Harris brothers' First Regiment came from the New York City area, including a man in their Company G, and one of them might have persuaded Joseph to go north. For whatever reason, he must not have been too daunted by the prospect of starting a new life in an unknown city, and by the end of the 1860s, he was living in Manhattan.

In 1870 Joseph was working as a waiter and living in a boardinghouse in a predominantly white Manhattan neighborhood. Also living there were two young Black families that had seven children between them, and one of the fathers was from Washington, DC.

For many Black residents, the memory of the 1863 Draft Riots in Manhattan would still have been raw, and newcomers undoubtedly would have heard of the notorious violence. The draft riots in New York had been some of the biggest and most violent riots in America. They were led by Irish immigrants who were initially protesting the wartime draft but whose rage soon shifted to Black residents. The rioters not only blamed them for the Civil War but also saw them as competitors for their jobs. As noted in chapter 5, more than a hundred Black people were killed, including eleven who were lynched. Houses were razed along with a Black orphanage.[7] In the following months, many Black residents living in Manhattan had either fled to other boroughs, especially Brooklyn, or to New Jersey. Joseph, however, had lived through a violent war and had served under white officers, and despite the earlier violence, he was apparently comfortable living near white residents.

Joseph soon met his future wife, Margaret Chase, who was originally from Philadelphia. They may have been introduced by a fellow soldier in his company of the First Regiment USCT who was also from Philadelphia. In 1871 Joseph and Margaret married; their marriage certificate not only cited their parents' names and their places of birth but also recorded them as a white couple. This confusion was consistent with the censuses and military records that described Joseph as having a light complexion. By the mid-seventies, Joseph and Margaret had two children, first a daughter and then a son.[8]

## Joseph Harris and the Pullman Company

The prosperity that followed the Civil War lasted for eight years until the Panic of 1873 triggered the worst depression in almost four decades. More than a hundred banks failed, and at least ten thousand businesses closed.[9] Railroad companies that owned 20 percent of the nation's railroad tracks went bankrupt. Although the economy took years to recover, once it did, the railroads resumed their expansion across the country and began to hire new workers to serve the increasing number of passengers. In 1878 Joseph Harris took advantage of the railroads' returning prosperity and began working as a porter for the Pullman Palace Car Company.[10]

Railroads had long since eclipsed canals as the major transportation system in the United States. When Joseph's great grandfather George Pointer had worked on the Potomac Canal in 1828, the United States had twelve hundred miles of canals and only seventy-three miles of rails. By 1860, however, it had thirty thousand miles of railroad tracks, and the railroad industry had decisively won the race against the canals.[11]

In 1862 the Pullman Car Company was founded by George Pullman in Chicago. After spending an uncomfortable night on a train, Pullman saw a business opportunity in improving passenger comforts on long railroad trips. The company's first car, named "The Pioneer," became well known because it was part of the funeral train that carried President Lincoln's body back to Illinois. By 1867 the Pullman Company was making "hotel cars" that included both eating and sleeping accommodations. The company not only leased these luxury cars to the many small, independent railroad companies but also supplied the cars with a staff of porters, conductors, and cooks and dictated how their jobs were to be performed.[12]

The Pullman Company was the country's first and largest company to employ Black porters, hiring "more Negroes than any business in America."[13] The porters the company initially hired were part of the first wave of Black urban workers after the Civil War.[14] From the beginning, George Pullman employed only Black men as porters, knowing he could hire them cheaply. A leading historian of the company said that Pullman preferred hiring formerly enslaved men with dark complexions who came from the Deep South because he wanted to replicate the traditional Southern house servant's role on his sleeping cars.[15]

Joseph, who had been raised free and had light skin, was not exactly what Pullman sought in a porter, but because of Joseph's service in the war, he probably had both a military bearing and the discipline that Pullman also wanted. Moreover, Joseph came well recommended by his commanding officer in the USCT, Col. John Holman, who had written personal recommendations for the soldiers who had served under him.

### The Life of a Pullman Porter

Apparently, Pullman porters such as Joseph often worked four hundred hours a month, and many nights they would get an average of only three hours of sleep. They also were often gone from home for a month at a time. Pay for porters was minimal. In 1879 Joseph's wages were $10 a month regardless of the number of hours he worked, and that was less than what he had made in the army fourteen years earlier. The pay did increase over time, but as late as 1915 when Joseph was still working for the company, the average Pullman porter's monthly wage was only $34.09. This salary was more than the income of most Black families but still a third of the wage white conductors received. Porters often had to fill in for conductors, but they were never compensated for the extra work.[16]

The company justified paying such low wages because tipping was allowed and encouraged as an incentive for porters to provide good service. Tips could vary, but a Pullman historian estimated that in the early years, the average tip for porters was a nickel and by the end of the nineteenth century a dime. Tips at this level did not add much to the salaries, and porters remained the lowest-paid members of the train car staff, including the cleaning crew.[17]

In addition to low wages and long hours, porters were often subjected to condescending treatment by the passengers. Passengers commonly called porters George, the name of the company's founder, rather than by their own names. They were sometimes addressed in even more demeaning terms, yet porters could never react to bad behavior. Any negative comment or complaint from a passenger, whether justified or not, could be cause for suspension. Should a passenger steal something from the train, the porter was the one held responsible.[18]

The Pullman Company wrote a manual of extensive and exacting rules that governed every aspect of the porters' work. The men were expected to learn them all, and company executives routinely hired undercover people called spotters to observe the porters at work. In some cases, a spotter had a quota of reports to fill, and it was not unusual for him to attempt to trick a porter into bending a rule. A negative report would go on the employee's record and could result in the loss of pay or a suspension. Porters watched out for spotters and warned one another when one was present.[19]

A Pullman porter was required to be polite and solicitous even if passengers were demanding and rude. A Langston Hughes poem titled "Porter" captures the constant servility required on the job, as the poet depicts a porter speaking of his daily work as "climbing up a great big mountain / Of yes, sirs!"[20]

Despite the low wages and uncertain tips, Joseph had a job that was both coveted by Black workers and highly regarded in the Black community. Sleeping car porters were considered "Aristocrats of Negro Labor" in an age when few Black people traveled.[21] Within Black society, the work of Pullman porters was comparable to that of teachers, lawyers, and funeral directors, and for many it became a step into the Black middle class.[22]

As a Pullman porter in the nineteenth century, Joseph Harris saw more of the United States than most people, white or Black. He saw the direct effects of the postwar expansion of American industry in the crowded urban railroad yards, and he served the masters of those industries in the Pullman sleeping cars. Through the windows of the moving trains, he could also see into the backyards of people living in shantytowns crowded along the tracks. Porters might have drawn the shades of the dining cars so that wealthy passengers would not have to see those who had been left behind by what Mark Twain had called the Gilded Age.[23]

Joseph's employee record with the Pullman Company is a single two-sided card that appears to be a summary of older records that have since disappeared.[24] It shows that he was employed during three separate periods and that he retired in 1921, but there is no explanation for why he left the Pullman Company three times. Possibly, as a literate veteran of the Civil War, Joseph found the work tedious and demeaning over a long period. Since Joseph lived

Pullman Company employee card for Joseph Harris. Available from the Pullman Company Records in the Newberry Library, courtesy of JoEllen Dickie.

in New York City, he may have found other work that was better compensated when he wanted to spend more time at home with his family. Former Pullman porters had little trouble landing good jobs in fine hotels and restaurants, where wages were better and would reflect the actual hours worked.[25] The first time he left the company was a year after the birth of his second child, so perhaps his family needed him at home.

The Pullman Company employee card for Joseph also demonstrates how the company dealt with its porters. With the company's extensive rules and network of spies, most porters' records showed violations and resulting sanctions.[26] Joseph's card had an entry that indicates he was suspended once in 1907 as a result of a passenger complaint. The reverse side of Joseph's employee card is a "Loss Record" that lists eight items lost by passengers while he was on duty. The list covers the years 1902 through 1908 and gives the name of the train car, the passenger, and the date of the loss, along with the item and its value. The items varied in worth from a necklace and a pocketbook of no stated value to a $500 pearl missing from a ring. Since no sanctions or reprimands are recorded in connection with these losses, presumably Joseph was not thought responsible.

The extended absences from home must have taken a toll on the porters' families and presumably strained many marriages. Joseph apparently was traveling when a census taker came to his Manhattan home in 1880. His wife, Margaret, was recorded as widowed or divorced, which may have been the way she felt, although in fact they remained married for many more years. Margaret was working as a waitress, perhaps needing extra income given the fluctuations in her husband's pay. She also had taken in a boarder, a woman in her sixties who may have been helping her with the two Harris children, who were then ages five and six. The following year Joseph left the Pullman Company, and it would be five years before he returned.

At the end of the nineteenth century, railroads were not only at the center of the American economy but also the focus of legal battles over segregation. Disputes over separate accommodations for white and Black rail passengers ended with an 1896 Supreme Court decision in *Plessy v. Ferguson* that approved the doctrine of "separate but equal" treatment of passengers of different color. The decision implicitly approved the segregation of American society more broadly and would not be overturned by the Supreme Court until 1954.[27]

The job of implementing the separate but equal treatment of passengers on the trains was delegated to the railroad conductors and porters who had to direct Black passengers to separate cars. Rail passengers in the District did not have to be legally segregated when they boarded a train because unlike states in the South, the District did not have any Jim Crow laws. When the train entered the state of Maryland ten minutes later, however, Black passengers would have to move to a separate car; therefore, they usually acquiesced to the inevitable separation at the beginning of the trip.[28]

In 1893 the economy suffered its third major collapse of the century. The economic panic of 1893 began with the bankruptcy of the Philadelphia and Reading Railroad, and the failure of 156 other railroad companies quickly followed. Many porters lost their jobs, and the ones who kept their jobs had their hours reduced and their wages cut on average by a third. In the next several years, one in five Americans lost their jobs, and four hundred banks closed. It became the deepest economic depression in the nineteenth century.[29]

The all-white American Railway Union made matters even worse in 1894 when it organized a nationwide railroad strike that shut down much of the passenger traffic, putting even more porters out of work.[30] The union, however, refused to include the grievances of Black porters. Not until another thirty years after Joseph's retirement did the Black porters formally organize themselves.

## Joseph's Return to the District of Columbia

Joseph left the Pullman Company in 1893, probably because of the effects of the economic depression on the railroads and the ensuing labor troubles, but he was also needed at home in the District. As noted, his father had died in 1891, leaving his mother a widow and dependent on her three sons who were still working in Georgetown. Two years later her situation became more precarious when her eldest son, John, died suddenly at age fifty-four, and then her youngest son, Lorenzo, moved to Buffalo.

Joseph thus probably returned to the District to help his mother temporarily and perhaps to be a source of income until the economy recovered and the Pullman Company rehired its porters. The depression, however, lasted for several years. In the 1900 census, Joseph was still on the family farm with his mother, while his wife and children continued living in New York. Joseph listed his occupation as a porter. According to the Pullman Company's records, he went back to work for the company in 1902 at the age of fifty-eight.

By the time Joseph returned to work, the railroads had recovered from the devastating depression following the Panic of 1893, and as their profits were increasing, they were consolidating.[31] Thus, when he went back to work, he could do so without having to return to New York because Washington had become a railroad hub. The two private railroad companies that formerly had separate stations on the Washington Mall had combined them at a new neoclassical building near Capitol Hill named Union Station.[32] The station's name was more prosaic than what most people might have assumed, because it referred to the uniting of the two private railroad stations, not the grander union among the American states.[33]

By the time Joseph rejoined the Pullman Company, Abraham Lincoln's son Robert Todd Lincoln had become its president after George Pullman's death in 1897. Lincoln continued to pursue the company's policy of fighting the formation of a porters' union, and although there is no record that he personally approved the printing of a pamphlet titled "The Pullman Porter, the Benefits of His Racial Monopoly," the company used it to counter the Black porters' attempts to unionize. In response, A. Philip Randolph, who was then leading the effort to organize the Black porters, replied witheringly, "Abraham Lincoln freed Negroes from economic exploitation as chattel slaves; whereas his son, Robert T. Lincoln, has lent his influence and name to the notorious exploitation of Negroes as Pullman slaves."[34] Finally, in 1925 the Brotherhood of Sleeping Car Porters was established, and twelve years later the union agreed to its first contract with the Pullman Company. Historians John Hope Franklin and Alfred A. Moss Jr. wrote, "It became the most significant step towards the unionization of African Americans in the United States."[35]

Working conditions for porters improved to some degree when the government assumed control of the railroads at the beginning of World War I. Wages increased to $405 annually, rules became less rigid, and some limits on working hours were established.[36] Joseph continued working through the war, but according to his employee card, a year after the war ended, he resigned at the age of seventy-five apparently because of a disability. His absence must have been temporary because the 1920 census showed him back at work, and according to his employment record, he did not retire permanently from the Pullman Company until the following year and before any protections had been negotiated by the porters' union.

Joseph was seventy-seven years old when he finally retired, an advanced age for the heavy work of railroad porters. His annual pay had increased to $810, exceeding the salary of some professionals such as schoolteachers, and although a pension was possible, it was rarely granted.[37] A notation of "Pension application refused" is scrawled diagonally across the face of Joseph's employee card, although no reason is given. The Pullman Company was reluctant to make good on its meager monthly pension and often refused to pay it. By 1926 the average pension was $18, but only porters who had at least twenty consecutive years of experience by the age of seventy received it. Although Joseph had worked twenty-eight years, they had not been consecutive, and his pension application may have been rejected for that reason.[38]

Joseph had moved to New York over two decades before his youngest brother, Lorenzo, did, and likely Joseph was a model for his brother when considering the move to Buffalo. Of course, the two had migrated under very different circumstances. Joseph had moved without a job or a wife, assuming that he would find both; Lorenzo had been married ten years when he and his wife moved because he was promised a substantial promotion. Joseph had gone to the largest city in the United States, where the Black population was just over 1 percent of the total. Lorenzo's move to Buffalo in 1893 was to a much smaller city, where African Americans were only a small fraction of 1 percent of the population.[39]

## Lorenzo Harris at St. Paul's Cathedral

When Lorenzo arrived in Buffalo, it was a thriving community built near the shores of Lake Erie and a very different city from the District, not only in climate but also in population and culture. Before the Civil War, it had been the western terminus of the Erie Canal and one of the northern terminuses of the Underground Railroad. In 1893 when Lorenzo and Celia arrived, the Black community was almost invisible, a significant change for a couple who had lived all of their lives in the District, where African Americans were 30 percent of the city's population.[40] If Lorenzo had any apprehension in making the move, it would have been mixed with the pride of becoming the sexton for the prestigious St. Paul's Episcopal Cathedral.

St. Paul's was an imposing sandstone Gothic structure that was the seat of the Episcopal bishop of the western New York diocese. Five years before Lorenzo's arrival, a massive gas explosion and fire had destroyed much of the church building, but by the time he arrived, the reconstruction was complete. Lorenzo assumed the sexton's responsibilities of a much larger church and gardens. He was an exception in his new role; at the time, more than 80 percent of men working as sextons in the United States were white.[41]

Although Lorenzo and Celia's move took place in the midst of the Panic of 1893, Lorenzo's new salary was $600 a year, or double his salary in Georgetown and more than double Joseph's base salary as a porter at the time.[42] Lorenzo was also paid extra for jobs beyond his regular duties, and before long he was earning enough at St. Paul's that he and Celia could afford to buy a home.[43]

Lorenzo and Celia bought a home in a primarily white neighborhood. The major immigrant group in Buffalo at the time had come from Germany after the Revolution of 1848, and German immigrants settled in neighborhoods where African Americans lived. Often such neighbors lived next door to each other, and it was not unknown for an African American and a German widow to share a house together. The Germans often had more skills and therefore better jobs than their Black neighbors, so they didn't feel competitive with them. They generally got along. Lorenzo and Celia's new bungalow on Garner Avenue was located in a neighborhood near the Niagara River that included several naturalized citizens as well as people who were second-generation Germans or English.[44]

Surprisingly, sextons of an Episcopal cathedral were not required to be Episcopalians. After working at the cathedral for five years, however, at the age of forty-three Lorenzo was confirmed in the church on the same day as the rector's young daughter. It was presumably at his own initiative, since the lack of it had not hindered his hiring. His confirmation was also an indication that he had settled into both his job and his new community. Three years later, the vestry of the cathedral made special note of his good work: "Lorenzo Harris is still the faithful and efficient Sexton of the parish."[45]

Lorenzo worked at the cathedral for the next twenty-six years. During his first decade in Buffalo, when his mother, Mary, was still alive, he would

St. Paul's Episcopal Cathedral in Buffalo, New York, in 1890. Courtesy of Library of Congress, Prints and Photographs Division.

occasionally return to Dry Meadows to visit her and his brother Joseph.[46] In 1919 when Lorenzo turned sixty-four, the cathedral newsletter announced his retirement to the congregation:

> After more than twenty-six years of service, which began September 12th, 1893, our faithful sexton, Lorenzo Harris, has felt compelled to resign the post which he has filled so satisfactorily for more than a quarter of a century. It is with much regret that I make this announcement through the columns of "The Chimes," and I know that there are hundreds of persons among the members of Saint Paul's congregation who will read these words with the same regret with which they are written. Our sexton will maintain a semi-official relation to the parish, and we shall often see his familiar figure, clad in a sexton's gown, at the services of the Church.[47]

The vestry board not only praised Lorenzo but also awarded him an honorarium, letting him choose either a lump sum or a small pension to be paid monthly for the rest of his life.[48] Lorenzo wrote the vestry board a letter of thanks and noted his pleasure in that "doing the best I could was taken notice of and has not been forgotten."[49] Wisely, he chose the monthly pension of $35, which was about two-thirds of his former salary, and he collected it until his death twenty years later.

After his retirement, Celia and Lorenzo led an active social life, as was occasionally noted in the local African American newspaper, the *Buffalo American*. Celia was part of a local literary group that researched selected topics, such as Japan and Liberia, and presented their findings to the group. They sometimes met in the Harrises' home, as reported in the newspaper.[50]

Lorenzo and Celia's greatest social achievement was probably a luncheon they gave honoring E. Thomas Demby, the first Black Episcopal suffragan bishop in the United States.[51] Demby had been born in Delaware in 1869 and attended several prestigious schools, including the District's Howard University, before he was consecrated as a bishop in the Episcopal Church in 1918. By the time he visited Buffalo in the fall of 1921, he was already well known for leading a movement to desegregate worship services in southern Episcopal churches where segregation was still practiced. The article about his visit made the front page of the *Buffalo American*, noting his busy schedule, which included the luncheon hosted by Celia and Lorenzo Harris at their home.[52]

The social column of the *Buffalo American* also periodically wrote about the numerous guests who visited the couple from Washington and Philadelphia.[53] Obviously the Harrises had achieved some prominence in the Black community of Buffalo, but they had also remained in close touch with family and friends. By the twentieth century, the trip to Buffalo was not difficult; in 1910 the main trunk lines of the Pennsylvania Railroad went from Washington to

Harrisburg, Williamsport, and then Buffalo, a much faster route than going through New York City. The couple may have encouraged family to visit them and see Niagara Falls, which was only twenty miles from their home. Lorenzo had also worked with his brother Joseph on paperwork related to the family farm, and he continued to be on the board of the Moses Society Cemetery of Tenleytown in the District where a number of family members had been buried.[54] Lorenzo and Celia never had children, but he must have felt close to his niece Mary "Minnie" Moten—the older daughter of his younger sister, Mary Moten, who had died in 1933—for he arranged in his will that his niece would inherit the Garner Avenue house upon his and Celia's deaths.[55]

Lorenzo worked at odd jobs for thirteen years after his retirement from St. Paul's, presumably to supplement his pension. City directories recorded him as working as a messenger, an elevator operator, a clerk, and even a night watchman, a job he held when he was eighty-one years old.[56] Celia Harris died in February 1939, and Lorenzo died nine months later of pneumonia at age eighty-four. Both he and Celia were buried in Pine Hill Cemetery in Buffalo, their adopted city of forty-six years. By the time they died, the size of the African American population in the city had grown to 24,600 people, but that was still only 3 percent of the city's population. One of the new Black residents of Buffalo was "Minnie" Moten Brown, who left Virginia to live in the Garner Avenue house that her uncle Lorenzo had left to her, and she was still living there in 1944.[57]

Both Joseph and Lorenzo were nineteenth-century forerunners of the twentieth-century migrations. By 1900, 350,000 Black southerners lived in the urban areas of the North, and in the first decade of the new century, 200,000 more African Americans would arrive from southern states.[58] Like most migrants from the South, Lorenzo never returned home permanently. The rate of return of southern Black migrants was only about 2 percent a year, while white migrants returned at three times that rate.[59] Joseph's return to his mother's home in Washington made him an exception.

During the second decade of the twentieth century, new restrictions on immigration from overseas abruptly reduced the number of available foreign workers for jobs in American industry. The restrictions on foreign migrants created a large demand for native-born workers to meet the military needs of World War I. As a result, half a million Black migrants from the South moved north. Although the economic devastation of the Great Depression (1929–39) subsequently cut the Black migrant flow in half, it began again during and after the end of World War II and became a tidal wave that changed the face of America.[60]

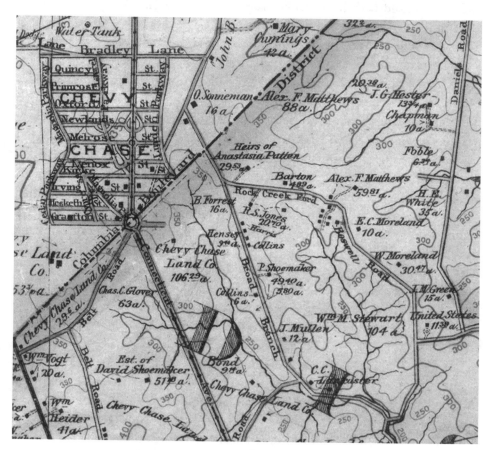

An 1894 Hopkins map of Washington, DC, and vicinity shows the first Chevy Chase Land Company development in Maryland. The Harris property is a dot marked "Harris" on Broad Branch Road, to the right of Chevy Chase Circle. Courtesy of Library of Congress, Geography and Map Division.

# 9

## Dry Meadows and the Encroaching City

When Joseph returned to Dry Meadows at the end of the nineteenth century, he was in his mid-fifties. For twenty-seven years he
had lived in New York, one of the most modern cities in the world.
Returning home was a journey back in time because the farm was
still on a country dirt road, and the family home lacked electricity
and modern plumbing. The one sign of progress was the new electric
streetlights lining the main road of Tenleytown, two miles away.[1]

As a Pullman porter since 1878, Joseph had traveled to more places
than anyone else in his family, but the Panic of 1893 and the resulting bankruptcy of 156 railroads brought dramatic changes to the
industry. In a period of major layoffs even by the surviving railroads,
Joseph took this time to visit his recently widowed mother for a few
months. His wife stayed in New York, so perhaps they considered his
stay temporary; but the economy and railroads took years to recover,
and his visit became longer than he may have planned.[2]

Returning to Washington also meant returning to a region marked
by pervasive racism. Fortunately, the racial violence that had spread
through much of the South after the collapse of Reconstruction had
not affected Washington. There had been no lynchings in the

District, although between 1875 and 1900, a total of nine Black men were lynched in the surrounding Maryland counties. Three occurred in Montgomery County, three in Prince George's County to the east of the District, and three in Ann Arundel County forty miles away. Each lynching was public knowledge, commonly shared by word of mouth, and extensively reported in the local newspapers.[3]

In 1888 a horse-drawn streetcar line had begun operating between Georgetown and Tenleytown, and two years later electric streetcars began running out to the District's boundary. A streetcar stop less than two miles from the Harris farm made it easier for the grandchildren in Georgetown to visit their grandmother Mary Ann and their visiting New York City uncle, Joseph. At the same time, modern transport began bringing white city residents out to the countryside. People from the District often visited the surrounding rural areas as weekend sightseers, but when the streetcars were later followed by telephones, electric lights, and postal service, the sightseers returned as prospective home buyers.[4]

The demand for better housing in the District had been increasing in the last decades of the nineteenth century, spurred by the growth in the federal government and the arrival of many people who wanted to influence it.[5] In response to the growing demand for housing, local land developers first began redeveloping downtown neighborhoods. Before the Civil War, the "West End" of the city had been an area where Black and white families had lived next to each other for decades, but soon after the war, developers began to transform the area. By the turn of the century, it had become an upper-class and segregated enclave within the District.[6]

Housing development moved slowly northward, transforming neighborhoods such as Kalorama and then reaching the more distant area where President Cleveland had his summer home. The area was soon called Cleveland Park and became an early "streetcar suburb." Reflecting the demand for housing that was affecting Tenleytown as well, a white citizen association was established in 1892. By the end of the century, twenty other associations throughout the District competed with each other for prospective white buyers who would increase their property values.[7]

The Chevy Chase Land Company

One of the most aggressive land developers in the District was the Nevada mining millionaire Francis G. Newlands. He had a surname appropriate for land development and had the money to make it happen. Having made his fortune out west, he quickly became one of the robber barons of the Gilded

Age. He was elected a US congressman from Nevada in 1893 and ten years later became a senator. He was also a white supremacist who publicly proposed exporting all African Americans to other countries, and in the interim he supported any government effort to restrict their rights. Mark Twain and Charles Dudley Warner's novel *The Gilded Age*, set in late-nineteenth-century Washington, DC, was populated with characters such as Newlands.[8]

By 1890 he and his partners had acquired more than seventeen hundred acres in northwest Washington and nearby Montgomery County, Maryland. One of their early land purchases was the 305-acre estate straddling the District-Maryland border that had belonged to the Charles Belt family. As noted in chapter 4, the Belt family had named their original land grant Cheivy Chace, and Newlands appropriated the name both for his land development company and the future subdivision that he would build. Unfortunately, the southeast edge of the Belt estate was not far from Broad Branch Road and the Harrises' farm. In 1891 the Washington newspaper *The Star* described the land acquisition by the Chevy Chase Land Company as "the most notable transaction that has ever been known in the history of suburban property."[9] While this description may have been an exaggeration, it probably felt that way to the Harrises and their neighbors as they watched the sale of land and the approaching development not far from their properties.

Newlands began construction of an ideal community for affluent white residents located just outside the District. To make it a reality, the company first had to improve transportation to the area so that potential buyers could easily reach the new development and return to their jobs in the city. For this purpose, it purchased the Rock Creek Railway and built a trestle bridge over the Rock Creek valley at Calvert Street, and it was instrumental in bringing electric streetcar service to Tenleytown and beyond. The company extended Connecticut Avenue five miles into Maryland, and the enormous project required extensively cutting rock and transferring tons of dirt. The company also built an artificial lake and amusement park near its Chevy Chase development for the new home buyers to enjoy.[10] In 1903 the magazine *House Beautiful* compared the new Maryland development, with its "handsome cottages" on streets planted with flowering trees, to an English park.[11]

The Chevy Chase Land Company also planned a subdivision of small affordable lots for domestic workers who would live near the elite residents of Chevy Chase. They called the proposed development, which was situated at the border of Maryland and the District, Belmont. But, as the company's marketing materials said, it also sought to protect Chevy Chase and its property values from "the encroachment of undesirable elements," whose meaning would have been clear to prospective buyers. Accordingly, when the developer whom the land company had contracted to build Belmont began to sell lots to African Americans, Newlands's company sued him, and the sales were blocked.[12] Newlands also likely considered the Broad Branch Black settlement, which was in the middle of his large project, undesirable.

Dry Meadows and the Threat of Development

Thomas Harris died in 1891 after the sale of the Belt property but before the housing projects under construction by the Chevy Chase Land Company reached the District of Columbia. Fortunately for the Harrises, the company had decided to develop the land that it owned in Maryland before turning its sights on the District, perhaps because the Maryland property was less developed and therefore easier to build on. An 1894 map of Washington and the vicinity shows the Harris property in the District in one of two clusters of small Black and white households, still surrounded by acres of land belonging to white farmers. Ominously, it also shows the large areas that the Chevy Chase Land Company had already purchased to the west and north of Dry Meadows as well as the company's new subdivision of land a mile away in Maryland.

Although the company had not begun subdividing its properties in the District for development, its aggressive purchasing of property must have prompted Mary Ann Harris to take legal action to guarantee that her children would own the Harris farm after her death. In 1898 when Mary Ann was seventy-eight years old, she formally divided the family's two-acre property equally among her four surviving children. By transferring the property to each of her children for a nominal $5 apiece, she guaranteed their inheritance. She also gave a clear signal to the land developers that she was not interested in selling. The transaction was published in the *Washington Post*, ensuring that the transfer in ownership of Dry Meadows became public knowledge.[13]

Whether the Harrises' land was called Dry Meadows when they bought it in the 1850s is unknown, but the name continued well into the twentieth century. The name was used in Mary Ann Harris's transfer of the property to her children and in two other real estate transactions: first in 1922 in a transfer involving Lorenzo's parcel and then in its final sale in 1928. Perhaps it was an apt description of the area's original appearance, as a meadow covered with hardy wildflowers that can survive drought, and the name endured even after Thomas Harris had changed the meadow into a farm to feed his family.[14]

Mary Ann Harris died sometime after transferring the farm to her children; although the date of her death is unknown, she did not appear in the 1910 census.[15] She had lived over eighty years, with the last sixty spent on Broad

Hugh Miller, Post Staff Photographer.
CANAL CHILD. Mary Moten, 73-year-old daughter of the Mary Harris who piloted President John Quincy Adams and his party up the old Potomac Canal to the ground breaking for the Chesapeake & Ohio Canal 100 years ago. She lives at 5803 Broad Branch road, Chevy Chase.

A 1928 photo of Mary Moten seated in front of her house on the Harris family's Dry Meadows property on Broad Branch Road. The inset photo likely depicts her mother, Mary Ann Harris. Originally published in the *Washington Post*, June 2, 1928, part of section called "Day's News in Camera Views"; photograph by Hugh Miller. © 1928 *The Washington Post*. All rights reserved. Used under license.

Branch Road on land that she and her husband first bought in the 1850s. She was the last living link between her children and her grandfather George Pointer, who had raised her in his cottage beside the Potomac River. She had told her children and grandchildren his stories about George Washington and other famous people of the eighteenth and nineteenth centuries. They must have been impressed, because more than twenty years after her death, they repeated those stories to a reporter from the *Washington Post*.

As noted in chapter 2, a reporter from the *Post* interviewed Mary Moten, Mary Ann Harris's daughter, for an article commemorating the hundredth anniversary of the ground breaking for the C&O Canal. Mary recounted the story she had heard about her then eight-year-old mother's helping to steer the canal boat that delivered President John Quincy Adams to the ceremonies that were held near George Pointer's old cottage. A photo shows Mary Moten sitting in front of the family's Broad Branch homestead, and in an inset photo the elderly Mary Ann Harris herself appears, smoking a pipe. Referred to as the "Canal Child," Mary Ann's life had spanned twenty-two presidencies, from James Monroe to Theodore Roosevelt, and she had lived through many of the major events in American history.[16]

### Changes at the Harris Farm

After the death of Mary Ann Harris, the greatest change at Dry Meadows was the death of her son-in-law, Armstead Moten. His wife, Mary Moten, was only forty-four years old when Armstead died at age fifty-seven in the spring of 1902, and perhaps it was unexpected as he had still been working at the turn of the century. At the time of his death, their four children ranged in age from sixteen to twenty-four years old, and three of them were living at Dry Meadows. Armstead's work as a cobbler had always provided the main financial support for their family, and although his wife, Mary, had responsibilities at the farm, she also worked as a domestic servant in neighboring white households. After his death, her earnings would not begin to make up for the loss of her husband's income. Although Mary was literate, she was largely limited to domestic work, as were many other African American women at the time. In 1910 more than half of all Black women of working age were formally employed, with most of them working on farms in rural communities. Of those women not in farming, 80 percent were working as either servants or laundresses.[17] A 1929 study in the *Monthly Labor Review* did not even bother to categorize their work because "it was safe to assume that they were all in domestic work."[18]

By 1904 three of Mary Moten's four children were married, and two had begun having children of their own. The elder Moten daughter, Mary, or "Minnie," lived in Alexandria, Virginia, with her husband and children, but the other three siblings—two with spouses—stayed with their mother on the Broad Branch farm. With the Chevy Chase Land Company's increasing land purchases in the area, however, there was no affordable land for them near Dry Meadows. To accommodate everyone, the family squeezed two more houses on the farm. The homes were probably small, two-story frame homes with a stoop in the front, similar to the one in the photograph in the *Washington Post*. All the Moten family members, including the women who were doing domestic work, contributed to the support of the farm.

By 1910 one house was occupied by Mary Moten's elder son, John Armstead, and his wife. John worked as a laborer for a private contractor, but his great interest was gardening. Mary's daughter Rosetta and her husband, Randolph "Rand" Harris, a wagon driver, lived in a second house with their three young children. Mary Moten's youngest child, William, who was newly married in 1910 and working as a wagon driver, shared a third house with his wife and his mother. Since two of these men were drivers, there may have also been a shed for horses and wagons.[19]

In fact, Mary Moten's children had built homes for their families on the land that legally belonged not only to their mother but also to their uncles, since Mary Harris had transferred equal shares of the land to her four surviving children. Mary's brothers Lorenzo and Lewis were by then long established in their own homes elsewhere—Lewis in Georgetown and Lorenzo in Buffalo—but apparently neither objected to Mary Moten's use of their land for new homes for her children. That the land continued to be viewed as a single property, to be used by the entire family, was shown yet again a few years later. Mary Moten's older brother Joseph, having returned to Dry Meadows around the time of his father's death in 1891, continued to live there after the turn of the century. When it became too crowded for him to continue living there, however, he apparently recognized the more compelling needs of his sister and her children. The 1910 census recorded Joseph as living nearby at the home of Edward Frazier, whose family had been neighbors of the Harrises for forty years. Joseph had deferred to the needs of his niece and nephews and moved off his own land to give them more space for their growing families. By

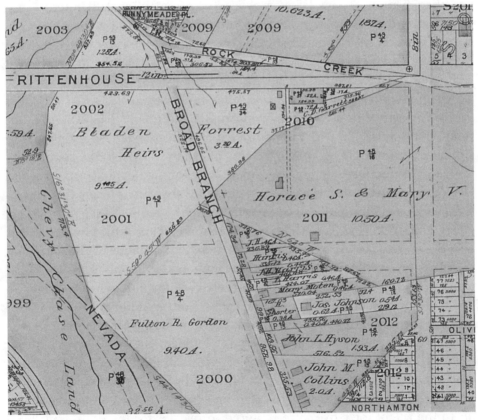

In this detail of *Baist's Real Estate Atlas of Surveys of Washington, District of Columbia*, the 1913 map shows the triangular Harris property divided into four parcels. It is still surrounded by large farm estates. Development of new lots on Oliver Street is visible at the lower right corner of the map. Courtesy of Library of Congress, Geography and Map Division.

1910 when Joseph went back to work as a Pullman porter based in the District, presumably he could visit his New York family easily, but he never again appeared in New York City records as a resident.

Despite the development of the nearby lands that was threatening the rural and multiracial community, the settlement on Broad Branch Road survived for two more decades. One elderly woman's recollection recorded in 1952 was that the Black residents of the area had been on good terms with their neighbors at the turn of the century and that "Willy" Moten, Mary Moten's son, used to play marbles with all of the white boys near Chevy Chase Circle. The election of 1914, however, would accelerate the developments that threatened Dry Meadows.[20]

Woodrow Wilson and the Approach of War

In 1913 Woodrow Wilson, who had been the president of Princeton University and the governor of New Jersey, was elected president of the United States; he was also the first southerner to occupy the White House since the Civil War. Soon after his election, he formally segregated the federal civil service. By then, Washington itself had become highly segregated. Although civil rights laws enacted during Reconstruction still existed in Washington, they were simply ignored. Restaurants and other public businesses refused to serve African Americans, and various associations and unions would not accept them. In response, the Washington branch of the National Association for the Advancement of Colored People became one of the largest in the country.[21]

In 1915 a fiftieth reunion of the Grand Army of the Republic took place in Washington. A volunteer organization of Civil War veterans formed shortly after the war, and the group had been instrumental in getting benefits for all veterans, both white and Black. Fourteen former members of the First Regiment of US Colored Troops attended the reunion, and a photo of the surviving members of the regiment shows the pride the men still took in their service. Most wore their war ribbons on their jackets and old military hats bearing the insignia of the Union army.[22] Some had canes, which was understandable since most of them would have been in their late seventies. Joseph Harris, who at seventy-one years old was still working as a Pullman porter, likely would have made every attempt to be there. As the old veterans posed for the photograph, they did not know that the country would soon be at war again.[23]

Once the United States declared war on Germany in 1917, American males up to the age of forty-five were required to register for the draft, and three of the Harris grandsons did so: Joseph's own son, Thomas, who was living in New York, and the two Moten sons in Washington. None of the three was

A fiftieth reunion of veterans of the First Regiment of the US Colored Troops in 1915 in Washington, DC. Carroll R. Gibbs and the Moorland Spingarn Center, Howard University.

taken, but their draft cards give a few descriptive clues about their appearance and their jobs. William Moten claimed no exemptions, although he was supporting his mother and his own family as a pharmacist's porter delivering medicine in Tenleytown, where he and his family were living. His draft record described him as a tall, slender, thirty-one-year-old man and a father of three children.[24] John was described as a forty-one-year-old man of medium build, and his stated profession was that of gardener working on his own property, which would have been the Dry Meadows farm. Their New York cousin Thomas was recorded as age forty-two and as a tall man of stout build who worked as a porter.

More than 350,000 African Americans ultimately fought in World War I, and virtually all served in segregated units, just as Joseph and John Harris had done in the Civil War. Racism was so well entrenched in President Wilson's government that when Black soldiers returned to Washington at the end of the war, they were ignored. The 480 Black soldiers of the First Separate Battalion had distinguished themselves in fighting abroad, and 25 of them were awarded France's distinguished Croix de Guerre. Despite that their bravery had been described in the *Washington Star* newspaper and that a ceremony had been held for returning white soldiers, the District held no parade to honor the Black soldiers' return and appeared to deliberately ignore their heroism. This snub was in contrast to the welcome that the District had extended to the returning First Regiment USCT at the end of the Civil War fifty-four years earlier.[25]

## The Moten Families in Reno, Tenleytown

By 1917 the families of Mary Moten's son William and her daughter Rosetta (now Rosetta Moten Harris) each had three children and had outgrown Dry Meadows. The two families moved from the crowded Harris land to the larger Black neighborhood of Reno in Tenleytown, leaving Mary Moten and her son John and his wife as the only Moten family members at the farm. That same year Joseph's wife, Margaret, finally moved from New York City to live with him on the farm, and the couple undoubtedly occupied one of the houses that had been vacated. Their grown son and daughter remained in New York.

The African American settlement of Reno had been part of Tenleytown since the Civil War when Fort Reno had attracted a community of people from Maryland and Virginia who were escaping slavery.[26] They built crude shelters near the fort and remained as squatters once the war was over. Eventually, two developers bought some of the land around the fort and laid out a new "Reno City" subdivision. Small lots sold for $25 with a down payment of $5.

The low prices meant that some of the former squatters were able to buy their own small plots, and by the turn of the century, Black residents made up three-quarters of Reno's population.[27]

Moving to Reno was a logical step for William's and Rosetta's families, as they would not be too distant from the Harris farm or their friends and neighbors on Broad Branch Road. The primitive homes of the first settlers of Reno had evolved into more substantial housing by the beginning of the twentieth century, and new unpaved streets had been laid out for the growing neighborhood. In the 1890s African American laborers had helped to rebuild the main road in Tenleytown, called the Rockville Turnpike, with a new sixteen-foot-wide strip of macadam to smooth the ride on the bumpy road.[28] Several small grocery stores, a barber shop, three Black churches, and a Black cemetery had all grown up to serve the Reno community.[29]

The move to Reno also meant that the Moten children would be much closer to their school. Less than half a mile from the center of Tenleytown, the Jesse Reno School had been built in 1903 to replace the dilapidated school for Black children, Grant Road Colored School.[30] A classic brick building with eight classrooms on two floors, the Reno School had been designed by the same municipal architect who had designed many other schools and fire stations in Washington, DC, and was an early example of the movement to "beautify" the capital city through the construction of new public buildings and parks.[31] Most important, the Reno School was a major contribution to the Black community. When the school closed in 1950, the city used the building for other purposes. In recent years, it renovated the building, which is now listed on the National Register of Historic Places.

Although living in separate (but proximate) neighborhoods, the Black and white residents got along well with one another, and their children often played together even while attending segregated schools. In 1899 the District installed a water reservoir, and fifteen years later a sewer line opened, although not all homes in Reno were connected to it. Sewage disposal thus remained a problem for many. Yet despite the unequal distribution of municipal services, Reno was considered a good place to live.[32]

## William Moten and the Funeral Home Business

William Moten had worked as a porter for a pharmacist named Thomas Armstrong for several years.[33] His job brought in regular money for his family, but he was ambitious and worked to develop a career as a funeral director. Early on he had studied embalming and received a certification from the Eckels College of Embalming in Philadelphia through its home study program.

William was still employed by the pharmacist in 1918, but he had started to practice undertaking as well when the worldwide influenza pandemic swept over the East Coast and hit the District particularly hard.[34]

Within ten months, more than three thousand Washingtonians had died of the flu, a mortality rate that was higher than that of other large American cities. The District government closed gathering places such as churches and theaters, and many firefighters and policemen were too sick to work. Even the statistician calculating the mortality numbers became one of his own statistics. There was such a shortage of coffins that the desperate head of the DC Health Commission stole a shipment that was destined for Pittsburgh. Given the high number of deaths, the undertakers must have been overwhelmed.[35]

The need for undertakers afforded an opportunity to William Moten to make his living in the profession for which he had trained. By 1921 he was no longer working at the pharmacy, and he listed his profession in a District directory as an undertaker. At the time, although there were funeral directors in both downtown Washington and in Georgetown, he was the only one in Tenleytown. The profession was strictly segregated, but establishing his own practice for African Americans in the area was the start of his lifelong career.[36]

In 1910 only 5 percent of the funeral directors in the United States were African American.[37] The next decade saw the funeral business move from small parlors, often in the funeral director's home, into modern funeral parlors. This development applied fully to African American funeral directors. Between 1910 and 1915, the estimated number of African American funeral directors in the United States more than doubled—going from five hundred to eleven hundred—and by the end of the 1920s, their number had reached three thousand even as the US death rate had dropped.[38] The growth in funeral directors would continue.

William Moten thus chose a promising profession for a young African American entrepreneur. Funerals for enslaved people had always been of central importance in their community, where, as one historian noted, "funerals gave enslaved African Americans a concrete and meaningful way to share grief, assert family ties, and build a spiritual and religious life." Even after emancipation, funeral traditions remained sacred to the African American community. A funeral was a homecoming celebration.[39] Funeral directors were equivalent to clergy because they were viewed as grief counselors in a time of need, and by the end of the nineteenth century, funeral directors were viewed as professionals in what was becoming a very profitable business.[40]

In an effort to gain a cachet of professionalism, US funeral directors founded a national trade association in the nineteenth century. Although initially open to both Black and white races in 1912, the group soon barred African American

The Independent Funeral Directors Ass'n and Guests.
Washington, D.C. Nov. 19 1936.    Scurlock, Photo

Photo of the Independent Funeral Directors Association of Washington, DC, and guests on November 19, 1936. Because he was vice president of the organization, William Moten may be seated in the front row. Courtesy of Scurlock Studio Records, Archives Center, National Museum of American History, Smithsonian Institution.

directors from membership. As a consequence, African Americans turned to the National Negro Funeral Directors Association, which in 1907 had grown out of Booker T. Washington's National Negro Business League.[41] By the 1920s, the association was in decline, however, and in 1924 the Independent Negro Funeral Directors Association was formed. The new organization, accepting the reality of Jim Crow segregation, sought aggressively to build the patronage of only African American customers. Strict segregation meant that the market for African American funeral directors was defined, yet this limited market seemed to be in their best business interests even as they fought racial prejudice.[42]

William Moten came into the profession at the right time, just as it was modernizing and becoming lucrative. In 1921, or four years after they moved to Reno, William and his wife were financially secure enough to buy their own home on Dennison Place. Thirty years later Moten's Funeral Home was on Prospect Street in Georgetown, where a number of Black families still lived and would be his clients. Later, he would move his business downtown.[43] He joined the Independent Funeral Directors Association of Washington, which by then had become the leading trade association for African American directors, and he eventually served as its vice president. He had made his way in a respected profession that, in contrast to the racist images that dominated American advertising, film, and radio, prided itself on its respectability, decorum, and affluence.[44]

## The Deterioration of Race Relations and the Riots in Washington

The end of World War I brought increasing unemployment to Washington after a reduction in the government workforce and the demobilization of the military. With the return of newly confident African American soldiers to the city and the work of people such as A. Phillip Randolph and Marcus Garvey, Washington's Black residents began demanding new rights, better economic opportunities, and the end of discrimination. White residents, not wanting any change in the status quo, resented the progress African Americans made.[45]

It would not be long before the racial tension in Washington exploded. In June and July 1919, a series of assaults on women, both Black and white, by Black men rocked the District. The police chief assigned a hundred of his men to investigate. Aided by many volunteers, they went throughout the city, rounding up hundreds of innocent Black men as possible suspects. One assault of a white woman took place in Maryland just over the District line, near Chevy Chase Circle, or about a mile and a half from the Dry Meadows farm where Joseph Harris and John Moten were living. Whether the men at the Harris farm or their neighbors were swept up in the arrests is not known, but surely the Black residents of Broad Branch Road and Fort Reno would have felt threatened.

The violence continued in the city as a white mob attacked one of the suspects, and within days an estimated five hundred guns had been sold in the District. In response, two thousand armed Black veterans confronted the police, who were then reinforced by white military troops.[46] The result was four days of rioting and violence, as Black residents stood their ground and defended their community. Arrests of African Americans were ten times greater than those of white people, but the thirty-nine total deaths resulting from the violence were distributed about equally between the two races. Rioting spread to other cities that summer, as the defiance of the African American community in Washington inspired other communities to resist white mobs.[47]

The causes of the conflict have been debated. A hundred years later, in a history of the riots by the *Washington Post*, the newspaper concluded that its reporting of the riots had been "highly provocative and shamefully irresponsible."[48] After the riots, the director of Negro Economics in the US Department of Labor suggested that one factor causing the violence was the growing

segregation of the races.[49] The same period saw increasing economic inse-
curity in the Black community. Although by 1890 home ownership among
African Americans had risen to 15 percent, twenty years later it had decreased
to 11 percent as segregation forced many homeowners in formerly integrated
neighborhoods to move to more segregated areas where they became renters.[50] The city of Washington, which had been integrated in the nineteenth
century, had become two separate cities—one Black and one white—by the
early twentieth century.

Six years after the riots, the situation had not improved. In August 1925,
the District commissioners permitted a downtown parade of members of the
Ku Klux Klan. The *New York Times* estimated that as many as fifty thousand
people marched down Pennsylvania Avenue in their white robes and pointed
caps, and then they held a ceremony at the Washington Monument. They
marched without their masks pulled over their faces because they had nothing to fear. The following year the US Supreme Court upheld the legality of restrictive covenants in real estate sales, meaning that African Americans could
be lawfully prohibited from renting or buying property in designated areas
such as Chevy Chase or Tenleytown.[51]

The deterioration of race relations directly affected the families of William
Moten and his sister Rosetta Harris, who had been living in Reno for almost
ten years. Rosetta and her husband, Rand, had rented a house in Reno not far
from where her brother William and his family lived. Rand worked as a laborer and later as a grocery store truck driver, while Rosetta, like her mother,
continued to do domestic work.[52] During the 1920s, however, their neighborhood came under increasing pressure from forces in favor of development
that are known today as gentrification.

The first displacement of Reno's residents began in 1928 with the construction of a new water reservoir, which by itself affected only a few Black
households. However, that same year the District commissioners authorized
the buying of property for the construction of a junior high school for white
children. A local citizens association in a 1930 newsletter announced the government's acquisition of more land as "good news, welcome to practically every reader of this paper." Of course, it was not good news for Reno's African
American residents, many of whom had lived in the area decades longer than
their white neighbors. As the government acquired Reno homes for both
parkland and schools, the Black residents who refused the government's offer
were threatened with the condemnation of their homes.[53]

The neighborhood's death knell was sounded, however, when a bill supported by local businessmen was introduced in Congress to condemn all the
homes in the predominantly Black community. The US government would
purchase fifty-two acres to build a public park commemorating the Civil War

Photo from the 1930s of African American homes in the Fort Reno neighborhood on Dennison Place, Northwest, the street where William Moten and his family lived. Homes were razed to build a park. Reprinted with permission of John P. Wymer photo collection, Historical Society of Washington, DC.

fort. Public statements in favor of the bill reflected the depth of white people's prejudice against the Black residents of the neighborhood. The president of the District Board of Commissioners urged passage of the bill, arguing that "this irregular, ill-devised subdivision constitutes a blight upon this part of the District." He added, "The territory surrounding is being developed by high class residences."[54]

Like Rosetta and her family, many of the African Americans in Reno were renters. As the government and speculators bought up the land, landlords stopped maintaining their rental homes, expecting them to be sold, and white residents then justified razing the neighborhood by pointing at the dereliction of the homes. In fact, however, many of the homes in Reno such as the one owned by William Moten were in good condition, but in the end, their condition did not spare them from being razed.

The citizens association of Tenleytown had been working since its formation in 1898 to redevelop the Reno neighborhood. The white residents of Tenleytown had been sympathetic to the South during the Civil War, and fifty years later, their neighborhood association continued to support the interests of their own white community members. When the bill to allow the government to reclaim the Reno area passed, it brought an end to what had been the thriving Black neighborhood.[55]

In her history of Tenleytown, Judith Helm wrote, "The [Black] social order at Fort Reno had been long-established; these feelings of community and status were lost when the residents moved, family by family, to other neighborhoods—most often to other neighborhoods that had no long-standing sense of community, family ties, or traditions."[56] In 1931 the newly constructed Alice Deal Junior High School opened, overshadowing the Jesse Reno School next door, and the all-white Woodrow Wilson High School opened four years later.[57] By 1935 following a number of their Reno neighbors, Rosetta and her husband had moved to Rosedale Street in the northeast section of the District, and eventually her brother John would move there too. William and his wife moved to a substantial 1875 building in the center of the District on Corcoran Street, Northwest, located about halfway between Dupont Circle and Logan Circle. All the families would remain in their new homes into the 1940s.

The Displacement of Cemeteries

The redevelopment of Reno displaced not only the current residents but also their families' graves. Reno's three Black churches were bought out, and the Black cemetery, which had served the community since 1880, was relocated to nearby Bethesda, Maryland. The original cemetery had been on a hill that had been known locally as Graveyard Hill, and the cemetery was referred to as both the Christian Cemetery and the Moses Cemetery. Located near a corner of the land where Fort Reno had stood, it was a little over a mile southwest of Dry Meadows.

The Harris and Moten families had a long connection with both the cemetery and the group that maintained it. When Mary Moten's husband, Armstead, died in 1902, his death record listed his burial place as the Christian Cemetery, which was run by a benevolent society called White's Tabernacle No. 39 of the Ancient Order of the Sons and Daughters, Brothers and Sisters of Moses, or the Moses Society. African American benevolent societies had begun in the nineteenth century to supply aid to people in need. Because of the importance of funerals, some of these societies began providing their members with funeral insurance and help with funeral rites and cemetery plots. The Moses Society also owned a meeting hall located in the same block as the Rock Creek Baptist Church, and it sponsored social gatherings that played an important role in the lives of many African Americans. In later years, William Moten was a particularly active member of the church and may have played a role in the Moses Society as well.[58]

In 1910 two Harris family members were trustees of the Moses Society when it applied for legal incorporation. Even though he had been living in Buffalo for seventeen years, Lorenzo Harris was listed in the society's incorporation documents as an elected trustee, as was Mary Moten's son John. Since family members were active in the Moses Society, it is probable that in addition to Armstead Moten, both Mary Ann Harris and her husband, Thomas, were among the 192 people who were buried in the Moses Cemetery between 1880 and 1910. By the time Lorenzo and John had become trustees of the society, the construction of new roads in Tenleytown had begun to threaten the old cemetery on Graveyard Hill, and the group decided to buy land for a new one.

The Moses Society located a suitable property along River Road in Bethesda, close to the border with the District and near the Macedonia Baptist Church that was serving the Black residents of that area. The opposition of white residents added further delays, however; it took ten years and congressional legislation for the graves in the Moses Cemetery to be moved to the new location. Unfortunately, the River Road location did not prove to be the final resting place of the graves.[59]

In the late 1950s, residential and commercial development near River Road once again forced the Moses Society to move the graves, this time to land located even farther out in Montgomery County. Within a few decades and following substantial suburban development, the memory of the River Road site was lost. Given the absence of any written records of the last move, little is known about the number of graves that were actually transferred. Recent research by local historians done in cooperation with the Macedonia Baptist Church confirms the cemetery's former location on River Road, and the group continues to work to get suitable recognition of this place where African Americans of both Reno and Bethesda were once interred.

A consequence of these multiple moves is that it is no longer possible to know exactly what became of the graves of any of the Harris family members who were buried at these locations. Because of the lack of documentation, it is thought that not all the graves at the River Road site were found and moved before the new development occurred, and the unmarked graves at the third site offer no help in identification. No historical marker or other sign identifies the sites of the Moses Society cemeteries where the Harris family members and other Black residents of Reno, Chevy Chase, and Bethesda were buried. The Macedonia Baptist Church, however, still occupies its old location on River Road across the street from gas stations and fast food stores that have grown up around it, and its members remain active to this day. At this writing the church seeks to regain possession of part of the land that the cemetery once occupied.[60]

## The Fight for Dry Meadows

At the same time that real estate developers were threatening the Reno settlement, they were also making a final assault on the small Black community on Broad Branch Road. By the early 1920s, almost all of the original white landowners had sold their properties surrounding the Harris farm to the Chevy Chase Land Company. The company had built a grid of roads on the nearby land and subdivided it into hundreds of small lots for suburban white buyers. The two-acre Harris farm was encircled by these numerous subdivided plots that had been carved out of the original Belt estate and other properties, and by 1925 about half of the lots already had houses built on them. Joseph Harris and Mary Moten would have heard the construction noise and seen the new homes marching toward the farm.

By then, Mary Moten and Joseph were the only two Harris siblings left on the family's land. Joseph was living with his wife, and Mary Moten was living with her son John and his wife, Annie. Their brother Lewis had died in Georgetown at the beginning of World War I, and their brother Lorenzo had been living in Buffalo for over thirty years. Faced with the rapid approach of the surrounding development, Joseph Harris and Mary Moten took steps to consolidate (or, perhaps more accurately, reunite) the title to their parents' farm. The issue concerned Lorenzo, who retained title to his half-acre parcel.

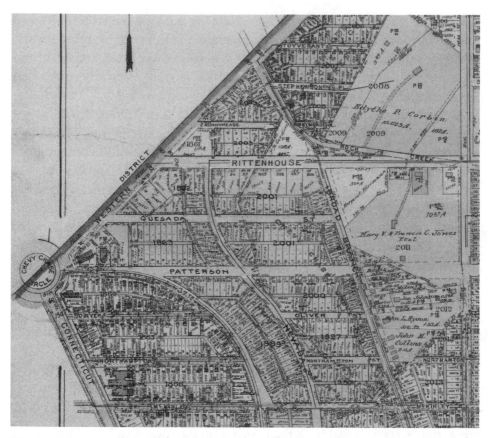

This detail from a 1919 plat map shows the extensive development by the Chevy Chase Land Company. The Harris property is a small triangle, located at the end of Patterson Street at the center right of the map and surrounded by newly developed housing. One piece of farmland backs onto their property. Courtesy of Library of Congress, Geography and Map Division.

Undoubtedly after discussions with his brother, in the fall of 1922 Joseph filed suit to have his name substituted for Lorenzo's on the subdivided parcel that his brother then owned. Lorenzo had been gone for many years and was unlikely to return or want use of the farm, and he had no children to inherit it. Lorenzo agreed to the change and allowed his parcel of Dry Meadows to revert to Joseph.[61]

When the Chevy Chase Land Company first began selling lots before the turn of the century, deeds did not have racial covenants restricting sales to white buyers, presumably because the company assumed that only the white "leisure class" could afford its homes. By the twentieth century, however, deeds in the Chevy Chase neighborhoods all contained restrictive covenants stipulating that buyers had to be white.[62] The courts then upheld the legality of the restrictive covenants in 1921. By 1924 the National Association of Real Estate Brokers, based in Chicago, adopted a code of ethics stating that "a Realtor should never be instrumental in introducing into a neighborhood . . . members of any race or nationality . . . whose presence will clearly be detrimental to property values in that neighborhood."[63]

Although Joseph Harris and Mary Moten, as long-standing property owners, were not threatened by the restrictive covenants in the deeds to the lands being sold around them, they were threatened by the government's power of eminent domain. Eminent domain, or the government's right to take private property for a compelling public use, had historically been part of British law and was included in the Fifth Amendment to the US Constitution. It allowed governments to build public roads and canals on land that belonged to private citizens. Land developers could not use eminent domain to take land for normal commercial purposes, such as the construction of private homes, but local or national governments could use it to acquire property to build public infrastructure, such as buildings and parks. In the hands of local powers seeking to push African American landowners out of the area, it would effectively eliminate the last vestiges of the Black communities on Broad Branch Road.

The new housing developments built by the Chevy Chase Land Company brought large numbers of white families to the area, and their children needed schools. Thus, in August 1928, while relying on its power of eminent domain for the purpose of building a white elementary school, the federal government paid $6,862.50 to Mary Moten for Dry Meadows. This forced sale ended the ownership of property that had been in the Harris family for about eighty years.[64]

Although eminent domain was the only way that the government could appropriate the Harris family's land, the government had to pay a fair market rate. The increasing demand for real estate in the suburbs of Washington during the first decades of the twentieth century had driven the value of the Harris farm from $600 in 1870 to almost $7,000 in 1928.[65] This price per square foot was actually higher than what was being advertised at the same time for land overlooking the Potomac River, land that undoubtedly had better views than Dry Meadows.[66] In today's dollars, the $7,000 price paid for the Broad Branch farm would be worth about $200,000.[67]

Mary and Joseph could not have known, of course, that when they sold their farm, albeit under compulsion, it had happened at the top of the real estate market. Renowned economic historian John Kenneth Galbraith said, "1928, indeed, was the last year in which Americans were buoyant, uninhibited and utterly happy."[68] "Utterly happy" did not describe everyone in America, but it might have felt like it in retrospect when Wall Street crashed the following year, sending banks and many businesses into bankruptcy. America would not fully emerge from the economic depression that followed for a decade. During that grim period, more than half of the Black population needed federal assistance, but so did a lot of white residents.[69]

In 1929 construction of the Lafayette Elementary School began on the land that had been the Harris farm. Ten years after the sale of Dry Meadows, the community of African American families was forgotten. A 1938 *Washington Post* article about the new elementary school reported, "Lafayette School which stands on the site of once barren ground is now the hub of a thriving community life."[70] In the space of a decade, four generations of the Harris family and their neighbors who had all been sustained by the "barren ground" for so many years had disappeared from the area's history.

Between 1890 and 1928, four Harris-Moten families, along with so many others, had been forced to move out of integrated neighborhoods to enable the government to build white schools. All of these schools still exist today: Western High School, now Duke Ellington School, in Georgetown; Wilson High School and Alice Deal Middle School in Tenleytown; and Lafayette Elementary School in Chevy Chase.

# Epilogue

The Harris and Moten families that were the last occupants of the Broad Branch farm did not move far from one another. Joseph Harris and his wife moved to Nineteenth Street, Northwest, in downtown Washington, close to Dupont Circle, and were less than a mile from Joseph's nephew William Moten, the funeral director. Joseph died two years later at the age of eighty-seven and was buried in the segregated Woodlawn Cemetery in Southeast Washington. Mary Moten was seventy-one when she signed the bill of sale for her parents' Broad Branch farm to the federal government. Although she thereafter largely disappears from the records, she presumably continued to live with her son John near Rosetta's family in Northeast Washington until her death in 1933.

John Moten worked as a gardener until the National Park Service hired him at the new Fort Reno Park, located on the same land where his younger brother's and sister's families had once lived.[1] During John's tenure with the Park Service, the director of the Office of Public Buildings and Public Parks in the District was Ulysses S. Grant III, the grandson of the Civil War general and American president. Despite his grandfather's strong record on race relations, the grandson sadly became one of the architects of segregation in the District of Columbia. As two historians of Washington have said, this descendant of the great Civil War general "spent a career embedding segregated housing patterns into D.C.'s residential geography."[2]

The growing racial isolation in Washington mirrored the increasing segregation in other cities in both the North and the South. There are different ways to measure segregation and racial isolation, but the cities all showed the same urban trends in the first half of the twentieth century. Soon after the Supreme Court's decision in 1948 declaring restrictive covenants unconstitutional, the trend in segregated housing in northern cities peaked, with segregation in southern cities culminating in the 1960s. The reintegration of formerly segregated neighborhoods followed, although slowly, one house at a time.[3]

World War II brought to an end the economic depression of the 1930s but not racial discrimination. All units in the US military remained segregated, just as they had been eighty years before in the Civil War and twenty-four years earlier in World War I. Public businesses and facilities such as parks and pools in the South discriminated freely against African Americans, and, as noted, discrimination in housing opportunities was both common and legal. Schools likewise remained segregated in southern states for many years, even following the Supreme Court's ruling in the fall of 1954 banning segregated schools as unconstitutional. Under the compulsion of the ruling, District schools, like many around the country, began the gradual process of desegregation.[4]

The 1960s brought a changing perspective. On August 28, 1963, more than 250,000 people joined a March on Washington for Jobs and Employment to celebrate the hundredth anniversary of the Emancipation Proclamation. Henry Louis Gates Jr. called the march "a phenomenal event."[5] It was the largest demonstration Washington had seen at that point, and, fortunately, the weather was unusually good for the hottest month in the summer.[6] William Moten was then seventy-six years old, and perhaps he and his three children walked to the Lincoln Memorial so that they might hear Rev. Martin Luther King Jr. and other leaders of the civil rights movement speak. William lived another seven years until his death in October 1970.

The year 1963 marked not only the centennial of the Emancipation Proclamation but also the 190th year after George Pointer's birth into slavery on a tobacco plantation ten miles up the Potomac River from Washington. Although he would not have known it, his birth was the beginning of his descendants' long journey through a tumultuous period in the history of the United States. As with many other African American families in Washington and elsewhere, the Pointer descendants emerged from an era of slavery to experience a thunderous victory in the Civil War, with its promise of

Reconstruction, only to face the withering of hope and increasing segregation for nearly a hundred years. At last, in the sixth decade of the twentieth century, George Pointer's descendants might have believed, along with Reverend King, that they were coming to the end of a long struggle and that it was time to dream of a better future for themselves and all their descendants.

As Langston Hughes wrote,

All this
A prelude to our age: Today
Tomorrow is another Page.[7]

*Appendix 1.* Letter Facsimile and Transcription of the Petition of Capt. George Pointer, September 5, 1829

What follows is the letter by George Pointer that started us on this journey. We reprint it in full here and provide a complete transcription after it.

Facsimile of George Pointer's eleven-page
letter written in 1829. Courtesy of the
US National Archives.

To the President, and directors of the
Chesapeake and Ohio Canal

Gentlemen—

I pray you to read the memmo=
rial and humble Petition of an old and
Obscure Citizen, I was born in the year A.D.
1773. 11th of October— in Frederick County Maryland,
I was born a slave and continued one for 19
years, a part of which time I had the honor
of being with the engineer and directors of the
old Potomack Canal Company, during that
Period, I had the good fortune to get in the good
graces of my master the engineer and the
Company, having been told recommended by
the engineer and directors for the faithful
Services Rendered them by me, my master
told me, that if I would pay him 300$
In a given time that I should be my
own man, which I did out of the
Hard earnings I Received from the company
I at that Period Occupied the Place where
my Little humble cottage now Stands, it
Being given to me by the Directors and

Company in 1787 – the chief engineer as well as I can Recollect was Mr. John Smith from Texeland, Whom General Washington as I Learnt employed to explore the Route of the Potomack Canal, it fell to my Lot to be his Servant during the Period of the Exploration, as well as I can Recollect Col. Gilpin of Alexandria was one of the directors Col. Herbert Lawyer Keith and Col. Fitzgerald – Mr. Vanhorn Pay master, Yearly in the month of October General Washington would come to view the Progress of the works, and well I Recollect that at every Squad of workmen he Passed he would give a dollar to, and I also well well Recollect that the Sections contained Two miles ¾ and ten Rods, I continued in that way during Mr. Smiths term Mr. Harbaugh was chosen Mr. Smiths Successor, I then was turned over to him and continued with him untill the Lower Canal was Finished, and then went on with him to the great Falls I continued with him till Capt Myers took his Place as engineer, I was directed by him

to take charge of five Boats that was to Run
the free Stone from Senica to the great falls
from day to day for the use of the Locks,
which duty it was well known I
Executed faithfully and to the satisfac
tion of Capt Meyers and the company
after the death of Capt Meyers Mr. Harbaugh
Took charge again, at that time the
Lower Locks was under way; in the
mean time flour came down so plenti
fully that More houses was established
for the reciption of produce, in the mean
time a machine was got under
way to Lower the flour down
for the boats to take it down, as the
Lock was not finished, we then made
a way from the falls to Sandy Landing
for the purpose of hawling boats down
to get them up to the machine to get
the flour to convey down, at that time
there was a change among the directors,
the next Engineer was Col. Dickens, the next
Gene. Smallwood Next Mr. Templeman
and Mr. John Lairas, the flour and
other produce came down so

167

profusely that the company thought it
expedient that Pilots should be chosen
to carry the western boats down, four was
chosen and among them was your
Petitioner humble Servant, in that ca
=pacity he continued for two seasons, after
which time they could with Pittsburgh
make out for themselves, at the same
time the company knowing that the boats
would be taken with a Return cargo
I was ordered to take some hands on the
Bed of the River for the purpose of making
ways &c for boats to Return, at that time
Mr. Harbaugh was about finishing the
Lower Locks, after they were finished I went
To Boating for my self and a continued in
that capacity untill new directors were
appointed and an enginer also, who was
Mr. Josias Thompson, the directors were
then Genl. Jno Mason Mr. Jonah Thompson
Col. Elie Williams and Mr. Jno Parna
Alden entered with Mr. Thompson in the
Erection of the New Locks at the
Little Falls Mr. Thompson went after that to
Explore the River antietam in order to

ascertain, whether it was navigable for Boats to come down in the Potomack. after that the directors thought it expedient that the Potomack Should be explored as there was a number of obstructions that hindred the Papage of boats up and down also, I was chosen by Mr. Thompson to Superintend the hands in Removing the Obstructions and making a good way For the Papage of Boats, which was Executed diligently and to the Satisfaction of him by me. I next went with the Directors and engineer to the Shenandoah River, I was left by Mr. Thompson to Superintend the navigation of that River Such as Removing dams and fish polls and many time Run the Risk of Loosing my Life by the inhabitants in the absence of the company for having Removed the Same for the Papage of boats agreeable to the direction of the engineer and Directors, We finished there and Returned Back, after that was compleated. Col Williams and Mr. Thompson Left

this Place for the Relocation of the Cumberland
Road to Wheeling, before they Started
they called on me to met the board
that had assembled at the lemon tavern
they then told the board that they thought
it inexpedient to employ any engineer on
the Potomack, as I had, had experience
enough to Superintend any work on the
Potomack that they might want done
Consequently I was named by Mr Ferney
Hoxell to Superintend any work that
might be wanting done and upon his
adoption I was appointed to Superintend
a Parcel of hands for the Purpose at that time
of building a Wall to throw the Water in
the canal at the great falls for boats to
come down in Low water, it was
finished to the utmost Satisfaction of the
Board, I next was ordered to Seneca
with 30 hands and made a Wall to
throw the Water into Seneca Canal & I
then commenced Running free Stone
from Seneca to the Little Rocks that were
then building, in Running the Stone
above mentioned on a certain day

there was a parcel of boats fast in Seneca
Falls with marble for the capitol, I could
not get by. consequently I had to run
out side. unfortunately my boat struck,
I was precipitated out of her, and a broken
Leg was the issue of it. I Laid in that
Situation four days without medical aid,
I However Saved the cargo and got it down
Safe to the Little Falls its place of destination
Next there was a complaint Lodged by the
Inhabitants of Cumberland, specifying that the
Inhabitants on the margin of the River had
Obstructed in a great measure the Passage of
Boats both down and up by building fish
Pots. I was ordered by the company to get
hands. go up. and tear down that in any
manner dammed the Water so as to obstruct
the Passage of boats, I went with hands, and out
Of 73. fish Pots I Pulled down 54. the rest
I Concived a benefit. as they backed the Water,
I came down and was Summoned before
the board to give an account of what I
had done, after my Statement was given in
It was approved of by the board, at that
Time I asked Leave of the board to build

me some fish potts out side of the navigation
of the Potomack Near the Spout of the Little
Falls; they thought it was wrong to grant
me that Liberty in as much as I had been
employed by the company to tear down a
Number that had been established above
on the Potomack, but they being informed
and Knowing at the same time that if
they granted me the Liberty that it could
not effect the navigation in no Respect
Immediately granted me the Liberty of
doing so, which I completed after Eight
hard years Labour, it was not Known at
that time that the Spout of the Little Falls could
Be Run by boals and if it could my dam
would not of ben any obstruction, I
Commenced building and as I have said
Before completed them in 8 years your
Petitioner has had the use of them for
Only 3 years the cost of building them
was at Least 400$ the fish that was
Taken in them was carried to the markets
of Geo Town and Washington
and they have not Paid him he
only having the use of them for three years

One half what they cost him —

the foregoing fish potts I built, that cost me
so much Labour and money, have been
taken down by Mr. McCord workmen
and the Stone of which, has been put in
his wall. I spoke to Mr. McCord about
Destroying me in that manner, and his
answer to me was that I was injured
Consadurably by it, but he could not
help it, and that the company ought
to Compensate me for it indeed, and
that my only course to pursue was
to apply to the company for Redress,
and I do hope that in the Futuerance
of their wealth that they will Remunerate
me for the Same, as they would of
added in equal degree to the support
of my self and an aged and distressed
family; also the Sheep Spring Island
which is no more for me as the wall that
was built opposite Mr. D. Bayards section
shuts me out entirely from it —

If made on the same Mona yearly from
13 to 14 Barrels of corn, but alas it is for
me no more at all, for goods sake Remu
= nerate me for the Loss I have sustained
Buy it which was almost our all ———

The Chesapeake and Ohio Canal is drawing
near my Little Cottage that I have occupied
for 43 years, unmolested both an aged
Wife and Some offspring but alas
none Left to assist us ——————

I do trust in God, the giver of all
things, that if the new Company, does
Dispossess us of our Little Humble Cottage,
that hitherto has not not been a detriment
to the old Canal Company nor anybody
Living, and which was given to me,
that they will give me Some Little
Place adjacent to the new Canal,
that they may upon it Support themselves
for the few days that they have to breathe
upon this earth ——— which is but few

God has prospered the old Canal
that the Father of his his Country
first brought into existence
and may he favour the new one
my well wishes the Company has
for its future Prosperity

Gentlemen, I have the honor
to be, with the greatest obligation
to you all, your very humble
and Obedient Servants

Capt. George Pointer

Sept. 5.th 1829

No. 1
To the President and directors of the Chesapeake and Ohio Canal
Gentlemen—

I pray you to read the memmorial and humble petition of an old and Obscure
Citizen, I was born in the year A.D. 1773. 11th of October in Frederick County
Maryland. I was born a slave and continued one for 19 years, a part of which
time I had the honor of being with the engineer and directors of the old
Potomack Canal Company. during that period, I had the good fortune to get in
the good graces of my master the engineer and the Company, having been well
recommended by the engineer and directors for the faithful Services rendered
them by me, my master Told me, that if I would pay him 300$ In a given time
that I should be my Own man, which I did out of the Hard earnings I Received
from the company; I at that period occupied the place where my Little humble
cottage now stands it Being given to me by the Directors and Company in
1787—the chief engineer as well as I can recollect was Mr. John Smith from
Scotland, whom General Washington as I learnt employed to explore the route
of the Potomack Canal, it fell to my Lot to be his servant during the period of
the Exploration, as well as I can recollect Col. Gilpen of Alexandria was one of
the directors Col. Herbert Lawyer Keith and Col. Fitzgerald—Mr. Vanhorn pay
master; Yearly in the month of October General Washington would come to
view the progress of the work, and well I recollect that at every squad of workmen he passed he would give a dollar to, and I also will well recollect that the
sections contained Two miles ¾ and ten Rods, I continued in that way during
Mr. Smiths time, Mr. Harbaugh was chosen Mr. Smith's successor. I then was
turned over to him and continued with him untill the Lower canal was finished, and then went on with him to the great falls. I continued with him till
Capt Myers took his place as engineer, I was Directed by him to take charge of
five Boats that was to run the free stone from Seneca to the great falls From day
to day for the use of the locks; which duty it was well known I Executed faithfully and to the Satisfaction of Capt Meyers and the company. after the death
of Capt Myers, Mr. Harbaugh Took charge again; at that time the Lower Locks
was under way; in the meantime flour came down so plentifully that ware
houses was established for the reception of produce, in the meantime a machine was got under way to lower the flour down for the boats to take it down
as the Locks was not finished, We then made a way from the falls to Sandy
Landing For the purpose of hawling boats down To get them up to the machine
to get the flour to convey down; at that time there was a change among the
directors, the next Engineer was Col. Dickens, the next Genl. Jn Mason, next
Mr. Templeman and Mr. John Laird; the flour and Other produce came down
so profusely, that the company thought it expedient that pilots should be chosen to carry the western boats down, four was chosen and among them was

your petitioners humble Servant,—in that capacity we continued for two seasons. after which time they could with little help make out for themselves, at the same time the company knowing that the boats would be laden with a return cargo I was ordered to take some hands on the Bed of the river for the purpose of making walls etc. for boats to return, at that time Mr. Harbaugh was about finishing the Lower Locks; after they were finished I went To Boating for myself and continued in that capacity untill new directors were appointed and an engineer also, who was Mr. Josias Thompson. The directors were then Genl. Jn. Mason Mr. Jonah Thompson Col. Elie Williams and Mr. Jn Laird; I then entered with Mr. Thompson in the Erection of the New Locks at the Little Falls, Mr. Thompson went after that to Explore the River antietum in order to ascertain whether it was navigable for Boats to come down in the Potomack; after that the directors thought it expedient that the Potomack should be explored as there was a number of obstructions that hindered the passage of boats up and down also; I was chosen by Mr. Thompson to Superintend the hands in removing the obstructions and making a good way For the passage of Boats. which was Executed diligently and to the Satisfaction of him by me. I next went with the Directors and engineer to the Shenandoah River. I was left by Mr. Thompson to Superintend the navigation of that river such as removing dams and fish potts and many time run the risk of Loosing my Life by the inhabitants in the absinence of the company for having removed the Same for the passage of boats agreeable to the direction of the engineer and Directors. We finished there and returned Back; after that was completed. Col Williams and Mr. Thompson Left this place for the relocation of the Cumberland Road to Wheeling; before they started they called on me to meet the board that had assembled at the Union tavern, they then told the board that they thought Inexpedient to employ any engineer on the Potomack, as I had had experience enough to Superintend any work on the Potomack that they might want done, Consequently I was named by Mr. Henry Foxall to Superintend any work that might be wanting done, and upon his adoption I was appointed to Superintend a parcel of hands for the purpose at that time of building a wall to throw the water in the canal at the great falls for boats to Come down in Low water; it was finished to the utmost satisfaction of the Board, I next was ordered to Seneca with 30 hands and made a wall to throw the water into Seneca Canal; I then commenced running free Stone from Seneca to the Little Locks that were then building; in running the Stone above mentioned on a certain day—there was a parcel of boats fast in Seneca Falls with marble for the Capitol; I could not get by. consequently I had to run Out Side. Unfortunately my boat struck, I was precipitated out of her, and a broken Leg was the issue of it. I Laid in that Situation four days without medical aid, I However Saved the cargo and got it down Safe to the Little falls its place of destination; Next there was a complaint lodged by the Inhabitants of Cumberland, specifying that the Inhabitants on the margin of the river had Obstructed in a great measure the passage of Boats both down and up by building fish Potts; I was ordered by the company to get hands, go up, and Tear all down that in any manner damed the water so as to obstruct the passage of boats. I went with hands and out of 73 fish potts I pulled down 44. the rest I conceived a benefit as they backed the water; I came down and was summoned before the board to give an account of what I had done, after my Statement was given in It was approved by the board. At that Time I asked Leave of the board to build me some fish potts out side of the navigation of the Potomack near the spout of the Little falls, they thought it was wrong to grant me that Liberty in as much as I had been employed by the company to tear down a number that had been established above on the Potomack, but they being informed and Knowing at the same time that if they granted me the Liberty that it could not effect the navigation in no respect; Immediately granted me the Liberty of doing so, which I completed after Eight hard years Labour, it was not Known at that time that the spout of the Little falls could Be run by boats and if it could my dam would not of been any ob-struction. I Commenced building and as I have said Before completed them in 8 years. Your Petitioner has had the use of them for only 3 years the cost of building them Was at Least 400$ the fish that was Taken in them was carried to the markets of Geo Town and Washington—and they have not paid him he only having the use of them for three years One half what they cost him—the foregoing fish potts I built, that cost me So much Labour and money have been Taken down by Mr. McCord & workmen and the Stone of which has been put in his Wall: I spoke to Mr. McCord about Destroying me in that manner, and his answer to me was that I was Injured considerably by it but he could not help it, and that the company ought to compensate me for it indeed, and that my only course to pursue was to apply to the company for redress, and I do hope that in the plentitude of their wealth that they will remunerate me for the same, as they would of added in equal degree to the support of my self and an aged and distressed Family; also the Shap Spring Island which is no more for me as the wall that was built opposite Mr. D. Bussards section Shuts me out entirely from it—

I made on the same Island yearly from 12 to 14 Barrells of corn, but alas it is for me no more at all; For gods sake remunerate me for the Loss I have sustained By it Which was almost our all—

The Chesapeake and Ohio Canal is drawing near my Little Cottage that I have occupied for 43 years, unmolested with an aged Wife and some offspring but alas none left to assist us—

I do trust in God, the giver of all things, that if the new Company does Dispossess us of our Little Humble Cottage, that hitherto has not not been a detriment to the old Canal Company nor anybody Living, and which was given to me, that they will give me Some Little place adjacent to the new Canal, that they may upon it support themselves for the few days that they have to breathe upon this earth—Which is but few God has prospered the old Canal that the father of his his Country First brought into existence and may he favour the new one, My well wishes the Company has for its future prosperity—

Gentlemen, I have the honor to be, with the greatest obligation to you all, your very humble and obedient Servant

Capt. George Pointer

Sept. 5$^{th}$ 1829

*Appendix 2.* The Family Tree of George Pointer

# The Pointer Family of Washington, DC

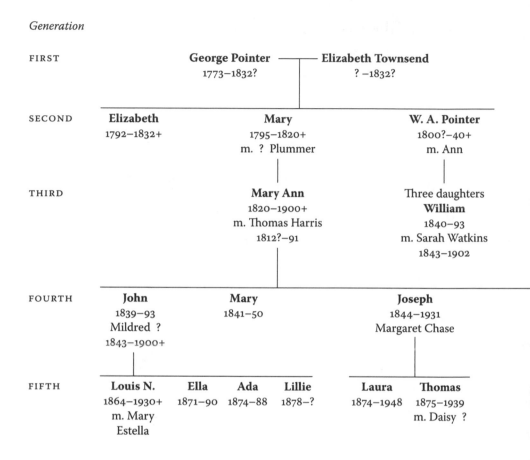

*Generation*

**FIRST**

George Pointer —————— Elizabeth Townsend
1773–1832?                    ? –1832?

**SECOND**

Elizabeth                Mary                W. A. Pointer
1792–1832+          1795–1820+          1800?–40+
                    m. ? Plummer            m. Ann

**THIRD**

                    Mary Ann            Three daughters
                    1820–1900+              **William**
                    m. Thomas Harris          1840–93
                    1812?–91            m. Sarah Watkins
                                            1843–1902

**FOURTH**

John                Mary                Joseph
1839–93            1841–50          1844–1931
Mildred ?                        Margaret Chase
1843–1900+

**FIFTH**

Louis N.    Ella      Ada      Lillie      Laura      Thomas
1864–1930+  1871–90  1874–88  1878–?      1874–1948  1875–1939
m. Mary                                              m. Daisy ?
Estella

**SIXTH**

*Note:* Most of the births and deaths on this family tree are approximate because of inconsistencies among different censuses and other data sources. Appendix 3 discusses the issues involved in using imprecise age data.

*Source:* The birth estimates for individuals on the family tree are generally extrapolated from the US Bureau of the Census, "Decennial Censuses." They can also be found at the National Archives, Record Group 29, Records of the Bureau of the Census, Washington, DC.

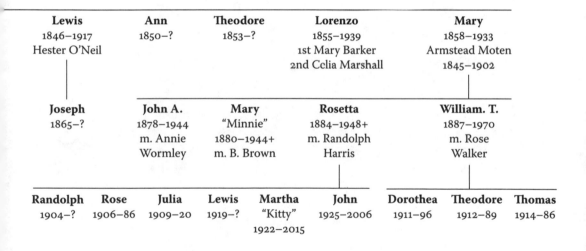

Lewis 1846–1917 Hester O'Neil | Ann 1850–? | Theodore 1853–? | Lorenzo 1855–1939 1st Mary Barker 2nd Celia Marshall | Mary 1858–1933 Armstead Moten 1845–1902

Joseph 1865–? | John A. 1878–1944 m. Annie Wormley | Mary "Minnie" 1880–1944+ m. B. Brown | Rosetta 1884–1948+ m. Randolph Harris | William. T. 1887–1970 m. Rose Walker

Randolph 1904–? | Rose 1906–86 | Julia 1909–20 | Lewis 1919–? | Martha "Kitty" 1922–2015 | John 1925–2006 | Dorothea 1911–96 | Theodore 1912–89 | Thomas 1914–86

# *Appendix 3.* The Adventure of Genealogy

Genealogy is more of an adventure than most people realize. Ask Tanya Gaskins Hardy. She grew up in Fairfax County, Virginia, and attended a segregated school just like other African American children her age. In the 1960s, Fairfax County Public Schools began to comply with the school desegregation decision in *Brown v. Board of Education* of 1954. In 1964 Tanya entered fourth grade at a predominantly white school that had better resources than her previous school. Those resources, however, did not make up for the level of attention and caring the students had received from their Black teachers, who believed in them and were committed to seeing them succeed in school over all else. The resources also did not make up for the whispering and funny looks Black students received as they walked through the integrated school. For Tanya, the loss of friends and fun in school was overwhelming. Tanya's father told her to "be a good girl and don't be afraid" at the new school where she would not see many others like her. He said, "You're there to learn all you can. If you have a problem, you come home and tell me. I'll take care of it."

Tanya's fifth-grade year took her to another school, brand new and closer to her neighborhood. The white teacher had an inviting spirit and attitude that displayed her caring for all of her students. "I felt much more comfortable in Mrs. Snyder's class and grew to love being there," says Tanya. It was a special after-school trip with her teacher that fired her interest in genealogy research.

History was a favorite subject, and after integration, Tanya began to ask her family members about how they went to school and what school was like, trying to make sense of what was happening to her. The answers she received led to more questions about her family's life and where her ancestors had lived. One day her fifth-grade teacher asked her about the old Black church that could be seen from the classroom window. Tanya shared that most of the Black families in the community attended the church. The teacher asked if Tanya would like to go with her to look at the old gravestones in the cemetery. That impromptu field trip sealed the deal for Tanya, and she began to read extensively and research "any and all" things about the history of African Americans and their families.

On becoming an adult, Tanya did not think she could make a career of being a historian, so she made the practical decision to become a special education teacher and administrator. History, however, became her avocation for the rest of her life. She used her family's biannual reunions in rural Virginia to learn about her ancestors from her oldest relatives, and after the reunions, she took a number of trips to their hometowns, looking for more detailed records of their memories.

In the 1980s, no public or family records were digitized, so everything had to be found in person, one document at a time. Old official documents were on microfiche, which had to be read in a machine that had no links or search functions, and information and notes had to be saved either in hard copy or on floppy and compact disks for future use. Marriage, death, and property records were often kept in local courthouses, and there Tanya's young child would play at her feet while she searched dusty manuscripts for clues to her family's past. Genealogy was a time-consuming avocation, but it was rewarding when the history of her ancestors slowly came into focus, little by little, as she followed clues. She found that her great-great-grandfather had walked to West Virginia from Buckingham, Virginia, after emancipation as he looked for work. She also discovered that her great-grandfather had been a shoemaker, and that helped explain why his grandson took on the profession many years later.

The digital age transformed genealogy research. The Genealogical Society of Utah had been founded in 1894 to help the Church of Jesus Christ of Latter-day Saints' members find their ancestors, and with the beginning of the digital age, the society developed software that made the volumes of information it had amassed searchable and accessible to everyone. A century after its foundation, the Genealogical Society of Utah created a large subscription-based genealogy database service, as did a number of other organizations.

When Tanya Hardy had completed as much as she could of her own family history, she offered to do the histories of her friends. In 2015 she was using the Ancestry.com software, looking for the ancestors of her partner, James Fisher, when an unknown woman reached out to her through the service. That woman was Clara Green, who was reaching forward into the twenty-first century to find the descendants of an enslaved man. In one day, that enslaved man born in the eighteenth century was verifiably linked to James Fisher in the twenty-first century.

The work of genealogical companies such as Ancestry.com has provided a gift to everyone interested in his or her personal history. Today a tidal wave of data is available on people who lived in the past, but still many challenges remain for anyone doing such research. The often unsystematic collection and storing of historical data means that many people are not captured in the official records. The challenges are even greater for African Americans because before emancipation the enslaved often had no last names and were not recorded by name. The many years of genealogical research and the more recent work of Clara Green and Barbara Torrey on the history of George Pointer's descendants have revealed both the strengths and weaknesses of using historical data and the joys of dealing with both. Tanya Hardy, now retired after forty-one years as an educator, is doing what she loves most. She began A View of the Past, a genealogy service that has many clients seeking her work.

Sources of Data

Over time statistical standards have evolved, and record keeping has become more systematic, but even today genealogical researchers should be aware of certain issues. In past centuries, many family research projects began with personal records such as Bibles with recorded births and deaths of family members over several generations. In addition, the US decennial censuses provide a strong but skeletal framework for most long-term family histories. Article 1 of the US Constitution requires a census of everyone, both citizens and noncitizens, living in the United States at least once every ten years. The resulting population counts are used to determine the number of members of Congress from each state and the number of members in the Electoral College. Today, it is also used to help allocate funding for federal programs. Before the Civil War, each enslaved person was counted as three-fifths of a person, but the census collected little or no information about the individual. Fortunately, since George Pointer became a free man in 1793, he is readily identifiable in the 1800 decennial censuses, and information on his descendants appears in every subsequent extant census.

These censuses were massive undertakings in a sprawling country.[1] Census takers, called enumerators, had to be recruited for every census district in the country. One of the qualifications was legible handwriting, but clearly in some cases there was compromise. The census data from 1790 to 1940 is open to the public in the National Archives in downtown Washington, DC, and online at Ancestry.com. To protect people's privacy, recent government data and records are not open to the public until seventy-two years after they are collected. Thus, the 1950 census will become available for the first time in 2022, and people who were born in the 1940s will then become statistically visible for the first time.[2]

Although the primary purpose of the decennial censuses was to count people for congressional apportionment, the censuses also collected other information, including age, sex, occupation, and race. Selected data, such as income, are collected periodically.[3] More information about the history of what the US Census Bureau has collected over time can be found on its website, www.census.gov.

The censuses are only the beginning of any family history search, however. Many other existing official records supplement the censuses, and for African Americans, records such as certificates of freedom, special surveys of free Black populations, employment taxes, and land records are especially valuable. Some of the richest data sources are military records, and in our research, these records gave us our first glimpse of what three of the Pointer descendants looked like. The records included physical descriptions, noting height, build, hair and eye color, and skin tone. They also provided information on dependents, birthplaces, current homes, and occupations. Military records often track a person's career in the military and his or her illnesses and death, as well as who collected the disability, death, and pension benefits. Past military records can be seen both in the National Archives and online at Ancestry.com.

## Data Issues

Challenges arise in using any data from the eighteenth and nineteenth centuries. They include varying ages or dates of birth for the same person or missing ages at marriage and death. The spelling of names of people and places varies considerably, and even the boundaries of states in the past were more flexible than we generally realize. Racial categories, too, changed over time. Not only are some people missing in every census and survey but some of the records are missing as well. Therefore, to address these challenges, we used a few general rules of evidence to provide both consistency and structure to the history of the Pointer family.

### Age

Many people born before the twentieth century didn't know how old they were. One poignant reaction to the lack of birth date information comes from Frederick Douglass. He said, "I have no accurate knowledge of my age, never having seen any authentic record containing it. . . . I do not remember to have ever met a slave who could tell of his birthday. . . . A want of information concerning my own was a source of unhappiness to me even during childhood."[4]

Age is an important factor in distinguishing between two people with the same name, particularly for people with common names. However, tracking individuals through censuses or surveys is sometimes a challenge when their ages may be recorded differently over time. Birth dates for the same person differ over time often because people didn't know their actual birth dates in the eighteenth and nineteenth centuries. In such cases, people guessed their ages, rounding to a close number. That sometimes created what is known as "age heaping," with more people reporting their age as fifty years old, for example, than would be biologically likely in a given year.[5]

In addition, many early censuses and surveys collected people's ages in broad ranges, such as zero to ten years old or twenty-five to thirty-four years old. In our work with early censuses, we generally picked the midpoint of a range to estimate a person's age unless other evidence could be used to determine the age more accurately.

Sometimes the household respondent in a census or survey is a person who may not have accurate information on the other people in the household. The census takers collected their information from whoever was at home at the time of their visit. For instance, in one year the census informant was the young daughter-in-law of the Pointer family in Annapolis; when the census taker knocked on the door, she was clearly the only adult at home and had no idea how old her in-laws were.[6] We made the assumption that if the person had the same name in the same small geographic area in the previous census and the age was within a ten-year range of a previous estimate, then it was the same person unless proven otherwise.

### Marriages

In the eighteenth and nineteenth centuries, marriages were often recognized by the community, but there was no systematic, formal process of recording them except in family genealogies.[7] In some southern states, most African Americans were not allowed the formality of marriage before the Civil War. Yet the census records of households show people living together for many years and raising children together. We assume that the mother and father were married de facto, if not de jure, by the time the first child arrived, although there is usually no evidence for that assumption. By the end of the nineteenth century, better records were kept on both marriages and divorces.

Marriages, formal or informal, usually resulted in the woman taking her husband's name, so keeping track of women from census to census is much harder. As a result, the histories of women in many family stories tend to fade after they reach marriageable age unless other available information can tie them to a specific household. In the story of the Pointers' granddaughter, we were lucky to find her after her marriage because an 1838 certificate of freedom linked Mary Ann Plummer Harris to her mother, Mary Pointer Plummer, and to her grandmother Elizabeth Townsend Pointer. The use of both their maiden and married names permitted us to tie the three generations together from the end of the eighteenth century to the beginning of the twentieth century.

### Deaths

In the eighteenth and nineteenth centuries, deaths were not systematically recorded except in the case of the 1850 Mortality Schedule of the decennial census. The 1850 census of the District of Columbia gave a detailed accounting of deaths of people between 1849 and 1850, including one of the Pointers' great-granddaughters. The Annapolis census of that same year, however, made an accounting of the mortality of white residents only. Good sources of information on deaths are church records, but sometimes they are lost or a graveyard and its records have been moved. At the beginning of the nineteenth century, a cabinetmaker in Georgetown kept a meticulous list of the coffins he made for both Black and white clients for over sixty years. His list provided evidence of the death of one of the Pointer grandchildren. His records were transcribed and later printed by the Washington Historical Society, and finding them depended on serendipity and an enterprising librarian.[8]

Diseases and premature deaths were rampant in the eighteenth and nineteenth centuries, and death rates from such causes were much higher than they are today. The history of epidemics in America helps to provide clues when someone in a family disappears. We can speculate about the endemic diseases and epidemics that are correlated with a person's disappearance, but often we have no direct evidence of what happened. People in previous centuries just tend to fade away in their family stories. We often registered the last known date of a person's existence followed by a (+) on the family tree, without knowing a precise date of death.

### Spelling of Names

Not only were a person's age and death statistically fluid in the past, so were their names. Tanya Hardy warns that people sometimes used their first name in one census and their middle name in the next one. What may look statistically like two different people can be the same one, and only using other evidence can sort out the confusion.

In addition to giving different names, people often spelled their names differently over time. In an official certificate of freedom for George Pointer's granddaughter, her name is spelled two different ways in the same three-paragraph legal document (see chapter 3). This did not seem to bother the judge or the court reporter, but the fluidity of spellings makes it challenging to track the same person across decades.

Fortunately, in this story we found only two ways to spell the patriarch's name, Pointer or Poynter. In addition, we encountered Wallis/Wallace, Moton/Moten, and multiple ways to spell Mary Ann. We assumed that if the pronunciation of a name was the same, although the spelling was different, that it was likely to be the same person when other evidence supported the identity of an individual. Most important for purposes of this history, however, is that no other Pointers/Poynters were in Washington, DC, or in surrounding Maryland counties in the eighteenth and the early nineteenth centuries.

In the first half of the nineteenth century, white Pointers can be found in various states, including Missouri, Kentucky, and Alabama, but African American Pointers not related to George Pointer did not appear in Washington, DC, until the second half of the nineteenth century. At that point, inferences about their relationships become much harder to make unless they were embedded in identifiable households.

Fortunately, two-thirds of this story takes place in rural areas where the populations were small enough that people could be confidently identified from decade to decade. The spelling of place names, however, was as fluid as the spelling of personal names. For example, there are as many ways to spell Potomac as there are letters in the name. Since it is an Indian name, the first settlers simply spelled it the way it sounded, but it sounded differently to each person. To avoid confusion, we used the spelling common today for both the river and the name of the company, recognizing that it is not precisely accurate historically.

### Geography and Neighborhoods

Map making was more of an art than a science in the eighteenth and nineteenth centuries, and the boundaries of the counties and states were more imprecise than they are today. In fact, the longitude of Washington, DC, was assumed to be exactly seventy-seven degrees west of Greenwich, England.[9] It was off by several miles, however. For whatever reason, George Pointer's household was always recorded in the District of Columbia census even though the Potomac Company's records clearly list his house a mile outside the District in Montgomery County, Maryland.

Early censuses did not record the addresses of most respondents, largely because most areas were rural and had no street addresses. Several times questions arose about whether the Pointers had moved between decennial censuses. A plausible way to decide was to look at their neighboring households in each census. Although we did not know the specific path of individual enumerators, when the names of the people in the neighborhood remained the same, we concluded that the Pointers had not moved.

Keeping track of the names of the Pointers' neighbors was also very useful in understanding the characteristics of their neighborhood. In this story, the neighborhoods of Pointers' descendants in both Washington, DC, and Annapolis were quite integrated in the nineteenth century but became increasingly segregated in the twentieth. Neighborhoods are an important local context for individual households, and the census data describe them systematically.

### Reliability of Sources

The reliability of evidence varies with the source, of course. We generally accepted census data and other government records, such as military records, as the most reliable information. Evidence from private sources may be just as reliable as public data if confirmed by alternative data, but if it could not be confirmed, we considered it circumstantial. For instance, the assumption that George Pointer's owner was William Wallace is based on the Potomac Company's records that listed a Wallis as the owner of a slave named Yellow George who worked at the same time that George Pointer was an enslaved worker for the company. George was not a common name among the enslaved, and light skin (yellow) was even more uncommon among the enslaved. The 1755 Maryland Census showed that over 90 percent of the young slaves manumitted were mulatto, and if that pattern continued for several decades, then we were comfortable concluding that George Pointer was biracial.

Chapter 1 has a detailed discussion of the subsequent evidence that supports our conclusion. Although all of the evidence is circumstantial rather than definitive, it strongly suggests that Pointer was the man named Yellow George who appeared on the Potomac Company's payrolls and who belonged to William Wallis. His lifelong friendship with William Wallace's middle son, a relationship that was confirmed after Pointer's death, was the final piece of evidence of his long-term and personal relationship with the Wallace family.

### Race

The classification of race in official data is as unstable as the concept itself.[10] Racial categories in the census shifted from decade to decade, based on the social usage of racial concepts rather than on any evidence from biological science.[11] Classifying people by the tone of their skin was common in the eighteenth and nineteenth centuries. It was usually done by outside observers, such as the census enumerators, and not by the individual being described. Racial descriptions of individuals varied by observer, so designations could change over time as the observers changed.

As social usage changed over the decades, the definition of the "Black" or "Negro" race in censuses varied. Racial designation began as "All other free persons not taxed" in 1790. In 1820 it became "free colored," and the term "mulatto" was added for the first time in 1850. By 1870 the census defined *mulatto* as including "quadroons, octoroons and all persons having any perceptible trace of African blood."[12] By 1890, in an attempt to clear up ambiguity, the US Census Bureau decided that a Black person was defined as someone with three-quarters or more of African American heritage, and a mulatto person was someone who had three-eighths to five-eighths of African American heritage. The attempt at clarification was, of course, not helpful in any way and reflected society's own confusion.

A detailed study of over fifteen hundred families in the Louisiana 1860 census found that at least 5 percent of the families were misclassified racially. For example, twenty-three Black families were listed as white, and fifty-three white families were listed as mulatto.[13] This suggests how arbitrary the categories were and how unreliable the racial data is. George Pointer was listed as white in the 1820 census, and at least two of his descendants were listed as white in subsequent censuses, although they were listed as Black in both earlier and later censuses. When the person is clearly embedded in the same family with the same name and approximate age, we assumed that the classification of race that was used most often over time was the most likely descriptor. Finally, in the 1960 census, the bureau began using mailed forms instead of individual enumerators to collect data, so people could define themselves however they wanted.

### Undercounted Population in the Census

One of the weaknesses of data collection in every century and in every country is the undercounted populations—that is, people who are missed and should have been included.[14] There are a number of reasons for undercounts including the absence of people when the enumerators visited or a deliberate avoidance of the census for whatever reason. Approximately 8–10 percent of the general population was not counted in the nineteenth-century censuses, but the undercount of the Black population was always higher than that of the white population. In 1870 the undercount was over 12 percent, and that year the bureau petulantly said, "The Census Office had no power over its enumerators save a barren protest and even this right was questioned in some quarters."[15]

Of course, some types of people are more often undercounted than others. Even as late as World War II, almost 20 percent of young, unmarried Black males were undercounted.[16] Although the undercount in recent years has declined considerably, it still exists in the twenty-first century and is carefully measured by post-enumeration surveys. For the historian, however, clearly the absence of an individual in a particular census or survey is simply evidence that the individual was not found. Only when a person never shows up again in any records can researchers tentatively consider that the person might have died.

### Missing Census Data

Not only are some individuals missing in every census but also, in some cases, an entire census is missing. For example, although George Pointer appeared in the Washington, DC, censuses of 1800, 1820, and 1830, he did not appear in the 1810 District census. Many records, including much of the 1810 census, were burned by the British when they invaded Washington during the War of 1812. More often, a census will be missing for a county but rarely for an entire state, although most states are missing the 1890 census, again due to a fire. Administrative records and storage facilities were simply not as safe in the nineteenth century as they were in the twentieth.

### Conclusion

By the twentieth century, data collection became more accurate. People tended to know the date of their births and recorded the date of their marriages. Unfortunately, as the statistics improved in the twentieth century, the number of people with similar names also increased. This adds a complication to research because it is harder to trace the relationships among many new people with similar names.

As with our own work on the Pointers and their descendants, we cannot be sure that we have not made errors or drawn the wrong conclusions. We may have missed critical links among people that we could or should have made. We were fortunate to have had George Pointer's letter as our starting point and then Mary Ann Harris's certificate of freedom, which linked three generations of women. The *Washington Post* article about Mary Ann and her daughter in 1928 gave us the confidence that we had correctly described the fourth generation. We were truly fortunate to have such strong independent sources linking that fourth generation to the living generations of the family today.

Given the previously mentioned data issues, it does take some courage to tell a family history that stretches over centuries. Most important, we need to be aware of the issues yet not be paralyzed by them. Tanya Hardy's rule is that once she hits a blank wall in tracing an ancestor's history, she puts her search for that person aside and takes up the search for someone else. Later, when she returns to the blank wall, she may have other clues about where to resume her search. Despite the frustration of genealogy research, she believes strongly that "looking for our ancestors is one of the best ways to honor them. The joy of bringing past centuries to life through the stories of individual families is worth all of the frustration it takes."

# Notes

## Introduction

1.  George Pointer, "Petition of Captain George Pointer to the President and Directors of the Chesapeake and Ohio Canal, September 5th, 1829," 1, Record Group 79, entry 262, National Archives, Washington DC (hereafter cited as Pointer, "Petition"). Within the last decade, the National Archives renumbered the entries of this group of records. Our citations reference the updated entries.
2.  The two literate brothers also lived more than a decade longer than their other brothers.
3.  Sacerdote, "Slavery," 217–34, as cited in Costa and Kahn, *Heroes and Cowards*, 213.

## Chapter 1

1.  Offutt, *Bethesda*, 5. See also Kinard, *Maryland, Colonial Census*; and the Wallace Family Papers, Wallace folder, Family Genealogy File, Montgomery County Historical Society, Rockville MD. Ancestors of the Elderslie Wallaces in Maryland came from Elderslie, Scotland. Their most famous ancestor was William Wallace, who led a revolt against the British in 1298 and is now known as Braveheart. The Wallace home in Maryland had originally been in the county of Frederick, but when Maryland redrew county lines in 1776, it became part of Montgomery County.
2.  River Road today still goes from Montgomery County, Maryland, into the District. In 1721 the Wallace family received a land grant of 1,721 acres from the colonial government, and the family named it Brothers' Industry. The boundaries of the land grant are on a hand-drawn map found at the Montgomery County Historical Society. Another land grant with the same name was in the town of Rockville.
3.  Kapsch, *Potomac Canal*, 226. Kapsch's book is an excellent history of the Potomac Company and contains excerpts from George Pointer's letter.
4.  Douglass, *Narrative*, 30.

5. Clark and Clark, *Spirit of Captain John*, 47, 55–57. Members of that original Presbyterian meetinghouse included Wallaces, Magruders, and Belts, whose extended families would be involved with George Pointer's descendants for many years. In fact, the land the Wallaces donated to the church may have been for the preacher's home several miles south of the crossroads in Potomac, Maryland, off Seven Locks Road.

6. Brugger, *Maryland*, 16; US Bureau of the Census, *Historical Statistics*, pt. 2, p. 1184; and Brackett, *Negro in Maryland*, 39.

7. Henson, *Life of Josiah Henson*, 6; and Henson and Stowe, *Truth Stranger than Fiction*, 17–18. Henson was the model for the book *Uncle Tom's Cabin* by Harriet Beecher Stowe. He grew up just outside present-day Rockville, Maryland.

8. MacMaster and Hiebert, *Grateful Remembrance*, 15. The barrels were called hogsheads.

9. Ecker, *Portrait of Old George Town*, 9.

10. Taggart, "Old Georgetown," 143.

11. Achenbach, *Grand Idea*, 29. His book is a wonderful history of George Washington's passion for the Potomac River.

12. Bacon-Foster, *Patomac Route to the West*, 18. Bacon-Foster quotes a letter from George Washington on July 20, 1770, to Thomas Johnson, who lived in Fredericktown, Maryland. Bacon-Foster says that "this letter was among the Potomac Co. papers. . . . Its present location is not known" (fn 33). Thomas Johnson eventually became one of the directors of the Potomac Company and the first governor of Maryland.

13. Bacon-Foster, 23, 27, 41. Virginia had ceded to Maryland the jurisdiction of the Potomac River as long as its citizens could have free navigation. The private scheme to build a canal was developed by John Ballendine. Washington's contribution was in Virginia currency and represented about 6 percent of the money raised.

14. Bacon-Foster, 44.

15. Achenbach, *Grand Idea*, 31.

16. Bacon-Foster, *Patomac Route to the West*, 51.

17. Potomac Company, *Proceedings, 1785–1828*, Record Group 79, entry 230, vol. A, October 18, 1785, 14, National Archives, Washington DC.

18. Potomac Company, October 4, 1786, 27.

19. Torrey and Green, "Old and Obscure Citizen," 307.

20. Komlos, "Toward an Anthropometric History," 307.

21. Walsh, "Rural African Americans," 328.

22. MacMaster and Hiebert, *Grateful Remembrance*, 59; and Walsh, "Rural African Americans," 338.

23. Pointer, "Petition," 1.

24. Potomac Company, *Correspondence and Reports, 1785–1825*, Record Group 79, entry 232, box 2, folder "1820–21."

25. Unrau, *Historic Resource Study*, 283. We know that the Pointers were alive because they were recorded in the 1830 census, but they were not recorded in 1840.

26. Kapsch, *Potomac Canal*, 68. Curiously, three decennial censuses listed the Pointer family household in the District of Columbia, although company reports clearly describe his cottage in Maryland, a mile outside the unmarked boundary between Maryland and the District. The discrepancy is likely because the census enumerators were using imprecise maps, if they were using maps at all.

27. Vallancey, *Treatise on Inland Navigation*, 1763; and Kapsch, *Potomac Canal*, 31, 79. The locks at the bottom of Little Falls canal still exist today. They are barely visible in the undergrowth along the banks of the river, just north of Fletchers Boat House at mile 3 of the C&O Canal.

28. George Washington's letters over this period are catalogued at National Historical Publications & Records Commission, "Washington Papers," Founders Online, NA, https://founders.archives.gov/?q=Author%3A"Washington %2CGeorge"&s=1111211111&r=1.

29. Pointer, "Petition," 1–2.

30. Bacon-Foster, *Patomac Route to the West*, 80. We assumed that Washington kept his shares because he had shares at the end of his presidency.

31. Kapsch, *Potomac Canal*, 72–73. The engineer was a Scotsman named James Smith, although Pointer calls him John Smith.

32. Pointer, "Petition," 2.

33. Achenbach, *Grand Idea*, 36.

34. Kapsch, *Potomac Canal*, 71–72.

35. Bacon-Foster, *Patomac Route to the West*, 66.

36. Kapsch, *Potomac Canal*, 72–73; Potomac Company, *Proceedings*, Record Group 79, entry 160, August 9, 1819, book A, 393, National Archives, Washington DC; and US House, *Report of the Committee*.

37. Kapsch, *Potomac Canal*, 86. The labor force data was for the year 1797, but it was unlikely to be much different a few years earlier. See also Kapsch, 214–15.

38. Great Falls Historical Society, "Patowmack Canal Company Employees," 10.

39. Distribution of names was based on a 1798 survey of slaves in Baltimore. Phillips, *Freedom's Port*, 88.

40. US Bureau of the Census, *Historical Statistics*, pt. 2, p. 1169. Great Britain took censuses in five colonies in 1755 and 1756, perhaps to determine how many men of draft age were available to fight in the French and Indian War. The age category of "young" included males aged sixteen years and under, or three years younger than George Pointer was when he was manumitted. The county data was published in Wright, *Free Negro in Maryland*, 85.

41. Great Falls Historical Society, "Patowmack Canal Company Employees," 10. The list of slave owners who rented slaves in 1792 included William Wallis. No other William Wallace or Wallis was recorded as living in nearby Maryland or Virginia at the time.

42. The contribution of William Wallace's white son to George Pointer's granddaughter is discussed in chapter 3.

43. Pointer, "Petition," 1.

44. Whitman, *Price of Freedom*, 175. This refers to slave sales in Baltimore, about forty miles northeast from the Wallace farm. The purchasing power calculation comes from Williamson, "Seven Ways"; Franklin and Moss, *From Slavery to Freedom*, 92; Wright, *Free Negro in Maryland*, 65; and MacMaster and Hiebert, *Grateful Remembrance*, 157.

45. Anderson, *Montgomery County Land*, 9. In fact, Wallace had bought an enslaved woman named Jenny on August 11, 1788.

46. Census records recorded the number but not the name of slaves, making it impossible to track specific enslaved people from census to census.

47. Brugger, *Maryland*, 169; and Wright, *Free Negro in Maryland*, 25.

48. Quarles, "Freedom Fettered," 301; and Fields, *Slavery and Freedom*, 12.

49. Anderson, *Montgomery County Land*. There were also forty-six documentations of slaves who moved into Montgomery County from outside of Maryland and the intention to free thirty-eight slaves sometime in the future.

50. Whitman, *Price of Freedom*, 44; and MacMaster and Hiebert, *Grateful Remembrance*, 155. The requirement for a bond to be posted was repealed in 1796.

51. Quarles, "Freedom Fettered," 301; Fields, *Slavery and Freedom*, 23; and Franklin and Moss, *From Slavery to Freedom*, 169.

52. Phillips, *Freedom's Port*, 90. The percentage refers to Baltimore between 1806 and 1816.

53. The geographical distribution of the family name of Pointer/Poynter comes from Ancestry.com. One enslaved male named Pointer lived in Greenbriar in western Virginia, 240 miles from Montgomery County, Maryland. In 1794 the Virginia General Assembly gave Richard Pointer his freedom "for displaying unusual valor by warding off by himself a company of Indians." Since this occurred after George Pointer was already a freeman, it seems unlikely that George took his name belatedly. Legislative Petitions, Greenbrier County, November 12, 1795, as quoted in Jackson, "Virginia Negro Soldiers," 247.

54. Phillips, *Freedom's Port*, 162 (estimate for 1850 in Baltimore).

55. Colonial law prohibited legal marriage of both enslaved and free Black people, and in the South this lasted until the Emancipation Proclamation. Therefore, almost no records exist of formal marriage among free Black people at the time. But given the longevity of the partnerships in this history, we assume they were married de facto, if not de jure. Corrigan, "Making the Most," 93.

56. Potomac Company, *Daybook*, Record Group 79, entry 240, December 10, 1804. The payrolls and the legal document are discussed in chapters 2 and 3.

57. The Wallace and Magruder families had been neighbors for almost a century and had intermarried. Major Magruder died in 1791. Dwyer, "Magruder's Folly," 40.

58. The William Wallace family's genealogy file in the Montgomery County Historical Society shows Charles as a single man. All the censuses between 1800 and 1860 do as well.

59. Bacon-Foster, *Patomac Route to the West*, 66.
60. Brown, "America's Greatest," 41–47.


## Chapter 2

1.  MacMaster and Hiebert, *Grateful Remembrance*, 156; and Rives, "Old Families," 57.
2.  Brugger, *Maryland*, 427; and Fields, *Slavery and Freedom*, xii.
3.  Calculated from census data and Franklin and Moss, *From Slavery to Freedom*, 98.
4.  Franklin and Moss, *From Slavery to Freedom*, 86; Brown, *Free Negroes*, 12–17; and Genovese, *Roll, Jordan, Roll*, 399.
5.  Torrey, *Portraiture of Domestic Slavery*, 57. Emphasis in original.
6.  Kapsch, *Potomac Canal*, 217.
7.  Pointer, "Petition," 3–4.
8.  Pointer, 4.
9.  Bacon-Foster, *Patomac Route to the West*, 88–89.
10. Bacon-Foster, 97.
11. Bacon-Foster, 168.
12. Mould and Loewe, *Remembering Georgetown*, 43.
13. diGiacomantonio, "To Sell Their Birthright," 37. It was called the 1801 Organic Law of the District of Columbia.
14. Wright, *Free Negro in Maryland*, 98.
15. Phillips, *Freedom's Port*, 90. Sixty percent of the 358 manumitted slaves who applied for freedom certificates in Baltimore between 1806 and 1816 did not have surnames. Johnston, *From Slave Ship*, 110. The census taker who recorded George Pointer and Free Hannah as neighbors classified his records as in the Georgetown District. No other Black Hannah was recorded in Georgetown that year.
16. Johnston, 110. Johnston says the relationship between Yarrow and Hannah is based on the circumstantial evidence of Hannah's daughter, Nancy Hillman, claiming Yarrow as her uncle.
17. Johnston, 107, 120. These relationships are based on evidence collected by James H. Johnston.
18. Fields, *Slavery and Freedom*, 31. He was owned by Thomas A. Brooke, a farmer and justice of the peace who lived a quarter mile east of the Pointer cottage. Torrey and Green, *Brookmont*, 210–12. Nace was the nickname for Ignatius, a popular name among Catholics.
19. The farmer who bought Nace was Francis Newman, Esquire. The Jesuit plantation St. Thomas Manor (now known as St. Ignatius Church and Cemetery), which was next door to Newman's plantation, was in Charles County in southern Maryland. Helen Hoban Rogers, *Freedom & Slavery Documents*, 2:127.
20. Maryland Province of the Society of Jesus, *Jesuit Plantation Project*. Of the 272 slaves sold, three were named Nace, but only one came from St. Thomas Manor

plantation, which was next door to Nace's owner. The approximate ages of the other two were younger than the estimated age of Nace, who had been sold by Thomas Brooke; however, the evidence is circumstantial.

21. In 1801 payments were made to George Pointer as well as to a "J. Pointer" and sometimes to a "John Pointer." The names John, George, or J. never appear together on the same date, and George Pointer was the only person, Black or white, with his surname recorded in the decennial censuses of Maryland or the District of Columbia between 1790 and 1830. Therefore, it is likely that George, John, and J. Pointer were the same man, and his name was recorded by a harried or half-literate clerk.

22. Potomac Company, *Proceedings*, Record Group 79, entry 230, vol. A, January 1801, 290, National Archives, Washington DC.

23. Potomac Company, *Daybook*, Record Group 79, entry 240, April 10, 1801, National Archives, Washington DC (hereafter cited as Potomac Company, *Daybook*).

24. Kapsch, *Potomac Canal*, 233, 217.

25. Kapsch, 121, 124.

26. Potomac Company, *Daybook*, entry 240, December 6, 1802.

27. Pointer, "Petition," 4.

28. Kapsch, *Potomac Canal*, 226. A comparison of the writing of some of the engineers and superintendents confirms that Pointer's handwriting was better.

29. Potomac Company, *Proceedings*, Record Group 79, entry 230, vol. A, May 11, 1802, 380, National Archives, Washington DC.

30. Potomac Company, *Daybook*, entry 240, December 10, 1804.

31. Kapsch, *Potomac Canal*, 124.

32. Pointer, "Petition," 4–5.

33. Bacon-Foster, *Patomac Route to the West*, 105.

34. Gallatin, *Report of the Secretary*, 77.

35. Mould and Loewe, *Remembering Georgetown*, 19, 27, 49, 50. When the District of Columbia was established in 1801, Georgetown was one of three cities within the District: Washington City, Alexandria, and Georgetown. The rest of the land that had been donated by Maryland was simply called Washington County.

36. Potomac Company, *Proceedings*, Record Group 79, entry 230, oversize volume, December 20, 1822, 5, "A Table shewing the Am't of tolls rec'd by the Potomac Company in each year from the 1st of August 1799 to the 1st August 1817," National Archives, Washington DC.

37. Pointer, "Petition," 4.

38. Rogers, *Freedom & Slavery Documents*, 1:64, 66; 2:179, 181, 185–86; 3:161. Between 1803 and 1819, he freed seven slaves.

39. Pointer, "Petition," 6–7. A history of Black laborers who helped build the US Capitol cites Pointer's petition and concludes that he "regularly brought building materials to the Federal City for the Capitol, Seneca Sandstone for the flooring and Potomac marble for columns shafts in House and Senate

Chambers." Pointer does not mention his contribution to the building of the Capitol in his petition. The historian may have misread Pointer's description of his accident. See Allen, *History of Slave Laborers*.

40. Guzy, *Navigation*, 23.

41. Kapsch, *Potomac Canal*, 246.

42. Potomac Company, *Proceedings*, Record Group 79, entry 230, vol. B, box 1, July 25, 1819, 380, National Archives, Washington DC.

43. Williamson, "Seven Ways."

44. Thorndale and Dollarhide, *Map Guide*, xxiii. Classification errors on race were not uncommon. These estimates came from an 1860 post-enumeration survey in Louisiana.

45. Pointer, "Petition," 10.

46. Kapsch, *Potomac Canal*, 294.

47. Kapsch, 292.

48. Potomac Company, *Miscellaneous Accounts, 1785–1828*, Record Group 79, entry 250, box 3 folder 1, July 22, 1828, National Archives, Washington DC.

49. Unrau, *Historic Resource Study*, 253.

50. Achenbach, *Grand Idea*, 251.

51. "Amid the Roar of Guns," *Washington Post*, August 2, 1891, 10.

52. Achenbach, *Grand Idea*, 249.

53. Guzy, *Navigation*, 96.

54. Rogers, *Freedom & Slavery Documents*, vol. 1. He occasionally bought and sold slaves in Georgetown.

55. Pointer, "Petition," 10.

56. Kapsch, *Potomac Canal*, 222. At least eight workers had worked multiple years, with the longest serving having worked seven years.

57. Pointer, "Petition," 10.

58. Pointer, 11.

59. We assume that the Pointers were still in their cottage because they had some of the same neighbors listed in the 1820 census. Maryanna French had fifteen slaves in 1820 and twenty in 1830 (when her name was spelled Marriann French). Nathan Luffboraugh, whose house still exists in ruins southeast of Pointer's house, had twenty-two slaves in 1820 and thirteen in 1830 (when his name was spelled Nathan Lofborough). The widow Henrietta Brooke was still living a quarter mile from the Pointers.

60. Hynson, *Free African-Americans*, 108. Elizabeth Pointer was recorded in a special Maryland census of the free Black population taken in 1832.

61. Province, *Free Negro Registers*, 105–6.

62. Fields, *Slavery and Freedom*, 45.

63. Georgetown University, Working Group on Slavery, Memory, and Reconciliation, "Holy Trinity Church Death Records."

64. Kapsch, *Potomac Canal*, 236. The engineer was Thomas Purcell.

65. Green, *Washington*, 1:135.

66. Wade, *Slavery in the Cities*, 141–42. As previously noted, it was also true that many of the enslaved were freed when they became disabled or aged because their value decreased as their health declined.

67. Atack and Passell, *New Economic View*, 429.

## Chapter 3

1.   McConnell, "Black Experience in Maryland," 406.

2.   Gates, *Life upon These Shores*, 44.

3.   Franklin and Moss, *From Slavery to Freedom*, 102. The law went into effect in 1808. British abolitionists who had been well organized for many years also outlawed the slave trade the same year.

4.   Franklin and Moss, 162–64.

5.   Torrey, *Martyrdom*, 28.

6.   Allmendinger, *Nat Turner*, 286–97.

7.   Lepore, *These Truths*, 205; and Asch and Musgrove, *Chocolate City*, 74.

8.   Green, *Secret City*, 35.

9.   Asch and Musgrove, *Chocolate City*, 74.

10.  Franklin and Moss, *From Slavery to Freedom*, 165, 286–97; and Berlin, *Slaves without Masters*, 285.

11.  Corrigan, *Social Union*, 109.

12.  Pointer, "Petition," 9.

13.  Wright, *Free Negro in Maryland*, 7.

14.  Brugger, *Maryland*, 212.

15.  Congress adopted the poem as the national anthem in 1931. The awkward poetry of the third stanza damns the Black men who had joined the British in the War of 1812.

16.  Brugger, *Maryland*, 212–13.

17.  Hynson, *Free African-Americans*, 108. George Pointer and his wife, Betty, were not counted in the census, suggesting that they may have already died, perhaps in the cholera epidemic. Their daughter Elizabeth was listed as forty-two years old, which is a few years older than she might have been based on other records.

18.  Berlin, *Slaves without Masters*, 203. Maryland provided $200,000 over twenty years; Virginia provided $90,000 over five years; and other states had smaller amounts.

19.  Phillips, *Freedom's Port*, 220. Not more than fifteen thousand people from the United States settled in West Africa.

20.  MacMaster and Hiebert, *Grateful Remembrance*, 157.

21.  Brackett, *Negro in Maryland*, 247.

22.  He was listed in the 1840 census as W. A. Pointer. His initials likely stood for William Alexander since his son was named William and his gradson was William Alexander.

23.  Donovan and Fletcher, *William King's Mortality Books*, 1:205.

24. Warden, *Chorographical and Statistical Description*, 10–11, 100.

25. Green, *Washington*, 1:143–44.

26. The Civil War records show that William Pointer, who was born in Washington County in the District of Columbia, was twenty-four years old in 1864.

27. Green, *Secret City*, 28.

28. Kytle, *Home on the Canal*, 44–50.

29. Zacharia Green, three households away from William Pointer, was paid for wheel-barrows, bacon, and powder. Alex Magruder provided legal services to the company. Wallace was paid for construction, and the Belts provided 228 pounds of bacon.

30. *C&O Requisition Book, 1828–1870*, Record Group 79, entry 349, vol. 1, National Archives, Washington DC.

31. Snyder, "Chesapeake and Ohio Canal," 14.

32. Foner, *Gateway to Freedom*, 193–95.

33. Mould and Loewe, *Remembering Georgetown*, 65.

34. Unrau, *Historic Resource Study*, 283.

35. The lockkeepers had changed, but their houses were noted in the censuses, verifying that it was the same neighborhood. In 1840 the neighborhood had been recorded in the District of Columbia census, but in 1850 it was counted for the first time in the far southwest corner of Montgomery County, abutting the poorly marked District boundary line. The two large landowners, the Brooke and the Loughborough families, were still there, however, and classified in Maryland.

36. McWilliams, *Annapolis City*, 153. Charles Wallace had been neighbors with the Magruder family for over fifty years. One of their extended family members had been a judge and then the mayor of Annapolis in the early 1840s. He returned home to Montgomery County when he retired, and he eventually died there.

37. McWilliams, 147, 174. Evidence for the move of the W. A. Pointer family to Annapolis is his son's enlistment papers in the US Colored Troops in Annapolis in 1864. He had been living in Annapolis for some time because he already had a wife and two children.

38. Green, *Washington*, 1:21; and McWilliams, *Annapolis City*, 381.

39. McWilliams, *Annapolis City*, 149; and Sprouse, *Along the Potomac River*, 24. The map was surveyed by US Coast and Geodetic Survey; the windmill began operating on September 4, 1760.

40. Brackett, *Negro in Maryland*, 241. It had cost the Maryland government over $100 per person to deport them to Africa.

41. Berlin, *Slaves without Masters*, 354. The fear was throughout the upper South, although this reference was specifically to Virginia.

42. Brackett, *Negro in Maryland*, 246; and Torrey, *Martyrdom*, 79.

43. McWilliams, *Annapolis City*, 140.

44. When he enlisted in the Union army, William A. Pointer said that he had been born in Washington County, DC, which is the census district where George Pointer's household was always located in the US censuses.

45. Green, *Washington*, 1:21.
46. Green, *Secret City*, 36; and Asch and Musgrove, *Chocolate City*, 78.
47. Lepore, *These Truths*, 225. The Jesuits' selling slaves is also discussed in chapter 2 of this volume.
48. Mann, "Horrible Barbarity," 3–13.
49. Northup and Wilson, *Twelve Years a Slave*.
50. Brackett, *Negro in Maryland*, 37.
51. Green, *Washington*, 1:143. We assume that the district courthouse for the District was used for Washington County business in the early days of the new city. Green mentions a grand jury for Washington County, but she does not say whether there was a separate courthouse.
52. Today, the courthouse still stands at Judiciary Square near the Capitol.
53. Province, *Free Negro Registers*, 105–6.
54. Brown, *Free Negroes*, 66.
55. See Wallace Family Papers. His younger brother was John Wallace, and his widow was fifty-five-year-old Harriet Vinson Wallace.
56. After the Civil War, Charles Wallace's nephew, Edward Wallace, became the head of the household.
57. Lepore, *These Truths*, 225. The roads going north were the Brookville and Old Baltimore Roads in Maryland.

## Chapter 4

1. Washington County was named in the 1801 Organic Law that formed the District of Columbia. The county's territory extended north from two roads that ran along the northern edge of the city called Boundary Street (now Florida Avenue) and Benning Road. It extended west to Georgetown and the Potomac River and beyond the Eastern Branch (now the Anacostia River). The Virginia land that was part of the District included the port of Alexandria and the county around it. The government eventually returned Alexandria and its county to Virginia in 1846. Green, *Secret City*, 33.
2. Green, 39.
3. Achenbach, *Grand Idea*, 263.
4. US Federal Census, "Mortality Schedule, 1850," microfilm series T655, roll 5, National Archives, Washington DC, https://search.ancestry.com/search/dbextra.aspx?dbid=8756.
5. Green, *Secret City*, 21.
6. US Federal Census, "Mortality Schedule." The census asked if anyone in the family had died in the previous year, the cause of death, and the length of the condition.
7. Helm, *Tenleytown*, 173.
8. The Seventh Street Turnpike is now called Georgia Avenue. The Harrises' neighbor and landowner John Hebbern and his family had been joined by Hebbern's brother and two other brothers, George and John Milbern, who

also became landowners nearby and lifelong friends of Thomas Harris. Thomas bought his land from them. The spelling of these names varies in the censuses over the years; early censuses include the spelling Hebborn, Hepbern, Milbern, Millbern, and Millburn. Twentieth-century property records show that the property the Harrises bought was previously owned by the Millberns.

9.  Brown, "Residence Patterns," 74.

10. Powell, "Statistical Profile," 277.

11. The censuses document the growth of the Broad Branch settlement. It is mentioned by name in Helm, *Tenleytown*, 173.

12. Kreisa, McDowell, and Finnigan, *Phase IB Archaeological Investigations*.

13. Torrey and Green, *Brookmont*, 16.

14. Although living in the District, they retained their Maryland ties and continued to be members of the Presbyterian Meeting House in Maryland that William Wallace, George Pointer's former owner, had helped establish.

15. The house survived into the twentieth century and was razed in 1907. Poole, "Ninian Beall," 7.

16. Massey and Denton, *American Apartheid*, 17–18.

17. Sharfstein, *Invisible Line*, 152.

18. Prewitt, *What Is Your Race?*, 14–28; US Bureau of the Census, *Historical Statistics*, pt. 1, p. 3; Brown, *Free Negroes*, 143, as calculated from the US Bureau of the Census, *Heads of Families*; and Corrigan, *Social Union*, 100–101.

19. Green, *Secret City*, 45–46.

20. Asch and Musgrove, *Chocolate City*, 93.

21. Lepore, *These Truths*, 284.

22. Green, *Secret City*, 48–49; and Howe, *What Hath God Wrought*, 653–54, 214.

23. Lepore, *These Truths*, 254.

24. Green, *Secret City*, 50.

25. Both of the Milbern brothers had married, with nine children between them, and they were listed as gardeners working on their own lands. Neighbor John Hebbern still lived on his property with his wife and three children.

26. In addition to John, Joseph, Lewis, and Ann, three more children were born: Theodore in 1853, Lorenzo in 1855, and Mary Ann in 1858.

27. The estimates come from the 1860 census and are updated to today's dollars based on Williamson, "Seven Ways."

28. The 1850 census records Charles Williams Jr. as a seventeen-year-old living with his family in Georgetown, suggesting he was born around 1833. He would have been about twenty-seven when he was recorded as a thirty-three-year-old living with the Harris family in 1860. The age discrepancy means that it is possibly another man by the same name.

29. Helm, *Tenleytown*, 95.

30. White property owners near the Harrises included Richard Jones, whose farm was close to Broad Branch Road. Jones had three children.

31. The household of George W. Parker was listed in the 1840 census next to Thomas Harris and Charles Belt.

32. US District Court for the District of Columbia, "Records Relating to Slaves, 1851–1863," microfilm serial M433, roll 3, Record Group 21, National Archives, Washington DC.

33. Asch and Musgrove, *Chocolate City*, 105; and Green, *Secret City*, 55–56.

34. McWilliams, *Annapolis City*, 166.

35. McWilliams, 166–68.

36. Helm, *Tenleytown*, 120.

37. Helm, 139, 114–15.

38. Offutt, *Bethesda*, 39.

39. Harrison, *Washington during Civil War*, 10.

40. US Senate, Committee on the District of Columbia, Petitions and Memorials, series 547, 37th Congress, Record Group 46, National Archives, Washington DC, found in Berlin et al., *Destruction of Slavery*, 1:178.

41. Colbert King, "154 Years after Emancipation, D.C. Had Grim, Unfinished Business," *Washington Post*, April 16, 2016.

42. Nalezyty, *Research Report*, 8, 10, 17–18, 39.

43. Belt, "Petition."

44. The Bowie children were George, Harriet, Andrew, Hamilton, and Eliza.

45. Winkle, "Emancipation"; and King, "154 Years." If Belt was given 40 percent of the value of his slaves, he would have been received $2,240. In today's dollars, it would have amounted to $53,088.

46. Sisters of the Visitation of Georgetown, "Petition."

47. Green, *Washington*, 261–62.

48. Helm, *Tenleytown*, 128–29.

49. They lived at 20 Fifth Street (now Q Street), Northwest, according to his draft registration.

50. Green, *Secret City*, 60–62.

51. Provost Marshal General's Bureau, "Consolidated Lists of Civil War Draft Registrations, 1863–1865," RG 110, entry 172, National Archives, Washington DC.

52. Gibbs, *Black, Copper, & Bright*, 20–40.

53. Leech, *Reveille in Washington*, 312–14.

## Chapter 5

1. National Park Service, *Historic American Landscapes Survey.* The bridge was near the Harris brothers' home. Pedestrians could cross the bridge since the aqueduct was drained during the war. An alternative way to get to the island was by ferry, but the fee might have discouraged the brothers.

2. Leech, *Reveille in Washington*, 313–14.

3.  Franklin and Moss, *From Slavery to Freedom*, 228. Several states had begun to recruit Black soldiers before the Draft Act was signed.

4.  Kaplan, *Walt Whitman*, as quoted in Steven, "1st US Colored Troops."

5.  Adjutant General's Office, *Compiled Military Service Records*. The recorded ages of the brothers differed slightly from those reported in the census, but both brothers may not have known their birth year, explaining why census ages were often inaccurate.

6.  Humphreys, *Intensely Human*, 9. The estimate was about one-third of white men were rejected for medical reasons, but that seems high.

7.  Gibbs, *Black, Copper, & Bright*, 240. William Harris lived with another member of the Harris family after the war, suggesting that he was a relative.

8.  Costa and Kahn, *Heroes and Cowards*, 65, 209.

9.  Gibbs, *Black, Copper, & Bright*, 31, 38–39; and Asch and Musgrove, *Chocolate City*, 41.

10. Gibbs, *Black, Copper, & Bright*, 44–46.

11. Kaplan, *Walt Whitman*, 1181, as quoted in Gibbs, *Black, Copper, & Bright*, 55.

12. Gibbs, 54–55.

13. Berlin, Reidy, and Rowland, *Black Military Experience*, 385–86; and US Colored Troops Division, Adjutant General's Office, letter, September 28, 1863.

14. Costa and Kahn, *Heroes and Cowards*, 21.

15. McPherson, *Negro's Civil War*, 206; and Gibbs, *Black, Copper, & Bright*, 84–85.

16. Adjutant General's Office, *Compiled Military Service Records*. The sutler was named George Seaton.

17. Adjutant General's Office, *Compiled Military Service Records*.

18. Costa and Kahn, *Heroes and Cowards*, 206.

19. Larsen, *Crusader and Feminist*, found in Gibbs, *Black, Copper, & Bright*, 55.

20. Dobak, *Freedom by the Sword*, 314–15. The general was Maj. Gen. Silas Casey.

21. Berlin, Reidy, and Rowland, *Black Military Experience*, 582–83; and US Colored Troops Division, Adjutant General's Office, letter, July 31, 1863.

22. Lincoln's order as quoted in Gibbs, *Black, Copper, & Bright*, 57–58.

23. Lepore, *These Truths*, 294.

24. The town had been occupied by Union forces in February 1862 because it was a transportation center. Despite the occupation, Confederate guerrillas were active in the area, and there was tension between local Black and white residents.

25. Berlin, Reidy, and Rowland, *Black Military Experience*, 493.

26. McPherson, *Negro's Civil War*, 206; and Gibbs, *Black, Copper, & Bright*, 198–200.

27. Humphreys, *Intensely Human*, 58–59.

28. Gibbs, *Black, Copper, & Bright*, 60–62.

29. Gibbs, 122–31. Unfortunately, soon after his arrival, Turner fell ill with smallpox and thus was not present for some of the regiment's early conflicts.

30. Gibbs, 67–69.

31. Gibbs, 201.

32. The First Regiment was transferred to the First Brigade, Hincks's Colored Division, XVIII Corps of the Army of the James. It was still commanded by General Wild.

33. Wilson, *Black Phalanx*, 340.

34. Berlin, Reidy, and Rowland, *Black Military Experience*, 587–88; and Secretary of War, Letters Received, Record Group 107, April 27, 1864, National Archives, Washington DC.

35. Wilson, *Black Phalanx*, 115; and Newton, *White Robes*, 11.

36. The troops of the First Regiment were with four other companies from the Tenth USCT Regiment and an artillery group from New York, for a total of about eleven hundred men.

37. Gibbs, *Black, Copper, & Bright*, 197.

38. Gibbs, 72–76. The Lee quotation is found in Asa Gordon, secretary-general of the Sons and Daughters USCT, "Afterword," in Gibbs, 197.

39. Dobak, *Freedom by the Sword*, 349–51; Gibbs, *Black, Copper, & Bright*, 76–81; and report by General E. W. Hincks, June 20, 1864, in Gibbs, 81.

40. Wheat, "Medicine in Virginia"; and Gibbs, *Black, Copper, & Bright*, 81–82.

41. Adjutant General's Office, *Compiled Military Service Records*, Miscellaneous Record Cards, 61–62, 63.

42. Costa and Kahn, *Heroes and Cowards*, 115.

43. Adjutant General's Office, *Compiled Military Service Records*, Miscellaneous Record Cards, 61–62, 63.

44. National Park Service, "Fort Reno."

45. Leech, *Reveille in Washington*, 419.

46. Brooks, *Washington, D.C.*, 159. It is unknown if two of the Harris children— Theodore, then eleven, or Ann, fourteen—were alive.

47. Offutt, *Bethesda*, 56.

48. "The Invasion!," *Washington Star*, July 12, 1864.

49. Leech, *Reveille in Washington*, 421–22.

50. Helm, *Tenleytown*, 155.

51. "Late and Important," *Washington Star*, July 13, 1864.

52. Leech, *Reveille in Washington*, 425.

53. William Pointer was born in 1840 in the house of his deceased grandfather, George Pointer. He was the first cousin of Mary Ann Harris and therefore the first cousin once removed of John and Joseph Harris.

54. See Ferraro, *Art of Dancing*.

55. Wilson, *Black Phalanx*, 397.

56. Du Bois, *Black Reconstruction in America*, 111.

57. As quoted in Eicher, *Longest Night*, 723.

58. *Philadelphia Press*, October 31, 1864, cited in Gibbs, *Black, Copper, & Bright*, 92–93.

59. Dobak, *Freedom by the Sword*, 398–99; and Adjutant General's Office, *Compiled Military Service Records*.

60. Barton's house and office at 437 Seventh Street, NW, was where she kept supplies for nursing the wounded. After the war, it became the office for her work in finding missing soldiers, and now it is a museum. Barton spent her last years in the 1890s in a house in the town of Glen Echo, Maryland, located along the C&O Canal and about two miles upstream from where George Pointer and his family had lived. It is now owned by the National Park Service.

61. Pryor, *Clara Barton*, 130; and Adjutant General's Office, *Compiled Military Service Records*.

62. Berlin, Reidy, and Rowland, *Black Military Experience*, 501–2; and Secretary of War, Letters Received, April 27, 1864.

63. Dobak, *Freedom by the Sword*, 413.

64. Humphreys, *Intensely Human*, 83.

65. Mark St. John Erickson, "Huge Hampton Military Hospital Spawned by the Civil War Opened This Week in 1862," *Daily Press*, August 14, 2018, www .dailypress.com/history/dp-nws-civil-war-hospitals-20120817-story.html.

66. Adjutant General's Office, *Compiled Military Service Records*, Miscellaneous Record Cards, 65. Joseph was mustered out in June 1865.

67. Gibbs, *Black, Copper, & Bright*, 100–102.

68. Williams, *Self-Taught*, 51–54.

69. Gibbs, *Black, Copper, & Bright*, 184.

70. Gibbs, 175; and Costa and Kahn, *Heroes and Cowards*, 195.

71. Gibbs, *Black, Copper, & Bright*, 164–66.

72. Gibbs, 166–67.

73. Gibbs, 170–73.

74. Costa and Kahn, *Heroes and Cowards*, 22.

75. Gibbs, *Black, Copper, & Bright*, 182. The rate was 63 percent.

76. McPherson, *Negro's Civil War*, 241. Fourteen percent of white soldiers died. The mortality rate of all Black regiments during the war was 21 percent: 37,300 Black soldiers died in the war out of the 178,985 who had enlisted.

77. The literacy rate within the regiment varied from company to company. Company F of the First Regiment had a 50 percent literacy rate among former slaves. See Costa and Kahn, *Heroes and Cowards*, 207.

78. Costa and Kahn, 189.

79. McPherson, *Negro's Civil War*, quoting James F. Jones, a Black soldier in the Fourteenth Rhode Island Heavy Artillery, 315.

80. Joseph's time in New York is discussed in chapter 7.

81. They were 30 percent more likely to do so. Costa and Kahn, *Heroes and Cowards*, 194–202.

82. Gibbs, *Black, Copper, & Bright*, 228–58.

83.  Blight, *Frederick Douglass*, 736.
84.  Gates, *Stony the Road*, 250.
85.  Asch and Musgrove, *Chocolate City*, 151.


## Chapter 6

1.   Costa and Kahn, *Heroes and Cowards*, 191. This quote referred specifically to former slaves, but it is applicable to all the Black soldiers.
2.   Green, *Washington*, 21, 267, 292, 295.
3.   Asch and Musgrove, *Chocolate City*, 123.
4.   Green, *Secret City*, 33.
5.   Helm, *Tenleytown*, 173.
6.   The increase is seen in comparing the 1860 and 1870 censuses. We don't know the route of the census enumerator, but the large number of households between the Harris and Belt homes in 1870 suggests an increased population density.
7.   His nephew was Samuel Spriggs.
8.   As recorded in the 1870 census.
9.   Quoted in Costa and Kahn, *Heroes and Cowards*, 66.
10.  Delivered on his second inauguration, March 4, 1865, and quoted in full in Sandburg, *Abraham Lincoln*, 94.
11.  Du Bois, *Black Reconstruction in America*, 223.
12.  US Senate, Committee on the District of Columbia, Petitions and Memorials, series 582, 39th Congress, Record Group 46, National Archives, Washington DC. Citation found in Berlin, Reidy, and Rowland, *Black Military Experience*, 817–18.
13.  Asch and Musgrove, *Chocolate City*, 144–47.
14.  Asch and Musgrove, 146–47.
15.  Asch and Musgrove, 146–51.
16.  Green, *Secret City*, 80, 91. Ninety-eight hundred white men and eighty-two hundred Black men registered to vote. See Mazur, *Example for All*, 145–47.
17.  Gibbs, *Black, Copper, & Bright*, 30–31, 82, 172, 191.
18.  Franklin and Moss, *From Slavery to Freedom*, 266–68.
19.  Foner, *Reconstruction*, 353, 355.
20.  Sharfstein, *Invisible Line*, 156–60; and Green, *Secret City*, 93.
21.  Du Bois, *Black Reconstruction in America*, 219.
22.  Harrison, *Washington during Civil War*, 133–34.
23.  Franklin and Moss, *From Slavery to Freedom*, 257.
24.  Green, *Secret City*, 88.
25.  Helm, *Tenleytown*, 225.
26.  The two Harris children were marked as attending school in the 1870 census, and the Grant Road Colored School was the closest to the farm. They were always listed in future censuses as literate.
27.  Kessler, "First School in Forest Hills."

28. Kessler, "Another School."

29. Foner, *Reconstruction*, 422.

30. Foner, 602.

31. Franklin and Moss, *From Slavery to Freedom*, 257.

32. Du Bois, *Black Reconstruction in America*, 708.

33. Kreisa, McDowell, and Finnigan, *Phase IB Archaeological Investigations*, 71–73. This 2014 archaeological dig at the property of Lafayette Elementary School, the previous site of the Harris farm, produced various nineteenth-century artifacts such as pottery, canning jar shards, pieces of glass oil lamps, and a clay pipestem.

34. Sacerdote, "Slavery," 217–34. Also referenced in Costa and Kahn, *Heroes and Cowards*, 213. This study followed the lives of Black Union soldiers who had been free and those who had been born enslaved.

35. US Bureau of the Census, *Negro Population 1790–1915*, 477.

36. Lepore, *These Truths*, 335.

37. Miller, "Destroyed by Slavery?," 1587.

38. Eblen, "New Estimates," 308.

39. Benefits of longevity in parents and grandparents are discussed in detail in Voland, Chasiotis, and Schiefenhövel, *Grandmotherhood*.

40. Helm, *Tenleytown*, 178–79, 184.

41. Harris, *Harder We Run*, 23–24.

42. Corrigan, *Social Union*, 124, 180.

43. Green, *Secret City*, 126–27.

44. Helm, *Tenleytown*, 184–85.

45. Mitchell, *Chronicles of Georgetown Life*, 54.

46. Helm, *Tenleytown*, 231–32.

47. Green, *Secret City*, 119.

48. Green, 121–28, 131–32, 145–48.

## Chapter 7

1. Clark, "Mills on the Potomac," 104–5; and Carter, "Henry Foxall."

2. Unrau, *Historic Resource Study*, 446–47.

3. Mould and Loewe, *Remembering Georgetown*, 52, 58–59, 109.

4. Ecker, *Portrait of Old George Town*, 180.

5. Mitchell, *Chronicles of Georgetown Life*, 8.

6. Lesko, Babb, and Gibbs, *Black Georgetown Remembered*, 16. The names of the streets of Georgetown changed in the early 1890s. Today the Herring Hill area is south of P Street, bordered by Rock Creek Park on the east and Twenty-Ninth Street to the west.

7. Mitchell, *Chronicles of Georgetown Life*, 90.

8. John and his family lived at 26 Monroe Street, now called Twenty-Seventh Street. After the street names changed, directories recorded them at 1337

Twenty-Seventh Street. The school was located on what is now Twenty-Sixth Street, between P and Q Streets.

9. Lesko, Babb, and Gibbs, *Black Georgetown Remembered*, 22–23.

10. Green, *Washington*, 1:325; and Freedmen's Savings and Trust, *Registers*, 1871. Most depositors were reimbursed some of their funds several years later.

11. Asch and Musgrove, *Chocolate City*, 150–56.

12. Mazur, *Example for All*, 232–38; and Asch and Musgrove, *Chocolate City*, 162.

13. Mitchell, *Chronicles of Georgetown Life*, 44–45.

14. Mitchell, 10. Ella was born in 1871, Ada in 1874, and Lillie in 1878, as recorded in the 1880 census. Lillie is not found in records after the 1880 census when she was two years old. We assume that the family rented their home. Censuses never registered John and Mildred as owning their property, although a census taker did not always ask Black residents about ownership and instead assumed they were renters.

15. Mould and Loewe, *Remembering Georgetown*, 63.

16. Green, *Secret City*, 147.

17. Mitchell, "History of Mt. Zion," in Lesko, Babb, and Gibbs, *Black Georgetown Remembered*, 155–59. There was no money to keep up the cemetery, and it fell into disrepair and suffered damage by vandals in the twentieth century. Now it is listed in the National Register of Historic Places.

18. The figures are from the year 1886–87, which was unlikely to be very different from 1890. See the US Civil Service Commission, *Fourth Report*, 688.

19. King, *Separate and Unequal*, 43–47, 233. The wage was an average for postal clerks. There were seventy Black employees of the Washington city post office who earned an average annual salary of $601.

20. W. T. Andrews and W. White, "Segregation in Government Departments," Reports of Investigations by the NAACP (1928), reprinted in King, *Separate and Unequal*, 235–40.

21. As noted in Washington city directories.

22. US Civil Service Commission, *Ninth Report*, 236–37, as reprinted in King, *Separate and Unequal*, 233. Numbers are for the year 1893.

23. King, 47.

24. Mitchell, *Chronicles of Georgetown Life*, 110, citing a study of past directories from Washington, DC. She was among 422 householders in Georgetown who had lived there since at least 1870, and fifteen years later she was one of 121 of such householders.

25. Green, *Secret City*, 64.

26. Future censuses never showed Lewis and Hester Harris as owning their home. An 1876 directory shows that they first settled at 204 Fayette Street, which is Thirty-Fifth Street today. Plat maps show that they lived at the corner of Thirty-Fifth and Reservoir Road, where the Duke Ellington School of the Arts is located now.

27. See https://gloverparkhistory.com/geography/maps-places-features/bryantown. The site's author, Carleton Fletcher says the spelling of Bryantown may have come from an early landowner named Bryan Duffy, who was a contractor, and that the spelling Brinetown came later.

28. Lesko, Babb, and Gibbs, *Black Georgetown Remembered*, 17.

29. Today the university has created and is maintaining a Georgetown Slavery Archive about its history with slavery.

30. Lesko, Babb, and Gibbs, 37–39.

31. Donovan, *Many Witnesses*, 340.

32. Ecker, *Portrait of Old George Town*, 180.

33. Corrigan, *Social Union*, 188–89.

34. A city directory for 1879 shows William Harris living at Lewis's Fayette Street address, but it was probably a temporary situation. Because nothing is known of Thomas Harris's background or about the other branches of his family, it is only an assumption that William was Lewis's cousin. It seems likely that he was because William had been a Georgetown resident before the war.

35. Mitchell, *Chronicles of Georgetown Life*, 79–81.

36. Lesko, Babb, and Gibbs, *Black Georgetown Remembered*, 41–42.

37. Mitchell, *Chronicles of Georgetown Life*, 81–82.

38. Mould and Loewe, *Remembering Georgetown*, 113.

39. One such developer, Frederick Huidekoper, also purchased a large tract of land called Burleith, where he intended to build large homes. When the area was finally developed in the 1920s, the homes constructed were relatively small, and the neighborhood took the name Burleith. See Lange, "Burleith History."

40. Construction began in 1891 on Fayette/Thirty-Fifth Street, and Western High School opened in 1897.

41. Lesko, Babb, and Gibbs, *Black Georgetown Remembered*, 41–42. The street where Lewis and Hester's family had lived was Fayette/Thirty-Fifth Street.

42. After living at 204 Fayette/Thirty-Fifth Street for five years, in 1885 they moved a few blocks north on the same street. Later they moved a block east to Thirty-Fourth Street.

43. Helped by a local store owner, Brown fit his two-hundred-pound, five-foot-eight frame into a wooden box whose largest side was three foot one. He drilled small air holes into the wood and used a beef bladder full of water for hydration. He spent twenty-seven hours in the box as it was routed first to Washington, DC, and then put on a steamship to Philadelphia, where it arrived at the Pennsylvania Anti-Slavery Society. Brown spent several years traveling in northern states, lecturing and enacting his escape, and he published a book about his life. See Brown, *Narrative of the Life*, 67–73.

44. For more on the Adams Express Company (now the Adams Diversified Equity Fund), see "Adams Express Company," Wikipedia, www.Wikipedia.org/wiki/Adams_Express_Company.

45. The 1910 census records a Joseph Harris, forty years old, working as a coachman for a family that lived on N Street. Although the age is not right, it seems likely he was Lewis's son.

46. The Risque home was at West 22 First Street, now N Street. Lorenzo's wife's name was Mary Baker.

47. The church is located at 3240 O Street in the heart of Georgetown.

48. Mould and Loewe, *Remembering Georgetown*, 120–21.

49. Andrew Stephen, "Georgetown's Hidden History," *Washington Post*, July 16, 2006.

50. Archives of St. John's Episcopal Church, Georgetown, District of Columbia, courtesy of Al Laporta, church archivist, in correspondence with the authors.

51. The first house was on Potomac Street; the second was at 3241 N Street.

52. Asch and Musgrove, *Chocolate City*, 300.

53. Green, *Secret City*, 121, 140–42.

54. At the turn of the century Lewis moved to 3618 P Street, on the western edge of Georgetown and not far from where he had first settled in the mid-1870s. The 1910 census showed him at that address, and presumably he was living there in 1917 when he died.

55. Lesko, Babb, and Gibbs, *Black Georgetown Remembered*, 42.

## Chapter 8

1. Franklin and Moss, *From Slavery to Freedom*, 308.

2. Gregory, *Southern Diaspora*, 12–13.

3. Hill, "Recent Northward Migration," 1–14. Refers to the year 1920.

4. US Bureau of the Census, *Negro Population 1790–1915*, 68, 218.

5. Harris, *Harder We Run*, 15.

6. Costa and Kahn, *Heroes and Cowards*, 194–202. Soldiers were more likely to move to cities where their fellow soldiers were from, as discussed in chapter 5.

7. Lepore, *These Truths*, 300.

8. Daniel Conner, a twenty-one-year-old brickmaker from Philadelphia, was in Joseph's Company G, First USCT. Perhaps before Joseph went to New York, he went to Philadelphia to visit his friend Daniel and met Margaret there. See Gibbs, *Black, Copper, & Bright*, 234. In New York City, Joseph worked as a waiter and boarded with a family headed by twenty-eight-year-old William Glover from Washington, DC, who was also a waiter. Glover's name is not found in the list of First Regiment soldiers. Joseph and Margaret had a daughter named Laura/Laurita in 1874 and a son who was named Thomas, probably after Joseph's father, in 1875.

9. Lepore, *These Truths*, 335.

10. Atack and Passell, *New Economic View*, 431. For Joseph's 1878 employment as a porter, see Pullman Company, Employee Service Card for Joseph Harris, Record Group 06/02/03, box 311, NY Penn Terminal, Newberry Library, Chicago IL.

Information is courtesy of Newberry librarian JoEllen McKillop Dickie. Joseph could have been employed earlier, but it cannot be determined because a fire destroyed all of the company's early archives in Chicago.

11. Achenbach, *Grand Idea*, 340.
12. Tye, *Rising from the Rails*, 10–11, 13–15.
13. Tye, 2.
14. Harris, *Harder We Run*, 60.
15. Tye, *Rising from the Rails*, 3. At its peak in the 1920s, twelve thousand Black men worked for the company.
16. Harris, *Harder We Run*, 38.
17. Tye, *Rising from the Rails*, 86–89.
18. Tye, 90–95.
19. Tye, 103–4.
20. Hughes, *Collected Poems*, 116.
21. Tye, *Rising from the Rails*, 77.
22. Tye, 73, 76.
23. Twain and Warner, *Gilded Age*.
24. Pullman Company, Employee Service Card.
25. Tye, *Rising from the Rails*, 76.
26. Tye, 104.
27. Kluger, *Simple Justice*, 71–73.
28. Asch and Musgrove, *Chocolate City*, 208.
29. Lepore, *These Truths*, 347.
30. Harris, *Harder We Run*, 41.
31. Atack and Passell, *New Economic View*, 444.
32. Architect D. H. Burnham's design for Union Station was inspired by the 1893 World's Columbian Exposition (World's Fair) in Chicago that demonstrated how to make beautiful buildings functional.
33. Asch and Musgrove, *Chocolate City*, 201.
34. Tye, *Rising from the Rails*, 110–111, citing Randolph, "Reply to Pullman Propaganda," 292.
35. Franklin and Moss, *From Slavery to Freedom*, 420.
36. Tye, *Rising from the Rails*, 86, 89.
37. Harris, *Harder We Run*, 78.
38. Per the publication of Brotherhood of Sleeping Car Porters, *Pullman Porter*, 14.
39. Rosenwaike, *Population History*, 63, 78. The Black population of New York City was 1.4 percent of the total population, and in Buffalo it was 0.3 percent.
40. The population percentages are drawn from the census of 1900. The timing of Lorenzo and Celia's move is assumed based on the date when Lorenzo began his employment at the cathedral.
41. US Bureau of the Census, *Negro Population 1790–1915*, tables 20 and 22, 550 and 526–27.

42. Per the archives of St. Paul's Episcopal Cathedral, Buffalo NY. All materials cited from the archives are courtesy of Wayne Mori, cathedral archivist, in correspondence with the authors.

43. Built in 1877, their house at 45 Garner Avenue was centrally located, two blocks south of what was then the Buffalo State Hospital and two blocks east of the Niagara River.

44. Horton and Keil, "African Americans," in Horton, *Free People of Color*, 170–84.

45. Evans, *History of St. Paul's*, 242; and the archives of St. Paul's Episcopal Cathedral.

46. An undated clipping from an unnamed District newspaper notes Lorenzo's ten-day visit to see his mother and brother in Chevy Chase. The clipping seems to date from 1899 because it says that after spending eleven years as a sexton at St. John's Church in Georgetown, Lorenzo was sexton "the last six years at Saint Paul's Cathedral, Buffalo."

47. *St. Paul's Chimes*, October 1919, in the archives of St. Paul's Episcopal Cathedral.

48. From authors' correspondence with Wayne Mori.

49. Letter, Minutes of Vestry, May 14, 1920, in the archives of St. Paul's Episcopal Cathedral.

50. The "Research Club" was reported in the *Buffalo American*, March 11, 1920, 2.

51. A suffragan bishop is subordinate to the bishop.

52. *Buffalo American*, October 13, 1921, 1; and *Buffalo American*, October 27, 1921, 4.

53. *Buffalo American*, March 20, 1920, 2.

54. Lorenzo's connection to the Moses Society is discussed in chapter 9.

55. The 1940 census shows Mary "Minnie" Moten Brown living at his house, and she is listed as the owner.

56. Ancestry.com, *US City Directories, 1822–1995*, for Buffalo.

57. The 1944 obituary for her brother John Armstead Moten lists her as living in Buffalo.

58. Harris, *Harder We Run*, 55–58.

59. Gregory, *Southern Diaspora*, 331. In 1935–40 1.8 percent of Black southerners living in the North returned home. Whether that would apply to the years at the turn of the twentieth century is not clear, although transportation was presumably easier for the return trips later in the century.

60. Harris, *Harder We Run*, 55–58; and Gregory, *Southern Diaspora*, 17.

## Chapter 9

1. Helm, *Tenleytown*, 247.

2. Lepore, *These Truths*, 347.

3. Brown, *Road to Jim Crow*, 313.

4. Helm, *Tenleytown*, 182, 370–74.

5. Twain and Warner, *Gilded Age*.

6. Asch and Musgrove, *Chocolate City*, 189.

7. Asch and Musgrove, 192–3; Helm, *Tenleytown*, 352.

8.   Asch and Musgrove, *Chocolate City*, 189–91, 220.

9.   *The Star*, January 1, 1891, as quoted in Helm, *Tenleytown*, 238.

10.  Anne Rollins, "Connecticut Avenue," in Elfin, Williams, and the Forest Hills Neighborhood Alliance, *Forest Hills*, 17–20; and Asch and Musgrove, *Chocolate City*, 191.

11.  *House Beautiful*, April 1903, cited by Alexander, "Some Recollections."

12.  Marc Fisher, "Chevy Chase, 1916: For Everyman, a New Lot in Life," *Washington Post*, February 15, 1999. The area where Belmont was to be developed is now an affluent commercial area called Friendship Heights, which is located right on the border of the District and Maryland.

13.  "Real Estate Transfers," *Washington Post*, October 5, 1898, 11. Twentieth-century maps show the property to be 2.3 acres.

14.  In Maryland the wildflowers most often found in dry meadows include purple coneflowers and tickseed sunflowers. See the Maryland Department of Natural Resources' website, "Creating a Wild Backyard—Wildflower Meadows," https://dnr.maryland.gov/wildlife/pages/habitat/wawildflowers.aspx.

15.  The authors did not find any death record for Mary Ann Harris. Censuses consistently show that she was born about 1820; however, her children's claim that she was ninety was recorded in the 1900 census, which is the last one in which she appeared. Her daughter said that she lived to be over a hundred years old. It is possible that the Harrises owned their property as early as 1850 although the census of that year did not indicate ownership. As Corrigan notes, census takers at that time were not likely to ask Black residents about property holding. Corrigan, *Social Union*, 177.

16.  "Days News in Camera Views," *Washington Post*, June 2, 1928, 20.

17.  US Bureau of the Census, *Negro Population 1790–1915*, 504, 509.

18.  Harris, *Harder We Run*, 65.

19.  Rosetta's husband was Randolph (Rand), John's wife was Annie, and William's wife was Rose but known as Maggie.

20.  Alexander, "Some Recollections of Old Chevy Chase, Unpublished. Moren, "Lafayette School."

21.  Green, *Secret City*, 166–69.

22.  *Gibbs, Black, Copper, & Bright*, 183.

23.  The men in the photograph are not identified, so one can only guess which one might be Joseph Harris. Knowing that he was seventeen years old when he enlisted and that the average age at enlistment was seven years older, he would have been one of the younger men. Since at the time the photograph was taken he was still working as a Pullman porter, it is unlikely that he is one of the men with a cane. Past records described him as light skinned and short in stature.

24.  Their three children were Dorothea, Theodore, and Thomas.

25.  Green, *Secret City*, 187–88. The parade and banquet honoring the First Regiment is described in chapter 5 of this volume.

26.  Originally named Fort Pennsylvania, Fort Reno was renamed in honor of Maj. Gen. Jesse Reno of the US Army who died in 1862 at the Battle of South Mountain in Maryland.

27. Helm, *Tenleytown*, 168, 173–74.

28. Helm, 202, 249–51.

29. "Tenleytown Neighborhoods & Subdivisions—Reno City," Tenleytown Historical Society of Washington, DC, www.tenleytownhistoricalsociety.org /neighborhoods/reno-city.php?neighborhood=2.

30. By the end of the nineteenth century, there were 150 students in the old Grant Road school building, which had a capacity for half that many.

31. The architect's name was Snowden Ashford.

32. Helm, *Tenleytown*, 327, 397–98.

33. Helm, 287.

34. William Moten's obituary in the *Washington Post*, October 3, 1970, stated that he ran his own business for sixty years, so he must have begun his career around 1910 when the funeral director industry was modernizing. He may have been apprenticed to someone and would have needed another job that provided regular income in the early years.

35. Iezzoni, *Influenza 1918*, 83, 147.

36. Helm, *Tenleytown*, 309.

37. US Bureau of the Census, *Negro Population 1790–1915*, 550, for the year 1910.

38. Smith, *To Serve the Living*, 67.

39. Smith, 31, 83.

40. Smith, 35, 36–38.

41. Smith, 53, 51.

42. Smith, 69–70, 47–48.

43. The 1954 city directory lists Moten's Funeral Home at 3354 Prospect Street in Georgetown. How long he practiced there is not known. His obituary listed his business at 2718 Twelfth Street, Northeast, in Washington.

44. Smith, 93–94.

45. Asch and Musgrove, *Chocolate City*, 231–32.

46. Gillian Brockell, "A Deadly Race Riot 'Abetted' by the Post," *Washington Post*, July 19, 2019, B1–B2.

47. Asch and Musgrove, *Chocolate City*, 234–36.

48. Brockell, "Deadly Race Riot," B1–B2.

49. Green, *Secret City*, 189–95.

50. Bureau of the Census, *Negro Population 1790–1915*, 462.

51. Green, *Secret City*, 99–206; and "White-Robed Klan Cheered on March in Nation's Capital," *Washington Post*, August 9, 1925, 1.

52. Rosetta's husband was no relation to her grandfather Thomas Harris.

53. *Top Notch* (Friendship Citizens Association newspaper), October 1930, quoted in Helm, *Tenleytown*, 479.

54. Helm, 476, citing a letter of Cuno H. Rudolph's dated February 3, 1926, Record Group 79, 55480/683, National Archives.

55. Neil Flanagan, "The Battle of Fort Reno," *Washington City Paper*, November 3, 2017, 19.

56. Helm, *Tenleytown*, 484.

57. Helm, 471–72.
58. Helm, 308. William Moten's obituary noted his membership in the church, and because he was a funeral director, he probably was active in the Moses Society.
59. Kathan, Whitley, and Rispin, "Tracing a Bethesda," 30–32. Within the deed of sale is a handwritten notation, "Mailed to John A. Morton [sic], Chevy Chase, Md. Feb. 4, 1911," in White's Tabernacle No. 39 Record of Incorporation, September 9, 1910, Book 27, 434, District of Columbia Archives, Washington, DC. Lorenzo Harris had moved to Buffalo in 1893, but apparently he remained a trustee.
60. Kathan, Whitley, and Rispin, "Tracing a Bethesda," 32. In the late 1960s, the construction of an apartment building and parking lot began in the approximate location of the cemetery. In the summer of 2020, construction of a storage unit building under way on part of the property has been protested by the church. See Matt Blitz, "'The Second Desecration of Our Ancestors': Activists Fight Construction near Historic Cemetery in Bethesda," dcist, July 8, 2020, https://dcist.com/story/20/07/08/moses-african-cemetery-bethesda-preservation-protests/.
61. The legal announcement of this process, "In the Supreme Court of the District of Columbia, Joseph H. Harris, Plaintiff, v. Lorenzo Harris et al., Defendants, Equity No. 40.549," recorded the name Dry Meadows. See Ford, "Legal Notices," 50:685. The authors have not found any property record from the period involving the parcel owned by the fourth brother, Lewis. It is assumed that upon his death in 1917, the parcel was inherited by Mary Moten, who was considered to be the owner when the government purchased it in 1928.
62. By the 1920s, most deeds contained restrictive covenants. See Marc Fisher, "Chevy Chase, 1916: For Everyman, a New Lot in Life," Washington Post, February 15, 1999, A1.
63. Massey and Denton, American Apartheid, 36–37.
64. See Document #1928 0806 0116, Office of Tax and Revenue, Recorder of Deeds of the District of Columbia.
65. The 1870 census estimated that the Harris household had $600 of assets, presumably most of which was their land and house. The actual government payment for the same property in 1928 was $6,862.50 as recorded in Document #1928 0806 0116.
66. Torrey and Green, Brookmont, 68. Perhaps the reason for the price difference was that the land overlooking the river was farther away from the amenities in Tenleytown than the Broad Branch settlement.
67. Of course, real estate values, especially in Chevy Chase, have gone up much more than the average change in the consumer bundle of goods. Williamson, "Seven Ways."
68. Galbraith, Great Crash, 23–27.
69. Asch and Musgrove, Chocolate City, 250.
70. Jay Walz, "Children Are Proud and So Are the Parents," Washington Post, May 22, 1938.

## Epilogue

1.  In 1942 John's World War II draft registration showed him living in Northeast Washington near his sister Rosetta, whom he listed as his closest living relative. Two years later he died at age sixty-six and was buried in Woodlawn Cemetery, where his uncle Joseph Harris had been buried thirteen years earlier. On his World War I draft papers, John Moten had listed himself as a gardener like his grandfather Thomas Harris.
2.  Asch and Musgrove, *Chocolate City*, 290.
3.  Massey and Denton, *American Apartheid*, 21, 47, 222.
4.  Green, *Secret City*, 308–11.
5.  Gates, *Stony the Road*, 255.
6.  Franklin and Moss, *From Slavery to Freedom*, 537; and "Arlington County, VA Weather History: Ronald Reagan Washington National Airport Station, August 28, 1963," Weather Underground, https://www.wunderground.com/history /daily/us/va/arlington-county/KDCA/date/1963-8-28.
7.  From "Prelude to Our Age," in Hughes, *Collected Poems of Langston Hughes*, 379.

## Appendix 3

1.  Anderson, *American Census*, 31.
2.  There is generally a two-year lag in releasing the earlier data.
3.  Anderson, 11.
4.  Douglass, *Narrative*, 2012, 3.
5.  Whipple's index is used to measure the tendency of respondents in censuses and surveys to round their ages or birth dates. In some cultures, people choose birth dates in auspicious years.
6.  This occurred in the Pointer family in Annapolis at the beginning of the twentieth century.
7.  Wright, *Free Negro in Maryland*, 243.
8.  Donovan and Fletcher, *William King's Mortality Books*, 1:205.
9.  Thorndale and Dollarhide, *Map Guide*, 396.
10. Omi, "Changing Meaning of Race," in Smelser, Wilson, and Mitchell, *America Becoming*, 1:243.
11. Gibson and Jung, "Historical Census Statistics," 3.
12. Sandefur et al., "Overview," in Smelser, Wilson, and Mitchell, *America Becoming*, 1:41.
13. Mills, "Ethnicity," in Taylor and Crandall, *Generations and Change*, 96.
14. Prewitt, *What Is Your Race?*, 106–11.
15. US Bureau of the Census, *Negro Population 1790–1915*, 27.
16. Thorndale and Dollarhide, *Map Guide*, xxii–xxiii.

# Bibliography

Achenbach, Joel. *The Grand Idea: George Washington's Potomac and the Race to the West.* New York: Simon & Schuster, 2004.

Adjutant General's Office, Records. *Compiled Military Service Records of Volunteer Union Soldiers Who Served with the United States Colored Troops, 1st US Colored Infantry.* M1819, Record Group 94. National Archives, Washington DC. www.ancestry.com/search/collections/1107/.

Alexander, Vida Ord. "Some Recollections of Old Chevy Chase." Unpublished. April 16, 1952. Chevy Chase Historical Society. Object ID 2009.1072.05. Chevy Chase MD. https://chevychasehistory.pastpefectonline.com/archive/C747EB4A-0571-4013-9839-607418794935.

Allen, William C. *History of Slave Laborers in the Construction of the U.S. Capitol.* Washington DC: Office of the Architect of the Capitol, 2005.

Allmendinger, David F., Jr. *Nat Turner and the Rising in Southampton County.* Baltimore: Johns Hopkins University Press, 2014.

Ancestry.com. *U.S. City Directories, 1822–1995.* Provo: Ancestry.com Operations, 2011.

Anderson, Margo J. *The American Census: A Social History.* New Haven: Yale University Press, 1988.

Anderson, Patricia Abelard, abstractor. *Montgomery County Land Record Miscellany, Libers A–E, Selected Abstracts, 1777–1794.* Damascus MD: GenLaw Resources, 2010.

Asch, Chris Myers, and George Derek Musgrove. *Chocolate City: A History of Race and Democracy in the Nation's Capital.* Chapel Hill: University of North Carolina Press, 2017.

Atack, Jeremy, and Peter Passell. *A New Economic View of American History from Colonial Times to 1940.* New York: W. W. Norton, 1994.

Bacon-Foster, Cora. *Early Chapters in the Development of the Patomac Route to the West.* Washington DC: Columbia Historical Society, 1912.

Belt, Charles R. "Petition of Charles R. Belt, 14 May 1862." Records of the Accounting Officers of the Department of the Treasury, 1775–1978. Record Group 217.6.5, National Archives. In Lawrence et al., *Civil War Washington.* www.civilwardc.org/texts/petitions/cww.00223.html.

Berlin, Ira. *Slaves without Masters: The Free Negro in the Antebellum South*. New York: Pantheon Books, 1974.

Berlin, Ira, Barbara J. Fields, Thavolia Glymph, Joseph P. Reidy, and Leslie S. Rowland, eds. *The Destruction of Slavery*. Series 1, vol. 1 of *Freedom: A Documentary History of Emancipation, 1861–1867*. New York: Cambridge University Press, 1986.

Berlin, Ira, Joseph P. Reidy, and Leslie S. Rowland, eds. *The Black Military Experience*. Series of *Freedom: A Documentary History of Emancipation, 1861–1867*. New York: Cambridge University Press, 1983.

Blight, David W. *Frederick Douglass: Prophet of Freedom*. New York: Simon & Schuster, 2018.

Brackett, Jeffrey Richardson. *The Negro in Maryland: A Study of the Institution of Slavery*. Baltimore: Johns Hopkins University Press, 1889.

Brooks, Noah. *Washington, D.C., in Lincoln's Time*. Edited by Herbert Mitgang. Athens: University of Georgia Press, 1971.

Brotherhood of Sleeping Car Porters. *The Pullman Porter*. New York: Brotherhood of Sleeping Car Porters, 1926.

Brown, Alexander Crosby. "America's Greatest Eighteenth Century Engineering Achievement: The Potowmack Company's Canal at Great Falls." *Virginia Cavalcade* 12, no. 4 (Spring 1963): 41–47.

Brown, C. Christopher. *The Road to Jim Crow: The African American Struggle on Maryland's Eastern Shore, 1860–1915*. Baltimore: Maryland Historical Society, 2016.

Brown, Henry Box. *Narrative of the Life of Henry Box Brown*. Manchester: Lee and Glynn, 1851.

Brown, Letitia Woods. *Free Negroes in the District of Columbia, 1790–1848*. New York: Oxford University Press, 1972.

———. "Residence Patterns of Negroes in the District of Columbia, 1800–1860." In *Records of the Columbia Historical Society*, 66–79. Washington DC: Columbia Historical Society, 1969–70.

Brugger, Robert J. *Maryland: A Middle Temperament: 1634–1980*. Baltimore: Johns Hopkins University Press in association with the Maryland Historical Society, 1988.

Carter, Elliot. "Henry Foxall Was Washington's First Defense Contractor." Architect of the Capital: Hidden History of Washington, DC. October 13, 2016. https://architectofthecapital.org/posts/2016/10/2/henry-foxall-early-defense-contract.

Chesapeake and Ohio Canal Company. *C&O Requisition Book, 1828–1870*. Record Group 79, entry 349, vol. 1. National Archives, Washington DC.

Clark, Allen C. "The Old Mills on the Potomac." *Records of the Columbia Historical Society* 31/32 (1930): 81–116.

Clark, Eugene, and Edythe Clark. *The Spirit of Captain John: A History of the Bethesda Presbyterian Church, Montgomery County, Maryland*. New York: Carlton Press, 1970.

Corrigan, Mary Beth. "Making the Most of an Opportunity: Slaves and the Catholic

Church in Early Washington." *Washington History* 12, no. 1 (Spring/Summer 2000): 90–101.

———. *A Social Union of Heart and Effort: The African-American Family in the District of Columbia on the Eve of Emancipation.* PhD diss., University of Maryland, 1996.

Costa, Dora L., and Matthew E. Kahn. *Heroes and Cowards: The Social Face of War.* Princeton: Princeton University Press, 2008.

Crosby, Alfred W. *America's Forgotten Pandemic: The Influenza of 1918.* New York: Cambridge University Press, 1989.

diGiancomantonio, William C., "To Sell Their Birthright for a Mess of Potage': The Origins of D.C. Governance and the Organic Act of 1801." Historical Society of Washington DC. *Washington History* 12, no. 1 (Spring/Summer 2000): 31–48.

Dobak, William A. *Freedom by the Sword: The U.S. Colored Troops, 1862–1867.* Washington DC: Center of Military History, US Army, 2011.

Donald, David Herbert. *Lincoln.* New York: Simon & Schuster, 1995.

Donovan, Jane. *Many Witnesses: A History of Dumbarton United Methodist Church, 1772–1990.* Georgetown DC: Dumbarton United Methodist Church, 1998.

Donovan, Jane, and Carlton Fletcher. *William King's Mortality Books.* Vol. 1, *1795–1832.* Westminster: Heritage Books, 2004.

Douglass, Frederick. *Narrative of the Life of Frederick Douglass.* Introduction and notes by Dale Edwyna Smith. New York: Barnes & Noble Sterling Publishing, 2012.

Du Bois, W. E. B. *Black Reconstruction in America, 1860–1880.* New York: Free Press, 1935.

Dwyer, Michael. "Magruder's Folly." *The Montgomery County Story* 52, no. 3 (Fall/Winter 2009): 40.

Eblen, Jack Ericson. "New Estimates of the Vital Rates of the United States Black Population during the Nineteenth Century." *Demography* 11, no. 2 (May 1974): 301–19.

Ecker, Grace Dunlop. *A Portrait of Old George Town.* Reprint. Richmond VA: Dietz Press, 1951.

Eicher, David J. *The Longest Night: A Military History of the Civil War.* New York: Simon & Schuster, 2001.

Evans, Charles Worthington. *History of St. Paul's Church, Buffalo, N.Y., 1817–1903.* Edited by Alice M. Evans Bartlett and G. Hunter Bartlett. Buffalo: Matthews-Northrop Works, 1903.

Ferrero, Edward. *The Art of Dancing, Historically Illustrated, to Which Is Added a Few Hints on Etiquette; Also, the Figures, Music, and Necessary Instruction for the Performance of the Most Modern and Approved Dances, as Executed at the Private Academies of the Author.* New York: Edward Ferrero, 1859.

Fields, Barbara Jeanne. *Slavery and Freedom on the Middle Ground: Maryland during the Nineteenth Century.* New Haven: Yale University Press, 1985.

Foner, Eric. *Gateway to Freedom: The Hidden History of the Underground Railroad.* New York: W. W. Norton, 2015.

———. *Reconstruction: America's Unfinished Revolution, 1863–1877*. New York: Harper Perennial Modern Classics, 2014.

Ford, Richard, ed. "Legal Notices." *Washington Law Reporter*. Vol. 50. Washington DC: Law Reporting Printing, 1922. https://babel.hathitrust.org/cgi/pt?id=hvd .hl4fsp&view=1up&seq=693.

Franklin, John Hope, and Alfred A. Moss Jr. *From Slavery to Freedom: A History of African Americans*. 8th ed. New York: Alfred A. Knopf, 2009.

Freedman's Savings and Trust Company. *Registers of Signatures of Depositors in Branches of the Freedman's Savings and Trust Company, 1865–1874*. M816, 27 rolls. National Archives, Washington DC. In *U.S. Freedman's Bank Records, 1865–1874*. Provo: Ancestry.com Operations, 2005.

Galbraith, John Kenneth. *The Great Crash, 1929*. New York: Houghton Mifflin, 1972.

Gallatin, Albert. *Report of the Secretary of the Treasury on the Subject of Public Roads and Canals*. Gloucestershire: Dodo Press, 1808.

Gates, Henry Louis, Jr. *Life upon These Shores: Looking at African American History, 1513–2008*. New York: Alfred A. Knopf, 2011.

———. *Stony the Road: Reconstruction, White Supremacy, and the Rise of Jim Crow*. New York: Penguin Press, 2019.

Genovese, Eugene D. *Roll, Jordan, Roll: The World the Slaves Made*. New York: Pantheon Books, 1972.

Georgetown University, Working Group on Slavery, Memory, and Reconciliation. "Holy Trinity Church Death Records, 1818–1867." Inventory GSA90. Washington DC. https://slaveryarchive.georgetown.edu/items/show/98.

Gibbs, C. R. *Black, Copper, & Bright: The District of Columbia's Black Civil War Regiment*. Silver Spring MD: Three Dimensional Publishing, 2002.

Gibson, Campbell, and Kay Jung. "Historical Census Statistics on Population Totals by Race, 1790 to 1990, and by Hispanic Origin, 1790 to 1990, for Large Cities and Other Urban Places in the United States." US Census Bureau Population Division Working Paper No. 76. Washington DC: US Census Bureau, February 2005.

Goldin, Claudia, and Hugh Rockoff, eds. *Strategic Factors in Nineteenth Century American Economic History*. Chicago: University of Chicago Press, 1992.

Great Falls Historical Society. "Patowmack Canal Company Employees: Great Falls, September 1797." Annual Reports, 1986–1988. Great Falls VA: Great Falls Historical Society, 1988, 9–14.

Green, Constance McLaughlin. *The Secret City, a History of Race Relations in the Nation's Capital*. Princeton: Princeton University Press, 1967.

———. *Washington*. Vol. 1, *Village and Capital, 1800–1878*. Princeton: Princeton University Press, 1962.

———. *Washington: A History of the Capital, 1800–1950*. Princeton: Princeton University Press, 1962.

Gregory, James N. *The Southern Diaspora: How the Great Migrations of Black and White Southerners Transformed America*. Chapel Hill: University of North Carolina Press, 2005.

Guzy, Dan. *Navigation on the Upper Potomac River and Its Tributaries.* Glen Echo MD: Chesapeake and Ohio Canal Association, 2008.

Harris, William H. *The Harder We Run: Black Workers since the Civil War.* New York: Oxford University Press, 1982.

Harrison, Robert. *Washington during Civil War and Reconstruction.* New York: Cambridge University Press, 2011.

Helm, Judith Beck. *Tenleytown, D.C., Country Village into City Neighborhood.* Washington DC: Tennally Press, 1981.

Henson, Josiah. *The Life of Josiah Henson, Formerly a Slave, Now an Inhabitant of Canada, as Narrated by Himself.* Boston: Arthur D. Phelps, 1849.

Henson, Josiah, and Harriet Beecher Stowe. *Truth Stranger than Fiction: Father Henson's Story of His Own Life.* Boston: J. P. Jewett and Company, 1858.

Hill, Joseph A. "Recent Northward Migration of the Negro." *Monthly Labor Review* 18, no. 3 (March 1924): 1–14.

Historic Chevy Chase DC and Northwest Neighbors Village. "Mapping Segregation: Illustrating Systemic Racism's Imprint on DC" (Zoom webinar). Featuring Mara Cherkasky of Prologue DC. September 24, 2020. https://www .historicchevychasedc.org/recent-news/mapping-segregation-a-public-history -project-illustrates-how-systemic-racism-shaped-our-city/.

Horton, James Oliver, and Hartmut Keil. "African Americans and Germans in Mid-nineteenth Century Buffalo." In *Free People of Color: Inside the African American Community.* Edited by James Oliver Horton, chap. 8. Washington DC: Smithsonian Institution, 1993.

Howe, Daniel Walker. *What Hath God Wrought: The Transformation of America, 1815–1848.* New York: Oxford University Press, 2007.

Hughes, Langston. *The Collected Poems of Langston Hughes.* Edited by Arnold Rampersad and David Roessel. New York: Vintage Books, 1994.

Humphreys, Margaret. *Intensely Human: The Health of the Black Soldier in the American Civil War.* Baltimore: Johns Hopkins University Press, 2008.

Hynson, Jerry M. *Free African-Americans of Maryland, 1832, Including Allegany, Anne Arundel, Calvert, Caroline, Cecil, Charles, Dorchester, Frederick, Kent, Montgomery, Queen Anne's, and St Mary's Counties.* Westminster MD: Family Line Publication, 1998.

Iezzoni, Lynette. *Influenza 1918: The Worst Epidemic in American History.* New York: TV Books, 1999.

Jackson, L. P. "Virginia Negro Soldiers and Seamen in the American Revolution." *The Journal of Negro History* 27, no. 3 (July 1942): 247–87.

Johnston, James H. *From Slave Ship to Harvard: Yarrow Mamout and the History of an African American Family.* New York: Fordham University Press, 2012.

Kaplan, Justin, ed. *Walt Whitman: Poetry and Prose.* New York: Library of America, 1982.

Kapsch, Robert J. *The Potomac Canal: George Washington and the Waterway West.* Morgantown: West Virginia University Press, 2007.

Kathan, David L., Paige Whitley, and Amy Rispin. "Tracing a Bethesda, Maryland,

African American Community and Its Contested Cemetery." *Washington History* 29, no. 2 (Fall 2017): 30–32.

Kessler, Ann. "Another School Once Stood at the Site of Murch Elementary." *Forest Hills Connection*, January 19, 2016. https://www.foresthillsconnection.com/style /forest-hills-history/another-school-once-stood-at-the-site-of-murch-elementary/.

——. "The First School in Forest Hills, DC Opened Almost 150 Years Ago." *Forest Hills Connection*, August 26, 2015. https://www.foresthillsconnection.com/kids /schools/the-first-school-in-forest-hills-dc-opened-almost-150-years-ago/.

Kinard, June, ed. *Maryland, Colonial Census, 1776* (database). Provo UT: Ancestry .com Operations, 2000. https://www.ancestry.com/search/collections/4247/.

King, Desmond. *Separate and Unequal: African Americans and the U.S. Government.* New York: Oxford University Press, 2007.

Kluger, Richard. *Simple Justice: The History of* Brown v. Board of Education *and Black America's Struggle for Equality.* New York: Vintage Books, 2004.

Komlos, John. "Toward an Anthropometric History of African-Americans: The Case of the Free Blacks in Antebellum Maryland." In Goldin and Rockoff, *Strategic Factors*, 297–329.

Kreisa, Paul P., and Jacqueline M. McDowell, with Kelly Finnigan. *Phase IB Archaeological Investigations Conducted for Improvements at the Lafayette Recreation Center in Washington, D.C.* Laurel MD: Stantee Consulting Services, July 2014.

Kytle, Elizabeth. *Home on the Canal.* Cabin John MD: Seven Locks Press, 1983.

Lange, Ann. "Burleith History." Washington DC: Burleith Citizens Association, 1998. www.burleith.org/burleith-history.

Larsen, Arthur J., ed. *Crusader and Feminist: Letters of Jane Grey Swisshelm, 1858–1865.* St. Paul: Minnesota Historical Society, 1934.

Lawrence, Susan C., Elizabeth Lorang, Kenneth M. Price, and Kenneth J. Winkle. *Civil War Washington.* Lincoln: Center for Digital Research in the Humanities at the University of Nebraska, 2015.

Leech, Margaret. *Reveille in Washington, 1860–1865.* New York: New York Review Books, 1941.

Lepore, Jill. *These Truths: A History of the United States.* New York: W. W. Norton, 2018.

Lesko, Kathleen M., Valerie Babb, and Carroll R. Gibbs. *Black Georgetown Remembered: A History of Its Black Community from the Founding of "The Town of George" in 1751 to the Present Day.* Washington DC: Georgetown University Press, 1991.

MacMaster, Richard K., and Ray Eldon Hiebert. *A Grateful Remembrance: The Story of Montgomery County, Maryland, 1776–1976.* Rockville MD: Montgomery County Government and Historical Society, 1976.

Mann, Alison T. "Horrible Barbarity: The 1837 Murder Trial of Dorcas Allen, a Georgetown Slave." *Washington History* 27, no. 1 (Spring 2015): 3–13.

Maryland Province of the Society of Jesus. *Jesuit Plantation Project at Georgetown University.* List of Slaves on Each Estate to Be Sold. Box 40, folder 10. Maryland Province Archives. Georgetown University Library, Washington DC.

Massey, Douglas S., and Nancy A. Denton. *American Apartheid: Segregation and the Making of the Underclass*. Cambridge MA: Harvard University Press, 1993.

Mazur, Kate. *An Example for All the Land: Emancipation and the Struggle over Equality in Washington, D.C.* Chapel Hill: University of North Carolina Press, 2010.

McConnell, Roland C. "The Black Experience in Maryland: 1634–1900." In *The Old Line State: A History of Maryland*, edited by Morris L. Radoff, 405–32. Baltimore: Twentieth Printing, 1971.

McPherson, James M. *The Negro's Civil War*. New York: Vintage Books, Civil War Library Edition, 1993.

McWilliams, Jane Wilson. *Annapolis City on the Severn: A History*. Baltimore: Johns Hopkins University Press, 2011.

Miller, M. C. "Destroyed by Slavery? Slavery and African American Family Formation Following Emancipation." *Demography* 55, no. 5. (October 2018): 1587.

Mills, Elizabeth Shown. "Ethnicity and the Southern Genealogist: Myths and Misconceptions, Resources and Opportunities." In *Generations and Change: Genealogical Perspectives in Social History*, edited by Robert M. Taylor Jr., and Ralph J. Crandall, 89–108. Macon: Mercer University Press, 1986.

Mitchell, Mary. *Chronicles of Georgetown Life: 1865–1900*. Cabin John MD: Seven Locks Press, 1986.

Mitchell, Pauline Gaskins. "The History of Mt. Zion United Methodist Church and Mt. Zion Cemetery." *Records of the Columbia Historical Society of Washington, D.C.* 51 (1984). Reprinted in Lesko, Babb, and Gibbs, *Black Georgetown Remembered*, 155–60.

Moren, Sharon. "Lafayette School." *Origins II* (Neighborhood Planning Council, Chevy Chase [MD] Historical Society) 59 (February 1976).

Mould, David, and Missy Loewe. *Remembering Georgetown: A History of the Lost Port City*. Charleston: History Press, 2009.

Nalezyty, Susan. *Research Report: The History of Enslaved People at Visitation: Learning, Reflecting, and Teaching*. Washington DC: Georgetown Visitation Preparatory School, 2019. https://www.visi.org/about/history-of-georgetown-visitation/history-of-enslaved-people-at-visitation.

National Park Service. "Fort Reno: Civil War Defenses of Washington, Rock Creek Park." Washington DC: Department of the Interior, June 25, 2019. www.nps.gov/places/fort-reno.htm.

———. *Historic American Landscapes Survey: Theodore Roosevelt Island*. Heritage Documentation Program, HALS No. DC-12, 9-20. Washington DC: Department of the Interior, 2007. http://lcweb2.loc.gov/master/pnp/habshaer/dc/dc1000/dc1044/data/dc1044data.pdf.

Newton, Michael. *White Robes and Burning Crosses*. Jefferson NC: McFarland, 2014.

Northup, Solomon, and David Wilson. *Twelve Years a Slave*. Auburn: Orton and Mulligan; London: Samson Low, Son & Company, 1853.

Offutt, William. *Bethesda: A Social History of the Area through World War Two*. Bethesda MD: Innovation Game, 1996.

Omi, Michael A. "The Changing Meaning of Race." In *America Becoming: Racial Trends and Their Consequences*, edited by Neil J. Smelser, William Julius Wilson, and Faith Mitchell, 243–63. Vol. 1. Washington DC: National Academies Press, 2001.

Phillips, Christopher. *Freedom's Port: The African American Community of Baltimore, 1790–1860*. Chicago: University of Illinois Press, 1997.

Pointer, George. "Petition of Captain George Pointer to the President and Directors of the Chesapeake and Ohio Canal, September 5, 1829," 1–11. Record Group 79, entry 262. National Archives, Washington DC.

Poole, Martha Sprigg. "Ninian Beall and Col. Joseph Belt." *Montgomery County Historical Society* 12, no. 3 (May 1969): 1–6.

Potomac Company. *Correspondence and Reports, 1785–1825*. Record Group 79, entry 232, box 2. National Archives, Washington DC.

——. *Daybook*. Record Group 79, entry 240. National Archives, Washington DC.

——. *Miscellaneous Accounts, 1785–1828*. Record Group 79, entry 250. National Archives, Washington DC.

——. *Proceedings*. Record Group 79, entry 160, August 9, 1819. Book A. National Archives, Washington DC.

——. *Proceedings*. Record Group 79, entry 230, vol. A, October 18, 1785. National Archives, Washington DC.

——. *Proceedings*. Record Group 79, entry 230, Oversize vol., December 20, 1822. National Archives, Washington DC.

——. *Proceedings*. Record Group 79, entry 230, vol. B, box 1, July 25, 1819. National Archives, Washington DC.

——. *Proceedings, 1785–1828*. Record Group 79, entry 230, vol. A, October 4, 1786. National Archives, Washington DC.

Potter, Stephen R. *Commoners, Tribute, and Chiefs: The Development of Algonquian Culture in the Potomac Valley*. Charlottesville: University Press of Virginia, 1993.

Powell, Francis J. "A Statistical Profile of the Black Family in Washington, D.C., 1850–1880." *Records of the Columbia Historical Society* 52 (1989): 277.

Prewitt, Kenneth. *What Is Your Race? The Census and Our Flawed Efforts to Classify Americans*. Princeton: Princeton University Press, 2013.

Province, Dorothy S. *District of Columbia Free Negro Registers, 1821–1861*. Westminster MD: Heritage Press, 2015.

Provost Marshal General's Bureau, Records. "Consolidated Lists of Civil War Draft Registrations, 1863–1865." Record Group 110, entry 172. National Archives, Washington DC. Accessed at Ancestry.com. *U.S. Civil War Draft Registrations Records, 1863–1865*. Provo, UT: Ancestry.com Operations, 2020.

Pryor, Elizabeth Brown. *Clara Barton, Professional Angel*. Philadelphia: University of Pennsylvania, 1988.

Pullman Company. Employee Service Card for Joseph Harris. Record Group 06/02/03, box 311, NY Penn Terminal. Newberry Library, Chicago IL.

Quarles, Benjamin. "Freedom Fettered: Blacks in the Constitutional Era in

Maryland, 1776–1810—an Introduction." *Maryland Historical Magazine* 84, no. 4 (Winter 1989): 299–304.

Randolph, A. Phillip. "Reply to Pullman Propaganda." *Messenger* 8, no. 10 (October 1926): 292.

Rives, Jeannie Tree. "Old Families and Houses—Greenleaf Point." *Records of the Columbia Historical Society* 5 (1902): 57.

Rogers, Helen Hoban, comp. *Freedom & Slavery Documents in the District of Colombia*. Vol. 1, *1792–1806*. Baltimore: Gateway Press, 2007.

——. *Freedom & Slavery Documents in the District of Colombia*. Vol. 2, *1806–1816*. Baltimore: Gateway Press, 2007.

——. *Freedom & Slavery Documents in the District of Colombia*. Vol. 3, *1816–1822*. Baltimore: Otter Bay Books, 2008.

Rollins, Anne. "Connecticut Avenue." In *Forest Hills*, edited by Margery L. Elfin, Paul K. Williams, and the Forest Hills Neighborhood Alliance. Images of America Series. Charleston SC: Arcadia Publishing, 2006.

Rosenwaike, Ira. *Population History of New York City*. New York: Syracuse University Press, 1972.

Sacerdote, Bruce. "Slavery and the Intergenerational Transmission of Human Capital." *Review of Economics and Statistics* 87, no. 2 (2005): 217–34.

St. John's Episcopal Church. Archives. Georgetown, Washington DC.

Sandburg, Carl. *Abraham Lincoln: The War Years*. Vol. 4. New York: Harcourt, Brace and Company, 1939.

Sandefur, Gary D., Molly Martin, Jennifer Eggerling-Boeck, Susan E. Mannon, and Ann M. Meier. "An Overview of Racial and Ethnic Demographic Trends." In *America Becoming*, edited by Neil J. Smelser, Willian J. Wilson, and Faith Mitchell, 1:40–102. Washington DC: The National Academy of Science Press, 2001.

Schlesinger, Arthur M., Jr. *The Almanac of American History*. New York: Putnam Publishing Group, 1983.

Secretary of War. Letters Received. Record Group 107. Letter, April 27, 1864. National Archives, Washington DC.

Sharfstein, Daniel J. *The Invisible Line: A Secret History of Race in America*. New York: Penguin Books, 2011.

Sisters of the Visitation of Georgetown, DC. "Petition of the Sisters of the Visitation of Georgetown D.C., 2 June 1862." Records of the Accounting Officers of the Department of the Treasury. Record Group 217.6.5, National Archives, Washington DC. In Lawrence et al., *Civil War Washington*. www.civilwardc.org /texts/petitions/cww.00569.html.

Smith, Suzanne E. *To Serve the Living: Funeral Directors and the African American Way of Death*. Cambridge MA: Belknap Press of Harvard University Press, 2010.

Snyder, Timothy R. "The Chesapeake and Ohio Canal and the Underground Railroad, Part 2." *Along the Towpath* (The Chesapeake and Ohio Canal Association) 43, no. 1 (March 2011): 14. http://www.candocanal.org/atp/2011-03 .pdf. From "Narrative of James Curry, a Fugitive Slave, January 10, 1840." Davis

Library Microforms Collection. University Of North Carolina, Chapel Hill. http://
docsouth.unc.edu/neh/curry/curry.html.

Sprouse, Edith Moore, ed. *Along the Potomac River: Extracts from the* Maryland
Gazette, *1728–1799*. Bowie MD: Willow Bend Books, 2003.

St. Paul's Episcopal Cathedral. *St. Paul's Chimes*. Archives, St. Paul's Episcopal
Cathedral, Buffalo NY.

Steven. "The 1st US Colored Troops at Roosevelt Island." *Civil War Washington,
D.C.* (blog), February 10, 2012. http://civilwarwashingtondc1861-1865.blogspot
.com/2012/02/1st-us-colored-troops-at-roosevelt.html.

Taggart, Hugh T. "Old Georgetown." *Records of the Columbia Historical Society* 11
(1908): 120–224.

Thorndale, William, and William Dollarhide. *Map Guide to the U.S. Federal
Censuses, 1790–1920*. Baltimore: Genealogical Publishing, 1987.

Torrey, Barbara Boyle, and Clara Myrick Green. *Brookmont: A Neighborhood on the
Potomac*. Bethesda: Signature Press, 2008.

———. "An Old and Obscure Citizen: Captain George Pointer and the Potomac
Company." *Maryland Historical Magazine* 107, no. 3 (Fall 2012): 305–19.

Torrey, E. Fuller. *The Martyrdom of Abolitionist Charles Torrey*. Baton Rouge:
Louisiana State University Press, 2013.

Torrey, Jesse. *Portraiture of Domestic Slavery, in the United States*. Philadelphia:
John Bioren, printer, 1817.

Twain, Mark, and Charles Dudley Warner. *The Gilded Age: A Tale of Today*. New
York: Penguin Books, 2001.

Tye, Larry. *Rising from the Rails: Pullman Porters and the Making of the Black
Middle Class*. New York: Owl Books, Henry Holt, 2004.

Unrau, Harlan D. *Historic Resource Study: Chesapeake and Ohio Canal*. Hagerstown
MD: US Department of Interior, National Park Service, August 2007.

US Bureau of the Census. *Bicentennial Edition: Historical Statistics of the United
States, Colonial Times to 1970*. Parts 1 and 2. Washington DC: Government
Printing Office, 1975.

———. "Decennial Censuses, 1790, 1800, 1820–1880, 1900–1940." Records of the
Bureau of the Census, Record Group 29. National Archives, Washington DC.
https://www.ancestry.com/search/categories/usfedcen.

———. *Heads of Families at the First Census of the United States Taken in the Year
1790: Maryland*. Washington DC: Government Printing Office, 1907.

———. *Negro Population 1790–1915*. Washington DC: Government Printing Office,
1918.

US Civil Service Commission. *Fourth Report of the U.S. Civil-Service Commission,
January 16, 1886, to June 30, 1887*. Washington DC: Government Printing Office,
1888.

———. *Ninth Report of the U.S. Civil-Service Commission, July 1, 1891, to June 30,
1892*. Washington DC: Government Printing Office, 1893.

US Colored Troops Division, Adjutant General's Office. Letters Received. Series 360,

Record Group 94. 35th USCT Regimental Books and Papers. National Archives, Washington DC.

US District Court for the District of Columbia. Records Relating to Slaves, 1851–1863. Microfilm publication M433, roll 3. Record Group 21. National Archives and Records Administration, Washington DC. https://www.ancestry.com/search /collections/2171.

US Federal Census. "Mortality Schedule, 1850." Microfilm series T655, roll 5. National Archives, Washington DC. https://search.ancestry.com/search/dbextra .aspx?dbid=8756.

US House of Representatives. *Report of the Committee of the District of Columbia to Whom Were Referred Sundry Memorials from the Inhabitants of Pennsylvania, Maryland, and Virginia Paying the Aid of the Federal Government towards the Improvement of the Navigation of the River Potomac.* House Report 111, 17th Cong., 1st sess., May 3, 1822.

US Senate. Committee on the District of Columbia. Petitions and Memorials, series 547. 37th Congress. Record Group 46. National Archives, Washington DC.

———. Petitions and Memorials, series 582. 39th Congress. Record Group 46. National Archives, Washington DC.

Vallancey, Charles. *A Treatise on Inland Navigation: Or the Art of Making Rivers Navigable.* Dublin: Printed for George and Alexander Ewing, 1763.

Voland, E., A. Chasiotis, and W. Schiefenhövel, eds. *Grandmotherhood: The Evolutionary Significance of the Second Half of Female Life.* New Brunswick NJ: Rutgers University Press, 2005.

Wade, Richard C. *Slavery in the Cities: The South, 1820–1860.* New York: Oxford University Press, 1964.

Wallace Family. Papers, unpublished. Family Genealogy File, Montgomery County Historical Society, Rockville MD.

Walsh, Lorena S. "Rural African Americans in the Constitutional Era in Maryland, 1776–1810." *Maryland Historical Magazine* 84, no. 4 (Winter 1989): 328.

Warden, David Bailie. *A Chorographical and Statistical Description of the District of Colombia: The Seat of the General Government of the United States.* Paris: Smith Rue Montmorency, 1816.

Warner, Ezra J. *General in Blue: Lives of the Union Commanders.* Baton Rouge: Louisiana State University Press, 1964.

Wheat, T. A. "Medicine in Virginia during the Civil War." *Encyclopedia Virginia.* Charlottesville: Virginia Humanities, April 27, 2016. https://www .encyclopediavirginia.org/Medicine_in_Virginia_During_the_Civil_War.

White's Tabernacle. No. 39, Record of Incorporation, September 9, 1910. Book 27, 434. District of Columbia Archives, Washington DC.

Whitman, T. Stephen. *Challenging Slavery in the Chesapeake.* Baltimore: Maryland Historical Society, 2007.

———. *The Price of Freedom: Slavery and Manumission in Baltimore and Early National Maryland.* Lexington: University Press of Kentucky, 1997.

Williams, Heather Andrea. *Self-Taught: African American Education in Slavery and Freedom*. Chapel Hill: University of North Carolina Press, 2005.

Williamson, Samuel H. "Seven Ways to Compute the Relative Value of a U.S. Dollar Amount, 1790 to Present." MeasuringWorth, 2020. www.measuringworth.com/calculators/uscompare/.

Wilson, Joseph T. *The Black Phalanx: A History of the Negro Soldiers of the United States in the Wars of 1775–1812, 1861–1865*. Hartford CT: American Publishing, 1888.

Winkle, Kenneth J. "Emancipation in the District of Columbia." In Lawrence et al., *Civil War Washington*. www.civilwardc.org/interpretations/narrative/emancipation.php.

Wright, James M. *The Free Negro in Maryland, 1634–1860*. Vol. 97, no. 3 of Studies in History, Economics, and Public Law (Columbia University). New York: Longmans, Green, 1921. Reprint, Whitefish MT: Kessinger Legacy Reprints, 2010.

# Index

# About the Authors

BARBARA BOYLE TORREY is the former executive director of the Division of Behavioral and Social Sciences and Education of the National Research Council at the National Academy of Sciences, Washington, DC. She has published many articles on economics and population dynamics, edited three books, and authored two local histories—*Brookmont: A Neighborhood on the Potomac* (2008) with Clara Green and *Slaves of the Harvest: The History of the Pribilof Aleuts* (1977). She lives in Bethesda, Maryland.

CLARA MYRICK GREEN is a retired teacher of secondary school French. She taught English in Tours, France, with a French government teaching assistantship and a Fulbright grant, followed by a thirty-four-year career teaching secondary-school French in Brooklyn Heights, New York, and in Bethesda, Maryland. In retirement she has written two articles and a local history in collaboration with Barbara Boyle Torrey titled *Brookmont: A Neighborhood on the Potomac* (2008). She lives in Bethesda, Maryland.